COMMUNISM
IN CENTRAL AMERICA
AND THE CARIBBEAN

HOOVER INTERNATIONAL STUDIES
Richard F. Staar, director

The Panama Canal Controversy
  Paul B. Ryan

The Imperialist Revolutionaries
  Hugh Seton-Watson

South Africa: War, Revolution, or Peace?
  L. H. Gann and Peter Duignan

Two Chinese States
  Ramon H. Myers, editor

The Clouded Lens: Persian Gulf Security
  James H. Noyes

Soviet Strategy for Nuclear War
  Joseph D. Douglass, Jr., and Amoretta M. Hoeber

Science, Technology and China's Drive for Modernization
  Richard P. Suttmeier

The End of the Tito Era
  Slobodan Stanković

Waiting for a "Pearl Harbor": Japan Debates Defense
  Tetsuya Kataoka

Afghanistan: The Soviet Invasion in Perspective
  Anthony Arnold

Communist Powers and Sub-Saharan Africa
  Thomas H. Henriksen, editor

The United States and the Republic of Korea
  Claude A. Buss

Communism in Central America and the Caribbean
  Robert Wesson, editor

COMMUNISM
IN CENTRAL AMERICA
AND THE CARIBBEAN

Edited by
ROBERT WESSON

HOOVER INSTITUTION PRESS

Stanford University | Stanford, California

HOOVER PRESS PUBLICATION 261

© 1982 by the Board of Trustees of the
   Leland Stanford Junior University
All rights reserved
International Standard Book Number 0-8179-7612-4
Library of Congress Catalog Card Number 81-82707
Printed in the United States of America

87   9 8 7 6

CONTENTS

TABLES

PREFACE

There is no need, in the present atmosphere, to justify offering these essays on the question of communism in the region of the Caribbean and Central America (with which Guyana has been included because of its strongly leftist politics). At a time when the balance of military power in the world is in question, the United States feels an increased sense of insecurity in the very region where its sway once seemed most complete.

The original concept of this book and its organization were the work of Dr. Richard F. Staar, principal associate director of the Hoover Institution, who withdrew from editorship in order to take up an ambassadorial appointment. Dr. William E. Ratliff assisted importantly in the early stages of the work.

The politics of the Caribbean–Central American region has always been turbulent, and events may bypass some of the perspectives offered here before the book can get to its readers. But we hope that this work will provide useful background information for a subject sometimes treated more emotionally than factually.

R. W.

INTRODUCTION

Latin America seldom impinges strongly on those who call themselves simply "Americans" except when they see a threat to their security. But when alien and hostile movements or ideologies appear to be advancing in this hemisphere, Americans take a grave view, not only because of the potential military threat but also because of a feeling that the United States is much more responsible for the nations of this hemisphere than for those of Africa or the Near East. This is especially true of the part of Latin America nearest our shores, the Caribbean islands and the small countries of Central America. Mexico is relatively large and strong, can fairly well manage for itself, and certainly wishes to do so. But the weak nations of the area are peculiarly subject to the influence of the United States, are commonly in need of assistance, and, in view of their sensitive location, are the object of U.S. concern.

Aside from the special case of Mexico, the Caribbean–Central American region looms largest in the awareness of the United States, and policies toward Latin America have often taken shape first and most strongly in this area. The era of U.S. intervention opened with the Spanish-American War of 1898, which resulted in the annexation of Puerto Rico and a protectorate over Cuba. In 1903 Theodore Roosevelt intervened to secure control of the site of the Panama Canal. The following year, he enunciated his "corollary" to the Monroe Doctrine: the United States would, in effect, protect the countries of the hemisphere—in reality, of the Caribbean–Central American region—because of their weakness. In due course, the marines were sent to restore order in the Dominican Republic, Haiti, and Nicaragua. They were most effective in organizing forces of order or national guards, which became the mainstay of those in power.

The Good Neighbor policy was proclaimed by Franklin Roosevelt, who renounced interventionism in 1933–1934. For some years thereafter the Caribbean–Central American region seemed less agitated and consequently received less attention. The strongest U.S. concern regarding Latin America in the late 1930s was the effort of Nazi Germany to win sympathizers in South America, especially in Chile, Brazil, and Argentina. During World War II, the Latin republics, except for nationalistic Argentina, generally cooperated with the United States and the United Nations. From the late 1940s until 1958, the United States paid scant attention to Latin America, whose problems seemed to be little more than a replay of the old record of coups and dictatorships relieved by occasional democratic regimes. In 1953–1954 there was a brief fear that Guatemala might be falling to communism, but the danger was rather easily liquidated.

In 1958, however, the United States witnessed with amazement and alarm the violently hostile reception of Vice-President Richard Nixon by the mobs of Lima, Caracas, and other cities on his goodwill itinerary of South America. Either the United States was widely hated, despite its wholly good intentions (the general feeling), or the communists had built up a surprisingly large following among the less privileged. Not long afterwards, a bearded young man with a small band toppled the dictatorship of Fulgencio Batista, who had enjoyed U.S. favor for many years; the nation was half-fascinated and shocked to hear Fidel Castro's battle cry of "Down with Yankee Imperialism." Castro shattered the seemingly impregnable U.S. domination of Cuba and led that country, through a series of confrontations with the United States, to communism and close economic and military association with the global adversary of America, the Soviet Union. Reluctantly the United States by degrees came to accept a situation that would a few years earlier have been regarded as completely unacceptable, the existence of a hostile regime off Florida, allied to a hostile great power.

If this disaster could occur so near, it seemed likely that the disease could spread; indeed, conditions seemed quite as propitious for communism in many countries of the mainland as they had been in Cuba. Fidel Castro fanned this fear by proclaiming his intent to revolutionize the Americas, and he did as much to this end as his resources permitted through propaganda and support for guerrilla movements similar to his own. The United States developed a new notion of the revolutionary potential of Latin America. The biggest response was the Alliance for Progress, intended to show Latin America, with the help of infusions of capital and progressive reforms, that there was a better, democratic way to prosperity and justice.

The Alliance for Progress foundered in its multiple contradictions. Castro's exported revolutionism, however, was no more successful. Brazil's drift to a leftist-nationalist, perhaps Castroite, state was cut off by a military coup in 1964. The situation in Latin America generally seemed to lose urgency, and the attention of the United States turned to Vietnam. The election of a Marxist, Salvador Allende, in 1970 as president of Chile, brought great hopes to some and frightened others; but he was replaced by a military dictatorship in 1973. This was the last major flare-up of leftist radicalism in South America.

Since 1973, South America has been perhaps more tranquil than in any previous period since gaining independence. In no country of the continent (except English-speaking Guyana) is a communist or pro-Soviet party a serious contender for power. There is not even much theoretical socialism or nationalism of the species that made a big issue of the expropriation of U.S. corporations in the 1960s. In Central America and the Caribbean, however, the situation is very different. Communist, or Marxist–Leninist, parties are strong in many countries; there is violent hostility among major population segments to the United States; and relations with or opposition to "imperialism" is a major issue. Until October 1980, a socialist with close ties to Cuba was prime minister of Jamaica, and in March 1979 a pro-Cuban, truculently anti-U.S. party took power in the island of Grenada. In Nicaragua, the Marxist–Leninist, or Castroite, group asserted hegemony over the movement that overthrew Somoza. Its rhetoric is sternly communist: the party that won the battle on behalf of the people claims the right to govern without troubling itself with elections or other "bourgeois" formalities. In El Salvador, a strong guerrilla movement threatened to topple a government favored by the United States and to establish a thoroughly revolutionary state. The Guatemalan guerrillas are much weaker but gaining strength in a contest between political extremes.

Under these conditions, leftists foresee an inevitable "popular" victory sweeping through Central America, while rightists perceive a domino situation more convincing than that touted in the 1960s for Southeast Asia. Cuban- (ultimately Soviet-) supported subversion might spread from one unstable country to the next. Not everything has gone the way of the left; the antisocialist Edward Seaga won a surprising victory in Jamaica and turned that country around, at least temporarily, to a course of friendship with the United States; and the "final offensive" of the Salvadoran leftists in January 1981 was defeated. But it seems clear that the United States, despite the problems of NATO, the Middle East, and so forth, must give more attention to the seething Caribbean–Central American area.

The Reagan administration has displayed some uncertainty. Its initial reaction was to stress strongly the military aspect of subversion, to see problems as caused primarily by Cuban (ultimately Soviet) logistic and political support for guerrilla movements, especially in El Salvador. Correspondingly, it emphasized military assistance as the solution. It soon realized, however, that it was necessary to take account also of economic frustrations in the region and that stabilization required better hopes for improvement without violence—a perception with which contributors to this volume agree. The United States has also made greater efforts to cooperate with the two Latin American countries best able to influence events in the region, Mexico and Venezuela, with the cooperation of Canada. It is to be hoped that such joint efforts may alleviate some of the problems described in the chapters of this book.

RICHARD F. STAAR

Director of International Studies
Hoover Institution

1 | MOSCOW, THE CARIBBEAN, AND CENTRAL AMERICA

W. Raymond Duncan

Moscow, in its quest for power in the Third World, finds the Caribbean and Central America a promising field for action.[1] Both the newly independent states and the older countries in the area are experiencing rapid, dramatic, and turbulent change. As the 1970s unfolded, the region erupted in political violence and socialist movements, typified by the 1979 leftist victories in Grenada and Nicaragua, the socialist experiments in Guyana and Jamaica, and guerrilla struggles in El Salvador and Guatemala.[2] The expansion in Cuban activities and the inadequacy of the U.S. response gave the Soviet Union an opportunity to project its presence in this strategic area, to pursue its national interests, and to spread socialism. Soviet efforts have not been in vain; several Caribbean and Central American countries look toward the Soviet Union and Cuba for increased economic, military, and political support in an effort to lessen U.S. influence.

Implications for the United States

Actual Soviet and Cuban *influence*, in contrast to their pronounced *presence*, in the region should not be overestimated. A number of intrinsic domestic, regional, and international factors constrain Soviet and Cuban power projection, including:

1. A rise in nationalist sentiments that militates against Soviet and Cuban overinvolvement;

2. The determination of Caribbean and Central American leaders to solve domestic social and economic problems through indigenous, rather than imported, models of change;
3. The desire of all political elites, including leftists, to avoid the pitfalls of the Cuban economic experiment;
4. The decline in Cuba's image as a revolutionary model among Latin American Marxists;
5. The Soviet Union's waning image within the Third World since its invasion of Afghanistan;
6. The continuing strength of the private sector, even where revolution has occurred, as in Nicaragua after the fall of Anastasio Somoza;
7. A strong attraction to Western, including U.S., financial assistance and technology, compared with the comparatively lower appeal of Soviet aid and goods; and
8. The rising importance of Mexico and Venezuela, due to their oil riches, in moderating regional conflict and in aiding the process of economic development.

These barriers to Soviet and Cuban penetration suggest that much of the region's revolutionary instability is produced less by external than by internal forces for change. These forces—discontent with the economic and political status quo, the rise of leftist revolutionary groups challenging entrenched landed and military elites, the emergence of centrist military reformers, the search for economic and technical support from non–North American sources, the distressingly high level of political violence—are deeply rooted in the region's economic and social inequities. Moscow and Havana manipulate these events where and when they can, but they do not cause them. Their influence is limited, yet by no means so limited as to justify complacency in the rest of the hemisphere.

The problem lies in the type of attention to give. Admittedly the region is in search of its own economic and political paths to development. But this evolution is occurring at a time of high tensions between the United States and the USSR. This situation makes Washington prone to perceive the region's instability as a security threat rather than as a quest for change through diverse economic and political models. It is difficult for Washington to keep Soviet and Cuban activities in perspective, to understand the roots of revolution, and to react so as to minimize political violence while helping to pave the road to economic development.

The transition from the Carter to the Reagan administration reflects the enormous difficulty of orchestrating U.S. policy effectively in response to indigenous change and the Soviet-Cuban presence. The Carter administration demonstrated growing awareness of the grass-roots trends at work in the Caribbean and Central America, the role that human rights might play in moderating the conflict associated with the breakdown of the traditional political order (especially in Central America), and the uses of American economic power to affect both regional and international events. Emergency economic aid to Nicaragua after the Sandinista revolution, for example, helped stabilize the government and reduced Soviet-Cuban influence. Yet the objectives of Carter policy were extremely inconsistent; the administration encountered great difficulties in reconciling the approaches of competing lobbies—the Pentagon, the National Security Council, the Central Intelligence Agency, and the State Department—to political instability and the Soviet-Cuban presence.

The Reagan administration, in contrast, in its early days in power emphasized military, as opposed to economic, aid to the region, thereby underscoring its concern with U.S. security in the context of renewed cold war tensions. At the same time, rather than associating revolutionary leftism with domestic economic and social strains, it stressed the role of Cuba and the USSR in fomenting instability. The U.S. approach to El Salvador vividly illustrates this. In February 1981 the U.S. State Department released a major report documenting the role played by Cuba (ostensibly with Soviet support) and other communist countries in the political unification, military direction, and arming of insurgents in El Salvador. Moreover, the administration's replacement of Ambassador Robert White stressed a new policy of increased military aid to the Salvadoran junta, the dispatch of more U.S. military advisers, and a cutoff of U.S. assistance to Nicaragua for its role in transshipping arms to El Salvador. In March 1981 Secretary of State Alexander Haig even stated that the Soviet Union had a "hit list" for the "ultimate takeover of Central America," with "the seizure of Nicaragua" constituting but the first phase.

As the Reagan administration's policy toward the Caribbean and Central America evolved, however, it appeared to place greater stress on the region's complex political, economic, and social forces as causes of revolutionary leftism and political instability. Perhaps under pressure from oil-rich Mexico and Venezuela, as well as from members of the U.S. Congress, President Reagan's advisers let the Salvadoran junta know of their unhappiness over the continued military and paramilitary violence, and in fact warned Salvadoran officials of their responsibility for the actions of the Salvadoran military and police establishments. At the same time, the Reagan administration increasingly emphasized the need for more economic aid to El Salvador because of the country's severe economic problems. As for Guatemala, the administration increasingly spoke of the connection between increases in U.S. military aid and improvements in human rights in that country, thus bringing more pressure to bear along nonmilitary lines. Nevertheless, the Soviet specter continued to haunt the administration.

Soviet Objectives

Soviet objectives in the Caribbean and Central America are relatively clear from the available evidence, and the assumptions underlying Moscow's policies can be inferred from the record. Moscow seeks to project its power into a major strategic arena historically dominated by the United States, to support Cuba and its activities in the region, and to weaken the influence of a still dominant North America, but not at the expense of a direct military confrontation. Certainly the USSR is not in a position to use overt military force, on which it has come to rely strongly, as in Angola, Ethiopia, and Afghanistan. But it can utilize radical nationalism in the Caribbean and Central America, with their long tradition of anti-Americanism. Moscow does so not only by courting local communist parties and Marxist groups and urging them to participate in broad united fronts, but by cooperating with a variety of governments in state-to-state diplomacy. The range of contacts have included military regimes, such as that of Panama's former strong man, Gen. Omar Torrijos Herrera; socialist governments, as in the case of Prime Ministers Michael Manley of Jamaica (prior to the October 1980 election of conservative Edward Seaga) and Forbes Burnham of Guyana; or Marxist/non-Marxist coalitions, as in Nicaragua after the fall of Anastasio Somoza in 1979.

The goal of power projection is to produce specific policy results. Moscow pays special attention to the Caribbean and Central American area, which includes Mexico and Venezuela, because it lies in what they view as America's "strategic rear."[3] A weakening of American influence there is likely to produce a shift in the world "correlation of forces" toward socialism. In the Soviet perception, the USSR has benefited from socialism's larger role in promoting Caribbean and Central American economic independence, even though capitalism remains strong.[4] Within this context the Soviets' pragmatic concern with the region is not unlike the United States' great power objectives; the difference being that to the extent Moscow achieves its goals, American power is indeed weakened. Among the Soviet objectives are access to increasingly scarce food and raw materials; logistical support for its civil-

ian and military maritime operations, for example, port and other facilities for fishing, oceanographic research, trade, and surveillance; and aid
and diplomatic relations with potentially important economic and political side effects.

In designating the Caribbean as a key world region in America's strategic rear, the Soviet Union is acutely aware of the area's geopolitical
and economic links to the United States. John Bartlow Martin, former
U.S. ambassador to the Dominican Republic, reports that a Soviet geo-
politician once remarked that the importance of the Caribbean to the
United States "can hardly be exaggerated. In military-strategic terms, it
is a sort of hinterland on whose stability freedom of United States action
in other parts of the globe depends."[5] This observation, combined with
Moscow's growing ties in the area, suggests a Soviet recognition that an
erosion of U.S. influence there has serious implications for Soviet-U.S.
competition in the Third World.

The Soviets seem to recognize the importance of the Caribbean and
Central America to the United States in terms of both power politics
and global interdependence. The Soviets are no strangers to the first
mode of thought, and they show growing awareness of the newer con-
ceptions of global interdependence that stress the vulnerabilities and
sensitivities of all states in an increasingly interdependent world.[6] The
Soviets understand the military significance of the region to the United
States quite clearly and, consequently, its importance as a potential setting for anti-U.S. military operations. Cuba's recent support of armed
struggle in Guatemala and El Salvador, and earlier in Nicaragua, illustrates this lesson in unmistakable terms. Moscow is equally aware that
the region is important to the United States as a source of raw materials,
such as bauxite, petroleum, sulphur, barium, graphite, and zinc.[7]

The Soviet leaders correctly perceive other strategic aspects of the
Caribbean and Central America. They recognize it as a locus of U.S.
investment and trade, whose loss would mean a reduction in U.S. economic power. The Soviets' civilian and military operations in the region
have made its role as a major sea route familiar to Moscow. Less directly
mentioned in the Soviet literature but an increasing problem for the
United States is the high rate of emigration from Caribbean countries,
particularly Cuba, Haiti, and Jamaica, resulting from unstable political
and economic conditions. North America, then, is sensitive and vulnerable vis-à-vis the Caribbean. The Soviets anticipate that their actions will
increase that vulnerability.

Soviet observers are convinced that a variety of trends at work in the
Caribbean and Central America are favorable to their long-range interests. They do not anticipate, however, that great inroads will come dra-

matically and quickly, that U.S. dominance in the region will diminish in the short run, turning the area into a communist base. They see the process of change occurring over an extended period of time—with set-backs along the way, as in Salvador Allende's Chile in 1973 or Jamaica's change of government in 1980—during which radical nationalism will dominate the process. The process includes, of course, Havana's turn to Marxism-Leninism in the early 1960s, the staying power of Fidel Castro, and the substantial growth in his influence during the 1970s in Africa, the Caribbean, and Central America.[8]

Beyond Cuba, the Soviets perceive other key trends at work during the 1970s and 1980s. Increased anti-U.S. nationalism, growing political leftism, and armed liberation movements are all part of this regional portrait of change. The old U.S.-dominated Pan-Americanism is on the wane. With the United States entangled in the energy crisis and economic difficulties, Soviet analysts view the Caribbean and Central America as a region in upheaval, with increasing opportunities for Soviet power projection.

The increased scope of Soviet activities in the Caribbean and Central America dates from May 1960, when the USSR formalized diplomatic relations with Cuba. Once Cuba established a revolutionary Marxist state in an area where Moscow's previous diplomatic efforts had seldom affected U.S. dominance, the USSR's relations with Cuba became one of its most significant ties in its greatly widened posture generally within the Third World. As Soviet scholars put it:

> The Cuban revolution was a shattering blow to the theory of "geographical fatalism" that for a long time had determined the policy of most of the Latin American countries. According to this theory, the territorial proximity of the Latin American states to the USA doomed them to permanent dependence and to following in Washington's wake. Cuba's experience has demonstrated that a revolutionary people can shake off imperialist oppression and, with the support of the socialist community, successfully withstand intervention, economic embargoes, achieve economic and political sovereignty and pursue an independent foreign policy.[9]

Cuba's importance in Moscow's Latin American posture is underlined by Soviet economic, military, and technical aid, which reached approximately $10 million per day by the late 1970s.[10] Cuba is essential to Soviet Third World activities in large part because of the closeness of Soviet-Cuban bilateral ties and the congruence of Soviet and Cuban policy aims. Clearly both countries benefit from their cooperation, not only in Central America and the Caribbean, but also in Africa and the

Middle East.[11] Additional benefits accrue to Moscow through Cuba's expanding activities in the Caribbean and Central American region, including technical assistance to Grenada, Guyana, and (formerly) Jamaica and moral and material support to national liberation movements in Nicaragua, El Salvador, and Guatemala.[12]

Since the Cuban connection was established in 1960, Moscow has greatly expanded its diplomatic activities in the region.[13] By 1980 the Soviet Union had established embassies, consulates, and trade offices in six countries (Costa Rica, El Salvador, Grenada, Guyana, Jamaica, Nicaragua) and nonresident ambassadors in Suriname and Trinidad-Tobago. Immediately after World War II, Soviet diplomatic, consular, and trade representation in the region was much more limited. East European and Cuban representation also grew throughout the area during the 1970s (see Table 1.1). The Soviet alertness to the opportunities presented by radical nationalism and political leftism has affected diplomatic contacts; thus, the USSR signed cooperative agreements with Grenada and Nicaragua after both states turned leftward in 1979. A Nicaraguan delegation led by Moisés Hassán, a member of the ruling junta, traveled to Moscow in March 1980. On March 22, 1980, authorities of the USSR Gosplan and the Nicaraguan Ministry of Planning signed an agreement of cooperation covering mining, light and food industries, joint development of Nicaraguan minerals, power engineering, transport, communications, and agriculture.[14]

Opportunities for Soviet influence in the Caribbean and Central America can be viewed from three major perspectives: (1) the general political setting in the countries in which Moscow can influence ruling or nonruling political leaders; (2) the underlying economic and social forces; and (3) regional and international issues that facilitate Soviet power seeking. Together these factors allow the Soviet Union to try to accomplish a number of ends, examined more closely below. They offer the Soviets a chance to project their presence through expanded diplomatic, aid, and trade contacts, to weaken U.S. power in a key part of the world, to establish logistical support facilities (as in Cuba), to gain access to food and raw materials, and to strengthen world socialism through extended contacts with Marxist representatives in and out of power. Effective and creative U.S. action to check these trends is enormously difficult. Yet this by no means suggests that the region will immediately fall under Soviet or Cuban domination. The area is, however, very likely to continue to plague U.S. foreign policy, with sufficient Cuban and Soviet involvement to undermine effective policy formation and consensus building among the executive branch, Congress, and public interest groups.

TABLE 1.1

COMMUNIST REPRESENTATION IN THE CARIBBEAN AND CENTRAL AMERICA, MARCH 1, 1980

	Albania	Bulgaria	China	Cuba	Czechoslovakia	East Germany	Hungary	Mongolia	North Korea	Vietnam	Poland	Romania	Yugoslavia	USSR
Bahamas				NRA										
Barbados	NRA	R	E	NRA	R				R			R	R	
Costa Rica				C	E,C,T	NRA	NRA,T	R	R	NRA	NRA	E,C,T	E	E,C,T
Dominican Republic							R				NRA			
El Salvador		T			T		T		R				T	T
Grenada				E	R	R				R		T		E
Guatemala														
Guyana		NRA	E,T	E	NRA	NRA,T	NRA,T		E	NRA	NRA	NRA	E	E
Haiti											L			
Honduras					NRA	NRA	NRA			NRA	NRA	NRA	NRA	
Jamaica		NRA	E	E	R	NRA	NRA	R	R	R	T	NRA	NRA	E
Nicaragua	R			E		E	R		R		NRA	R	R	E
Panama		R		E		R	NRA	R			NRA	NRA	E	
St. Lucia				NRA					R			NRA		
St. Vincent														
Suriname			E	NRA	R	NRA	R					R	NRA	NRA
Trinidad-Tobago			E	NRA			R					NRA	NRA	NRA

KEY: E-embassy; L-legation; C-consulate; T-trade office; NRA-nonresident ambassador; R-relations, but no representatives exchanged.
SOURCE: U.S. State Department, Bureau of Intelligence and Research, Latin American Division.

Caribbean Political Dynamics

The political dynamics of Caribbean and Central American countries understandably attract Soviet interest. Only three countries in the Caribbean were independent in 1960; thirteen had reached that status by 1980. Each government, deeply aware of its colonial past, carefully avoided new forms of neocolonialism and imperialism. The pattern on achieving independence was to search for ways to maximize independence in a complex international economic and political system that continued to make these states highly vulnerable to external pressures. Leftist currents—the drive to change existing economic and social conditions to favor the "common man," a tendency to use state control over economic processes, and greater stress on social, cultural, and economic rights than on civil and political rights—readily emerged.[15] Externally the emphasis centered on trade and aid diversification, as much independence of action as possible, and a growing identification with other Third World countries in opposition to the developed countries of the North—which meant the United States in the Western Hemisphere.

Leftism in the Caribbean includes a wide range of Marxist-Leninists, socialists, ethnic nationalists, and moderate reformers. Falling into the Marxist category are the People's Progressive Party (PPP) of Guyana, the Puerto Rican Socialist Party (PSP), the Jamaican Communist Party, and the Jamaican Workers' Party (both formed in the late 1970s).[16] Within the socialist category are Michael Manley's People's National Party (PNP) of Jamaica and Forbes Burnham's People's National Congress (PNC) of Guyana, both of which have courted, and been courted by, the Cubans and the Soviets. The ethnic nationalists, curiously, are found also within Guyana's PNC and PPP; the former is composed largely of blacks, the latter is essentially East Indian in membership. The New Jewel Movement, which came to power in Grenada in March 1979 under the leadership of Maurice Bishop, combines leftist ideological orientations and some "black power" concepts;[17] the Democratic Labor Party of Trinidad-Tobago is primarily East Indian in membership. Finally, leftist moderate reformers are illustrated by Dr. Eric Williams, prime minister of Trinidad-Tobago and head of the People's National Movement until his death in March 1981.

The Caribbean, in short, is alive with variants of political leftism and radical nationalist leaders, whose policies are attractive to the Soviet Union and Cuba. Michael Manley moved Jamaica strongly toward socialism between 1972 and 1980, but not fast enough for Marxists within his PNP and within Jamaica's two communist parties, but much too fast and with disastrous results, according to the conservative Jamaican Labor Party (JLP), headed by Edward Seaga, who came to power in October 1980 on an anticommunist platform. Manley enjoyed close relations with Cuba and Fidel Castro and was courted by the Soviet Union; he traveled to both countries, and Fidel Castro visited Jamaica in October 1977. Cubans worked in Jamaica from 1975 until Manley's defeat.[18] Seaga's party made much of the danger of communism.[19]

Guyana under Forbes Burnham is closely linked to Cuba and has ties with the USSR. Cuban assistance to Guyana is on a lesser scale than that to Jamaica and is complicated by Cuba's desire to cooperate with the major opposition party—the PPP, headed by Marxist Cheddi Jagan. Grenada is the most recent Caribbean government to turn leftist. Soon after the coup in March 1979, Prime Minister Bishop invited the Cubans to provide arms, military advisers (most of whom had left by mid-1981), and about 300–350 construction workers to build a new airport, and the Soviet Union and Grenada quickly exchanged embassies.[20] Other areas of leftist discontent include Surinam, St. Vincent, St. Kitts–Nevis, Dominica, St. Lucia (where leftists came to power in July 1979), and Puerto Rico.

The Soviets and Cubans pay special attention to the Puerto Rican independence movement, and Cuba allows its spokesmen to use Havana radio. As *Pravda* notes:

> In the past few years, the Puerto Rican people's courageous struggle has found ever broader support around the world. The United Nations Commission on Decolonialism has repeatedly adopted resolutions affirming the Puerto Ricans' inalienable right to self-determination and independence ... The people of the world demand that the U.S. fulfill the provisions of the historic Declaration on the Granting of Independence to Colonial Countries and Peoples and put an end to colonialism in Puerto Rico.[21]

Cuba meanwhile attempts to promote the independence of Puerto Rico in various ways, including conferences of solidarity with the Puerto Rican independence movement, making Cuba the home of a permanent representative of the Puerto Rican Socialist Party, and frequent support for Puerto Rico in the Afro–Asian–Latin American Peoples' Solidarity Organization, which is headquartered in Havana. The Cuban government has played a pivotal role in getting the question of Puerto Rican independence brought before the United Nations.[22]

While much of the external Marxist influence in the Caribbean is Cuban, the Soviets are certainly present. Soviet influence is exercised directly through diplomatic, trade, cultural, technical, and cooperative planning agreements, and indirectly through Cuba (the Soviet Union underwrites much of Cuba's diplomacy). The Cuban approach to diplomatic relations in the Caribbean now harmonizes with the Soviet line and techniques, unlike the situation in the late 1960s when Havana advocated armed struggle only. Expansion of Cuban relations in the Caribbean complements the Soviet cause and objectives in many respects, although Cuba has its own reasons for its brand of diplomacy.

Central American Politics and Soviet Relations

In Central America the traditional order is changing rapidly and violently. The transition, so clear in Nicaragua, El Salvador, and Guatemala, is marked by assassinations and murders on a scale unknown in the Caribbean, due largely to the different political cultures and political systems of Central America. The Caribbean, to be sure, has political violence, as in the gang warfare of downtown Kingston, Jamaica, but in Central America death occurs in the thousands—within *single* countries—as leftists seek to produce change and as the wealthy, military-backed rightists work to prevent this.

The English-speaking Caribbean inherited systems of legitimate self-government and parliamentary rule; Central America observes traditions of Spanish authoritarianism and violent political combat. When Central American leftists challenge their government and the groups it represents, the tradition is to use bullets rather than ballots. This perhaps explains why Cuba pursues not only peaceful diplomacy in Central America, but also supports armed liberation with propaganda, training, and arms support, as vividly underscored by the February 1981 U.S. Department of State white paper on Cuban and other communist involvement in leftist military and political activities in Central America. The public record, moreover, does not indicate any Soviet attempt to chastise Cuba for this activity, as it did during the late 1960s when the USSR criticized the Cuban attempt to export revolution to Latin America.

A brief overview of political dynamics in Central America highlights the situations amenable to Cuban and, indirectly, Soviet power seeking. The new Nicaraguan Government of National Reconstruction, for example, is guided by nationalism, pragmatism, and Marxist theory. After more than three decades of rule by the U.S.-supported Somoza family and eighteen months of civil war, which caused nearly 50,000 fatalities, the Marxist- and nationalist-inspired Sandinista National Liberation Front overthrew the Somoza dictatorship in July 1979.[23] On the eve of Somoza's overthrow, virtually all segments of Nicaraguan society were allied with the Sandinistas against Somoza and his National Guard. The new Nicaraguan government faces extraordinary development problems. Building a consensus and legitimizing its rule and combining private enterprise with a strong public sector are two key issues.

Acutely sensitive to forms of neocolonialism and past U.S. dominance, the new Nicaraguan government is attracted to Cuban and Soviet ties. This is not simply because Castro supported the Sandinista guerrillas, who dominate the National Directorate of the government, during the Nicaraguan civil war in 1978–79.[24] Cuba has offered types of aid that Nicaragua can use and afford—1,200 teachers and several hundred medical specialists and other types of technicians. So, too, has the Soviet Union; the planning accord of March 1980 and later agreements to exchange radio and television programs directly benefit the Nicaraguan economy. Nicaragua's ties with Cuba and the Soviet Union represent a shift away from U.S. dominance and toward alternative aid and trade links—an important move for Nicaraguan decision makers, who are trying to shake off the legacy of the past. Indeed, members of the Sandinista directorate apparently arranged the mechanics of the shipment of Cuban arms to the guerrillas in El Salvador—perhaps without the knowledge of the full directorate. This traffic, in any event, led the Reagan administration to suspend aid to Nicaragua in February 1981.

Yet the Nicaraguan government demonstrated a strong concern for continued U.S. financial aid and a desire not to alienate the United States in the future. In response to the curtailment of U.S. economic aid, the Nicaraguan government appointed a new ambassador to the United States in March 1981, Arturo Cruz Porras, a banker and business leader, in order to communicate Nicaragua's hope to stay on good terms with Washington. To fathom the reasons and significance of Nicaragua's turn toward Cuba and the Soviet Union, one must understand Sandinista aspirations to develop the country as an indigenous movement working in a native historical setting.

In El Salvador, too, leftist-inspired guerrilla groups are challenging the old order. Over nine thousand people were killed in the conflict between the extreme left and the right in 1980. Neither the old military government of Gen. Carlos Humberto Romero nor the two "reformist" juntas that have held power since Romero's overthrow in October 1979 have been able to control the opposing groups or introduce needed changes peacefully, despite a serious attempt at agrarian reform. By early 1981 the leftist organizations fighting against the civilian-military junta headed by Christian Democrat José Napoleón Duarte had organized a coordinating group, the Revolutionary Democratic Front (FDR). Their efforts were not completely successful; a January 1981 leftist offensive failed to unseat the junta, and the peasantry seemed interested more in peace rather than in continued fighting.[25] The United States accused the Cubans of using Honduras as a staging zone to equip and train insurgents for fighting in El Salvador and of transshipping weapons through Nicaragua.[26] These events led Secretary of State Haig to propound his Soviet "hit list" thesis.

The substantial Soviet coverage of the Salvadoran conflict excoriated the right wing for its violence against the left, denounced the governing junta as reactionary, and accused the United States of backing the terrorism of the "oligarchs" and "reactionaries" and of preparing for armed intervention.[27] By mid-1980, El Salvador's main opposition coalition, the FDR, began a major public effort in Western Europe and Latin America to gain financial support for its armed struggle against the U.S.-backed junta, a move that did not embarrass the Soviets or Cuba.[28]

Opposition between extreme right and left also characterized the Guatemalan political setting by 1980, raising again the potential specter of Cuban, if not direct Soviet, support. Like other Central American countries, violence and political instability are part of Guatemalan history, but not quite at the systematic and organized level visible in the late 1970s. Undoubtedly stimulated by events in Nicaragua and El Salvador, certainly impelled by the severe government repression since President Lucas García assumed power in July 1978, and perhaps even affected by leftist currents in Caribbean politics, active guerrilla groups were estimated in strength from 7,000 to 20,000. They reportedly began to coordinate their efforts and were attempting to ally with non-Marxist factions represented in the broad-based Democratic Front Against Repression. The guerrilla groups involved included the Guerrilla Army of the Poor, the Armed People's Organization, the Rebel Armed Forces, and the Guatemalan Workers' Party.[29] Of major significance were the growing numbers of Indians, historically passive in political warfare, joining the leftists. Cuban propaganda, as might be expected, continued to support the leftist movement. Its news media lauded guerrilla activities, condemned the "bloody Romeo Lucas García regime and its imperialist and local oligarchic backers," and strongly criticized U.S. military aid to the government.[30] The Soviet Union demonstrated acute sensitivity to U.S. media charges that it was "intensifying" its efforts, with Cuban assistance, to penetrate Guatemala, as well as Costa Rica and El Salvador. Moscow argued instead that Guatemala and the other Central American countries were

> experiencing an upsurge in the national liberation movement and heightened sense of national identity, shedding the heavy shackles of political

and economic dependence on the United States. Having swept away, in a tenacious and bloody struggle, the Washington-imposed dictator, the people of Nicaragua are building a new life in conditions of freedom. The positions of U.S. imperialism are showing cracks in El Salvador.[31]

It is not to be assumed that "Cuban-style" or "Soviet-dominated" governments will soon dot the Central American or Caribbean landscape. Each country's internal political system reflects its unique historic roots, operating style, and nationalist sentiments. Each country needs continued Western financial support to achieve its development goals. But already established leftist governments in such countries as Guyana, Grenada, and Nicaragua and national liberation movements in El Salvador and Guatemala continue to offer possibilities for an expansion of Soviet and Cuban presence. Even if Cuba's and the USSR's activities do not greatly increase their influence, they concern many people in the Caribbean and Central America and condition U.S. policy responses.

Underlying Economic and Social Forces

Radical nationalist and leftist political dynamics in the Caribbean and Central America, although produced by historical economic and social forces, intensified during the 1970s. Slow economic growth, partly produced by increased oil prices after 1973 in combination with other domestic and international factors, plague both areas. Economic systems tend to be small in scale, depend on one or two export commodities, are burdened by large foreign indebtedness, and suffer from structural dualism (the existence of a high-wage, capital-intensive modern sector, usually owned and controlled by foreign-based multinational corporations, alongside a low-wage, labor-intensive traditional sector). The modern sector is characterized by mineral extraction, processing industries, and other capital-intensive production; the traditional economy by handicrafts, services, and agriculture. Historically the economies have been vulnerable to external forces and highly dependent, a situation that arouses leftist antagonism toward neocolonialism and imperialism.[32]

Continued low rates of economic development are caused by, and produce, other economic and social pressures. The region suffers from high rates of inflation and unemployment and low per capita income. Inflation ran at approximately 20 percent in El Salvador and Nicaragua during 1980; in the Caribbean it averaged between 11 percent (Bahamas)) and 35 percent (Jamaica) during the late 1970s.[33] Many of the Caribbean islands have unemployment rates of 25 percent overall and of nearly 50 percent among young people. Unemployment in urban

Nicaragua exceeds 35 percent. Gross national product per capita is low: figures for 1977 are Haiti $230, Honduras $410, El Salvador $550, Guatemala $790, and Jamaica $1,150 (the comparable figure for the United States is $8,520).[34] Income maldistribution is notorious in Central America. The bottom 20 percent of the population in El Salvador receives 2 percent of the national income; the top 5 percent receives 38 percent.[35] Guatemala has a similar concentration of wealth. In some areas the pattern is changing. In 1974 the lowest 60 percent of Jamaica's income earners received 24 percent of all individual income, up from 18 percent in 1958 and 20 percent in 1963. In contrast, the top 5 percent accounted for 24 percent of total income in 1974, down from 29 percent in 1963.[36]

Demographic problems are part of this classic picture of underdevelopment. Large numbers of hopeful peasants flood the cities, only to face grim prospects. Urban growth rates between 1960 and 1977 ranged from a low of 1.0 percent in Barbados to 7.1 percent in Jamaica, with figures of 4.6 percent for Honduras, 5.1 percent for Nicaragua, and 3.8 percent for El Salvador.[37] The population growth rate, furthermore, is high, averaging over 2.0 percent in a number of countries, including the Bahamas, the Dominican Republic, and Guyana. El Salvador averaged 2.9 percent, Guatemala 2.0, and Nicaragua 3.3 percent annually between 1970 and 1977. Much of the population is young, as well as unemployed. In 1973, over 50 percent of the populations of the Dominican Republic, Guyana, Haiti, Jamaica, and Trinidad-Tobago were nineteen years or younger, placing correspondingly heavy burdens on the economic and political systems. (The figures for the United States and Canada were 37 and 40 percent.) Illiteracy is a by-product of these conditions, which makes Cuban offers of educational assistance extremely attractive. Central America is especially disadvantaged in this respect; adult literacy in the late 1970s was estimated at only 57 percent in Nicaragua, 62 percent in El Salvador, and 46 percent in Guatemala. Haiti ranks lowest, at 23 percent.

Another source of social conflict in the region is ethnic-racial tension. Caribbean and Central American nations comprise complex ethnic-racial groupings, each having a unique self-perception, each antagonistic to other groups within the same country, and each typically occupying a distinct socioeconomic niche. The existence of economic inequality between racial groups impedes the formation of legitimate political systems. This is especially true in Central America, but in both areas makes it difficult to achieve a consensus on development.

Light skin color typically carries higher status within the Central American area. Indian peasants are further down the economic ladder than mestizos in Guatemala; lighter skinned blacks are better off than darker blacks in Panama. In the Caribbean area, Guyana is about equally divided between blacks and East Indians and is split thereby along party lines. Blacks and East Indians also constitute the major racial groups in Trinidad-Tobago, with East Indians predominantly rural and blacks dominating the country's urban settlements and employment. Whites and light-skinned nonwhites traditionally have controlled Jamaica's politics and economy. These multiracial settings make nation-building extremely difficult, especially given the degree of economic underdevelopment. The situation complicates the attempt of the Soviet Union and Cuba to increase their influence in the area, but may give Cuba, itself multiracial with ties to black Africa, a distinct advantage.

These enormous economic and social strains on Caribbean and Central American political systems account for the tendency of radical nationalist or leftist governments to turn for help to Cuba and the Soviet Union, as well as to Western Europe, other Latin American states, especially Mexico and Venezuela, and the United States. They also suggest a reason for the high level of conflict, especially in Central America. Rising numbers of young people entering labor markets ill-equipped to absorb them, urban squalor and totally inadequate public utilities and housing, and extreme poverty in the countryside all contribute to the frustration, crime, violence, and escalating political conflict.

The contrast in wealth, so clear in El Salvador and Guatemala, naturally causes the elites to fear leftist extremism and look to the military for protection; peasants, workers, and students are determined to change the status quo through new foreign and economic policies, frequently with a socialist or Marxist orientation. If they can get arms from Cuba, they are likely to take them. But the attainment of political power by leftists does not guarantee an end to civil conflict or smooth economic development. Given the enormity of the economic and social strains, leftist-oriented governments may well look to both Marxist and non-Marxist sources for educational and technical help. It is not so strange, then, that Nicaragua welcomed Cuban teachers while actively seeking U.S. aid.

Regional and International Trends

To the Soviets, the deteriorating economic and social setting and the consequent radical nationalist and leftist domestic and foreign policies produce significant opportunities for regional and international relations. Among the favorable regional trends are (1) expanded aid, technical cooperation, and trade relations with the USSR and its socialist client-states of Cuba and Eastern Europe; (2) increased domestic control over natural resources; (3) the creation of regional economic and development organizations that include Cuba and exclude the United States; (4) less domination of the inter-American system by the United States and a general decline of U.S.-controlled Pan-Americanism through the Organization of American States (OAS); (5) wider participation in the non-aligned movement directed by Cuba; and (6) a growth in national liberation movements, for example, those in El Salvador and Guatemala and in Belize and Puerto Rico—areas still under colonial rule.

The Soviets perceive this pattern of events as a positive opportunity to expand socialism and Soviet national interests. Regional anti-imperialist pressures presage a general erosion in the economic and political bases of North American strength and the evolution of a new setting in which to project Soviet power and to strengthen long-range Soviet security interests. The pattern includes, of course, the desire of independent, ex-colonial, leftist Caribbean or Central American states to cooperate and trade with and receive aid from the Soviet Union and Soviet client-states. The principal factor in this pattern is the Cuban revolution, which, to cite Soviet analysis, "broke the chain of imperialist opposition in the American continent and gave a powerful impetus to the struggle of its people for complete national liberation."[38] This event is important not only for its impact on the expansion of socialism, but for other reasons as well.[39]

New Soviet, East European, and Cuban cooperative and trade links with the Caribbean and Central American countries help assure access to food and raw materials, a distinct pattern in Moscow's relations with Third World countries. Increased Cuban or East European access also helps Moscow indirectly by relieving financial burdens on the Soviet Union. Among other activities, the Soviets are exploring for oil in 15 developing countries and concluded a mining agreement with Nicaragua in 1980. Moscow's search for alumina and bauxite in Guinea and India parallels its offer to build an aluminum plant in Guyana. The Soviet Union assists some 40 developing countries in fishing in return for offshore fishing rights, including Cuba, for whom Moscow has built an enormous fishing and maritime fleet.[40] Moscow and Jamaica signed a joint cooperative agreement covering sea navigation and fishing; Jamaica agreed to service Soviet fishing vessels.[41] Romania and Costa Rica have signed a protocol on cooperative exploration of minerals and commercial exchanges, and Czechoslovakia, East Germany, Poland, and the USSR have offered to buy $10 million worth of bananas a year from Panama.[42] Behind these developments, as the Soviets well know, lie a stress on nationalizing foreign corporations and local control over natural resources and a growing interest in trade diversification to enhance development opportunities. The frequency of Soviet discussions of these trends and Soviet trade patterns indicate the USSR's eagerness to take advantage of the situation.[43]

The Soviets view the economic and development organizations recently created in the region as essentially anti-imperialist. In the words of one Soviet observer, these are part of the "mounting anti-imperialist struggle for democracy" and transcend the effort to restore local control over natural resources and to liquidate the domination of foreign capital through nationalization.[44] Three organizations viewed in Moscow as weakening "imperialism's position" are the Latin American Economic System, which includes Cuba; the Caribbean Free Trade Association; and a joint Caribbean shipping company of eight countries.[45]

While Moscow does not leap to the conclusion that North America's economic and political grip has slipped, it does envision cracks in the old, U.S.-dominated system of Pan-Americanism. The Soviets note several major events during the 1970s that challenged U.S. control. Among them were pressure from Caribbean, Central American, and other Latin American countries to lift OAS economic sanctions against Cuba; the worsening of relations between the United States and Latin American countries reported by several U.S. fact-finding missions; the United States' inability to mobilize the OAS to settle the Nicaraguan crisis of 1978–79; and the rejection of inter-American military intervention in that affair by, among others, Barbados, Costa Rica, Grenada, Jamaica, Mexico, Panama, and the Dominican Republic.[46] Another gratifying trend must be the displeasure of several Caribbean states, including Mexico and Venezuela, with the continuing U.S. tendency to use military force in the face of crises instead of using economic aid and trade to avert crises before they develop. Venezuela, for example, charged that by landing 1,800 marines at the U.S. naval base at Guantanamo Bay, Cuba, in October 1979, Washington had once again overreacted to the presence of Soviet troops in Cuba with "an excessive demonstration of force" in the Caribbean.[47]

One result of Cuba's hosting of the Sixth Summit Meeting of Nonaligned Countries in Havana in September 1979 was the election of Fidel Castro to head this organization until 1982. Moscow regards this event as highly significant, given its close relations with Cuba and what Castro's leadership would mean for the USSR—the fidelity of which was shown when Havana resisted U.N. pressure to condemn the Soviet invasion of Afghanistan. The event was also important in a symbolic sense: once isolated Cuba now become a major leader of the developing countries, including the 21 Latin American and Caribbean countries in attendance at the Havana affair.

The nonaligned meeting provided a forum for Caribbean and Central American leaders to demonstrate their independence of the United States. At the same time, the meeting made possible a demonstration of Caribbean and Central American solidarity regarding major regional issues and the struggles of developing countries in Africa, Asia, and the Middle East. The Soviets, then, could feel encouraged by positions taken at the meeting that they, too, supported and that affirmed their reading of the nature of regional and international affairs in an area so close to the United States. Moscow must have been heartened when Michael Manley and Maurice Bishop heaped praises on Fidel Castro; Panamanian President Aristides Royo welcomed Grenada, Nicaragua, and Suriname into the movement to join Guyana, Jamaica, Panama, Trinidad-Tobago (Belize has special status); Maurice Bishop condemned imperialism and neocolonialism; and Juan María Bras, general secretary of the Puerto Rican Socialist Party, praised Grenada's liberation and the Nicaraguan victory over Somoza.[48]

Moscow is certain that the potential for national liberation movements in Central America and the Caribbean has not been exhausted. The Soviet media support guerrilla movements in El Salvador and Guatemala and have not condemned Cuba for weapons shipments to El Salvador as they might have done in the late 1960s when armed struggle versus peaceful change was the issue dividing Havana and Moscow. They are attentive to the situation of Belize and Puerto Rico. Although the Soviets felt that the overthrow of Salvador Allende in Chile (1973) was a setback, they (or at least some observers) find the recent turn of events in Nicaragua promising.[49] To the USSR, the Caribbean and Central America form a special region within Latin America that is moving in a favorable direction.

Constraints to Soviet Influence

A balanced assessment of Moscow's opportunities in the Caribbean and Central America requires an examination of factors constraining the expansion of Soviet influence. The Soviet presence in the Caribbean and Central America does not necessarily mean an enormous degree of immediate influence. A number of case studies of Soviet–Third World relations demonstrate this point, and a similar argument can be made for the Caribbean and Central America.[50] This is not to argue that the Soviet presence in the region will not have a detrimental effect on U.S.

interests. The Soviets do support trends that might in the future disrupt oil supplies, decrease access to important raw materials, and encourage the growth of logistical support facilities for the Soviet fleet. The argument is rather that in the short run Soviet influence is less than might be expected. These countries are unlikely to become Soviet economic dependents or members of the Soviet bloc, as has Cuba, despite the crisis atmosphere created in Washington around Soviet troops in Cuba, the Nicaraguan civil war, and Cuban support of El Salvadoran leftists.

Constraints to Soviet influence can be categorized as economic, political, and social. Specifically they involve (1) comparatively greater U.S. and Western financial power in aid and trade relations; (2) the relative attractiveness of Western technology; (3) mounting economic problems in Cuba, which erode the island as a perceived model for other countries; (4) growing opposition among nonaligned Third World states to Soviet economic aid and military practices; and (5) the strength of nationalist and ethnic sentiments in the area.

The comparatively greater economic power of United States and Western aid can be demonstrated easily enough. Over the years, the United States has provided about $14.8 billion to Latin America, with sizable amounts going to the Dominican Republic, Guatemala, Panama, and more recently, to the Caribbean states, including Jamaica and Nicaragua.[51] Beyond direct U.S. aid, many of these countries also draw upon the Inter-American Development Bank and the International Monetary Fund, and other sources of Western aid.[52]

Moscow extended a total of only $964 million to all of Latin America (except Cuba) between 1954 and 1978,[53] compared with $7 billion to the Middle East, $5 billion to South Asia, $3 billion to North Africa, and $1 billion to sub-Saharan Africa for the same period. The Caribbean and Central America, notwithstanding Soviet interest and goals in the region, are areas where Moscow has been constrained by its overall aid capabilities.[54] Cuba is, of course, an exception; Moscow provided subsidies for bilateral trade deficits amounting to $3.8 billion between 1960 and 1974 alone.[55] The size of support for Cuba makes it difficult for the USSR to aid other countries in the area. The attention leftist governments in the region give to U.S. and other Western financial sources indicates the strength of non-Soviet foreign aid. Even the socialist government of Michael Manley called for private foreign investment to promote development.

The Soviets recognize Western financial strength. In the current Soviet debate over Latin American conditions and trends, one school of thought perceives "progressive forces" on the ascendancy. A second line of argument is more pessimistic, depicting the region as "dependent on capitalism," where foreign control and U.S. multinational interests prevail.[56] This second image suggests doubts over Moscow's capacity to influence economic development along socialist lines in the Caribbean and Central America. It does not preclude, however, a limited financial investment to take political advantage of opportunities to try to encourage trends favorable to the USSR.

The region continues to favor U.S. and Western technology over Soviet technology. Certainly Soviet technology finds some acceptance in the region—a nuclear power plant in Cuba, hydroelectric projects in other parts of Latin America, fishing arrangements with Guyana and Jamaica. But the communist countries are hampered by the region's preference for Western goods. Of the $2.4 billion in credits extended by communist countries to Latin America between 1958 and 1977, only $525 million had been drawn by 1977.[57] Overall communist trade with Latin America has been in deficit for over a decade, and despite intensive communist campaigns to sell machinery and equipment, the region still prefers to buy from Western producers.

By the late 1970s, Cuba's economy was in great difficulty, as Castro admitted in a speech of December 1979. It was still dependent on sugar after twenty years of revolution, while poor productivity and absenteeism still plagued the labor sector. The wave of refugees fleeing socialist Cuba in May 1980 reported food rationing, lack of consumer goods, low pay, and high prices. Cuba's economic condition, combined with mass attempts to flee the island, marred the image of socialist Cuba as a Soviet-sponsored experiment in rapid development. This image must be assessed along with the more positive aspects—doctors, technicians, and schoolteachers—of Cuba's other connections with the Caribbean and Central America.

Cuba's leadership of the nonaligned movement should not be interpreted as automatic power and influence for Moscow. Havana, to be certain, emphasizes the Soviet bloc as the "natural allies" of developing states.[58] It continued to espouse this position indirectly after the Soviet Union invaded Afghanistan in late 1979. But reactions to this invasion and other aspects of Moscow's Third World posture suggest that even with Cuba running interference, the Soviet Union is still not on an all-win course in its race for the allegiance of the nonaligned countries.

Recent events highlight the less-than-perfect Soviet record with developing states. Cuba's attack on U.S. imperialism at the nonaligned meeting in Havana did not meet with complete acceptance; not only did a rift develop between Tito and Castro over the movement's direction and alignment, but President Royo of Panama noted that it was "only fair to recognize the balanced, equitable and understanding action taken by President Carter" in signing the new Panama Canal treaties.[59] The U.N. vote to censure Moscow over Afghanistan included the Bahamas, Barbados, Costa Rica, the Dominican Republic, El Salvador, Guatemala, Guyana, Haiti, Honduras, Jamaica, Mexico, Panama, St. Lucia, and Trinidad-Tobago—a sizable representation from the Caribbean and Central America that left just Cuba and Grenada on the other side.[60] Cuba's withdrawal of its bid for a Security Council seat after losing the votes of several Third World countries as a result of the Soviet invasion of Afghanistan illustrates another negative aspect of the Soviet-Cuban relationship. Meanwhile, the meetings of the New International Economic Order—in which the Caribbean and Central American states participate—are increasingly critical of the USSR for its relatively low financial commitment and unconcern for their development needs.[61] In the past, Moscow has regularly claimed that the needs of a developing country were the responsibility of the "imperialist" and "colonialist" countries that originally put the Third World states into their under-developed position and continue to keep them there.

The Third World states, including the Caribbean and Central American countries, are likely to step up their demands on the USSR, but there is no guarantee that Soviet capacity to meet these needs will also increase. A growing world population, declining energy resources, and decreasing raw materials together suggest continued world poverty and a sharpened awareness of global interdependence—with southern nations deeply concerned about their development future. Moscow's own economic troubles are notorious. Demands from energy-seeking client-states are escalating. Moreover, the USSR does not belong to any major international lending institution, which further weakens its donor capacity. The global setting and Moscow's role within it vis à vis the Caribbean and Central American developing states do not necessarily augur well for Soviet economic relations.

Nationalism in Central America and the Caribbean will also affect foreign policy directions and relations with the Soviet Union. The Caribbean and Central American states are not homogeneous nation-states like Japan or Germany. They are mixed ethnic-racial groups joined together into sovereign states. "Nationalism" suggests a homogeneous ethnic nation; the states of this area are not "nations" in this sense.

Yet many of these states are determined to minimize external control as much as possible and to plot as independent a course in world affairs as they can. They are just as acutely sensitive to Soviet or Cuban as to U.S. neocolonialism and imperialism. At the same time, ethnic-racial groups are achieving new self-identities and a growing sense of dignity in common group causes. Given these two distinct factors, these countries will not succumb easily to Soviet or Cuban neoimperialism. They are, however, likely to accept Soviet and Cuban aid—when they can get it on reasonable terms and if it serves their interest to do so.

The United States' power to influence the Caribbean and Central America is shaped by complex processes of change at work in the region. The region's political and economic problems do not lend themselves to simple, single-factor solutions.[62] The result is an impressive menace to U.S. interests, a combination of waning hegemony and ineffective policy responses. What Washington once considered a relatively secure area has now become a regional security threat. The area's expanding links with the USSR and Cuba symbolize the increased U.S. isolation within the "Caribbean lake."

Moscow's presence is part of a larger problem: the U.S. failure to deal effectively with revolutionary change spawned by underdevelopment.[63] Many reasons account for this failure. The region's geographic location led the United States to take it for granted for too long, notwithstanding sporadic attempts to deal with the economic and social realities affecting American strength. Executive and congressional obstacles continue to impede much-needed foreign aid legislation, as do events in distant countries that divert attention from America's own backyard. Interest groups meanwhile resist effective trade policies with the region; and the natural public fear of communism so close to U.S. shores complicates the matter further.

As long as these roadblocks to effective economic policy remain, it seems likely that Soviet involvement will continue. The opportunities will still be there, and a growing Soviet presence will make the formulation of effective foreign policy even more difficult. What is needed is the capacity to decouple events in the region from the Soviet and Cuban connection, at least insofar as underlying causes rather than overt symptoms are involved. While the United States cannot afford to be sanguine, the Soviet presence does not mean that the region is about to fall under Moscow's control.

The changes symbolized in the Caribbean and Central America by Soviet diplomacy are even broader than might be imagined. First, the transstate[64] ties of revolutionary governments in the region appear to be growing due to a consolidation of aspirations and ideologies, with continued isolation of the United States. Second, the types of opportunities available to Moscow in Grenada, Guyana, and Jamaica (under ex–Prime Minister Manley) in the Caribbean and in Nicaragua, El Salvador, and Guatemala in Central America could spread to Costa Rica,

Honduras, and Panama, as well as to the smaller Caribbean islands. Third, events in this region affect Mexico and Venezuela, both of which are deeply concerned about revolutionary changes.[65] The success of U.S. foreign policy in the Caribbean and Central America will affect its relations with these two key energy producers. The fate of the Caribbean and Central America is not unlinked to other events in Latin America.

Moscow's policies in the Caribbean and Central America indicate the growing need to forge a creative North American response to the region's development problems. The results to date are admittedly slim, yet the signs of a new awareness in Washington clearly exist. In recent testimony, William G. Bowdler, then assistant secretary for inter-American affairs, for example, stressed the need for stronger economic commitments to the Caribbean and Central America due to dramatic and rapid changes in the old order and their impact on U.S. security.[66] One major aspect of this complex process of change to which the U.S. government should expand its links and understanding is the increased radicalization of Catholic priests and nuns, especially in the Central American region.[67] The policy process remains plagued by bottlenecks, too little total aid, problems with trade, and confusion over what groups to aid and exactly how to do it. We can only hope that Soviet policy in the region will at least stimulate the U.S. to innovative rather than counterproductive responses.

Notes

1. For studies of recent Soviet policy in the Third World emphasizing the quest to project Soviet power and influence and, to a lesser extent, the desire to spread socialism, see *The Soviet Union and the Third World: A Watershed in Great Power Policy? Report to the Committee on International Relations, House of Representatives,* May 8, 1977; Alvin Z. Rubinstein, ed., *Soviet and Chinese Influence in the Third World* (New York: Praeger Publishers, 1975); Roger Kanet, ed., *The Soviet Union and the Developing Countries* (Baltimore: Johns Hopkins University Press, 1974); W. Raymond Duncan, ed., *Soviet Policy in the Third World* (New York: Pergamon, 1980); and Robert Legvold, "The Super Rivals: Conflict in the Third World," *Foreign Affairs* 57, no. 4 (Spring 1979): 755–78.

2. For background reading on domestic forces in the region and on American foreign policy responses, see Richard Millett and W. Marvin Will, eds., *The Restless Caribbean: Changing Patterns of International Relations* (New York: Praeger Publishers, 1979); W. Raymond Duncan, "Caribbean Leftism," *Problems of Communism* 27 (May–June 1978): 35–57; Royce Z. Shaw, *Central America: Regional Integration and National Political Development* (Boulder,

Colo.: Westview Press, 1979); Basil A. Ince, *Contemporary International Relations of the Caribbean* (Trinidad: University of the West Indies, Institute of International Relations, 1979); and Richard R. Fagen, "Dateline Nicaragua: The End of the Affair," *Foreign Policy* 36 (Fall 1979): 178–91.

3. See V. Vasilyev, "The United States' 'New Approach' to Latin America," *International Affairs* (Moscow), 1971, no. 6 (June): 43. For an analysis of this conceptualization, see Leon Gouré and Morris Rothenberg, *Soviet Penetration of Latin America* (Miami: University of Miami, Center for Advanced International Studies, 1975), pp. 5–6.

4. Soviet observers describe the nature of the present epoch as one in which socialism has become a world system, in which the socialist community "has firmly grasped the historical initiative . . . securing a further change in the balance of strength and continuing to crowd capitalism." See V. I. Popov, I. D. Ovsyany, and V. P. Nikhamin, eds., *A Study of Soviet Foreign Policy* (n.p., Soviet Union, 1975), pp. 18ff: also V. G. Bushuyev, *Latin America–Irreversible Processes* (Moscow: Znaniia, 1973), pp. 19–20, quoted in Gouré and Rothenberg, *Soviet Penetration*, p. 3. For the Soviet impact on Latin America, see C. Klochkovsky, "The Struggle for Economic Emancipation in Latin America," *International Affairs* (Moscow), 1979, no. 4 (April): 39–47.

5. John Bartlow Martin, *U.S. Policy in the Caribbean* (Boulder, Colo.: Westview Press, 1978), p. 138.

6. For the Soviet conceptualization of global economic interdependence, see Robert Legvold, "The USSR and the World Economy: The Political Dimension," in *The Soviet Union and the World Economy* (New York: Council on Foreign Relations, 1979), pp. 1–16. Also Elizabeth Kridl Valkenier, "The USSR, the Third World, and the Global Economy," *Problems of Communism* 34 (July–August 1979): 17–33.

7. See Martin, *U.S. Policy*, pp. 5–11, 138–44 for an analysis of American strategic interests in the region. Also James D. Theberge, *The Soviet Presence in Latin America* (New York: Crane, Russak & Company, 1974), chap. 4, for an analysis of Soviet interests in the area.

8. "Cuba's Role in the World," *International Affairs* (Moscow), 1980, no. 2 (February): 141–42, outlines many of Cuba's policies that make it so important to the USSR, including the island's help to liberation movements in Africa and Latin America.

9. Popov, Ovsyany, and Nikhamin, *A Study of Soviet Foreign Policy*, p. 151.

10. Moscow extended many types of economic aid to Cuba after 1960, including direct subsidies for Havana's trade deficits with Moscow, payment for Cuban sugar above the prevailing world market price, lowered prices for Soviet petroleum products, supplies of military equipment, and direct credits for economic development. Subsidies to cover bilateral trade deficits amounted to about $3.8 billion between 1960 and 1974; Moscow paid three to five times more than the prevailing world market prices for Cuban sugar during the 1960s

and provided several hundred million dollars in credits for economic development in the period. Arms transfers from Moscow to Havana amounted to several billion dollars in the 1970s. For a discussion of Soviet aid to Cuba and Cuban indebtedness to the USSR, see Jorge L. Dominguez, "Cuban Foreign Policy," *Foreign Affairs* 57, no. 1 (Fall 1978): 83–108.

11. By 1978, 38,650 Cuban military technicians were in Africa (the bulk in Angola and Ethiopia) and 1,150 in the Middle East (Iraq and South Yemen), supported by Soviet weapons, equipment, and transport. In addition, Cuban economic advisers were in Africa and the Middle East by 1978. See U.S., Central Intelligence Agency, National Foreign Assessment Center, *Communist Aid Activities in Non-Communist Less Developed Countries, 1978* (Washington, D.C., 1978), pp. 4, 14–15.

12. On the scope of Cuba's expanding relations with the Caribbean and Central America, see Tad Szulc, "Radical Winds in the Caribbean," *New York Times Magazine,* May 25, 1978, pp. 18ff; U.S., Congress, Senate, Committee on Foreign Relations, Subcommittee on Western Hemispheric Affairs, *Latin America: Hearings* (Washington, D.C.: Government Printing Office, October 4–6, 1978); U.S., Congress, House, Committee on Foreign Affairs, Subcommittee on Inter-American Affairs, *Economic and Political Future of the Caribbean: Hearings* (Washington, D.C.: Government Printing Office, July 24, 26, September 20, 1979); and U.S., Congress, House, Committee on Foreign Affairs, *Caribbean Nations: Assessments of Conditions and U.S. Influence. Report of a Special Study Mission to Jamaica, Cuba, the Dominican Republic, and the Guantanamo Naval Base, January 3–13, 1979* (Washington, D.C.: Government Printing Office, July 1979); and Duncan, "Caribbean Leftism." In March 1980, Franklin Kramer, deputy assistant secretary of defense, told a House subcommittee considering aid to El Salvador and Honduras that "Cuban influence in El Salvadoran and Honduran leftist organizations is long-standing, and there are clear indications the Cubans are assisting these groups in their attempt to overthrow the current government of El Salvador" through arms shipments (*Democrat and Chronicle,* [Rochester, N.Y.], March 26, 1980, p. 12A).

13. On the historic development of Soviet-Cuban ties, see Wyatt Mac-Gaffey and Clifford R. Barnett, *Twentieth Century Cuba* (New York: Anchor Books, 1965); and Andrés Suárez, *Cuba: Castroism and Communism, 1959–1966* (Cambridge, Mass.: Massachusetts Institute of Technology Press, 1967).

14. Radio Moscow, March 22–23, 1980, in *Foreign Broadcast Information Service (FBIS),* March 27, 1980. By April 1980, Moscow had added an embassy in Grenada (see statement submitted by Miles R. R. Frechette, director of Cuban affairs, U.S. Department of State, Bureau of Public Affairs, to the Subcommittee on Inter-American Affairs of the House Foreign Affairs Committee, April 17, 1980: Policy Statement no. 167, U.S. State Department, p. 2).

15. Duncan, "Caribbean Leftism," p. 33.

16. The Jamaican Communist Party (JCP) was founded in 1975, the Jamai-

can Workers' Party (JWP) in 1978. Both parties support Michael Manley's People's National Party, and the formation of both parties stimulated charges from the conservative Jamaican Labor Party that Cuba was fast at work subverting Jamaica. A representative of the Communist Party of the Soviet Union attended the founding congress of the JWP. This is not unusual given Moscow's consistent efforts to maintain fraternal relations with communist parties and Marxist guerrilla movements in the Caribbean and Central America, while working simultaneously through normal state-to-state channels with established governments of the same states. On the formation of the JWP and JCP, see Richard F. Staar, ed., *Yearbook on International Communist Affairs, 1980* (Stanford: Hoover Institution Press, 1980), pp. 371–72.

17. See *Keesing's Contemporary Archives*, June 29, 1979, pp. 29689–691, for background on the New Jewel coup of March 1979 in Grenada; see also George C. Abbot, "Grenada: Maverick or Pace-Maker in the West Indies?" *World Today*, April 1980, pp. 154–62; and for additional information, see coverage in *FBIS* and *Granma*, "Weekly Review in English," e.g., the March 9, 1980 issue, which carried an interview with Richard Jacobs, Grenadian ambassador to Cuba, on the first anniversary of the Grenadian revolution. The Cubans may have known of the New Jewel Movement's plan for a coup; there appears to be no evidence that they engineered it (Frechette testimony, p. 2).

18. Other Jamaican party officials have traveled to the USSR, such as the PNP's D. K. Duncan in March 1980 (*FBIS*, March 19, 1980; *Kingston Daily Gleaner*, March 11, 1980). Cuba's help to Jamaica involves assistance in improving Kingston's water supply, housing, and school construction, modernizing agricultural and fishing techniques, and medical and construction training—with Cuban doctors going to Jamaica and Jamaican youths going to Cuba (Frechette testimony, p. 2).

19. See Oakland Ross, "Jamaica at the Brink," *World Press Review*, April 1980, p. 32. Reports of an increased number of people at the Soviet Embassy in Kingston during 1979 did not help to allay these fears (see testimony of John A. Bushnell, deputy assistant secretary of state for inter-American affairs, before Subcommittee on Inter-American Affairs, House Committee on Foreign Affairs, July 24, 1979, *Economic and Political Future of the Caribbean*, p. 32).

20. Frechette testimony, p. 2; *Granma*, "Weekly Review in English," March 9, 1980, noted the work of twelve Cuban doctors; help in engineering, medicine, and agriculture; aid in water conservation; training in the fishing industry; and a pledge from Cuba to Grenada of eleven fishing boats, two of which had been delivered by March 1980.

21. *Current Digest of the Soviet Press*, January 16, 1980, p. 21.

22. See *Granma*, September 15, 23, 1976; and Ruben Berrios Martinez, "Independence for Puerto Rico: The Only Solution," *Foreign Affairs* 55, no. 3 (April 1977): 561–83.

23. For background information on the civil war, see *Keesing's Contemporary Archives*, September 7, 1979, pp. 29805–810; and William M. LeoGrande,

"The Revolution in Nicaragua: Another Cuba?" *Foreign Affairs* 58, no. 1 (Fall 1979): 28–50.

24. Available evidence suggests that Cuba supported the Sandinistas during 1979 through clandestine arms shipments (Frechette testimony, p. 2). Costa Rica and Panama also supported the Sandinistas.

25. The groups constituting the front were the Popular Revolutionary Bloc, the Front of United Popular Action, and the Popular Leagues–February 28. Total membership in the three factions is estimated as 75,000. (See *Facts on File*, January 18, 1980, p. 38.)

26. Testimony of Franklin Kramer, deputy assistant secretary of defense, *Democrat and Chronicle* (Rochester, N.Y.), March 26, 1980. State Department officials agreed with this estimate (see *Facts on File*, March 28, 1980, p. 220).

27. See *FBIS*, March 31, 1980; February 8, 1980; and February 5, 1980. In the words of *Pravda* (March 26, 1980), "Washington is behind the conspirators. It is the United States that is vigorously urging El Salvador reaction toward a Pinochet-type putsch." The March 24, 1980 assassination of Archbishop Oscar Arnulfo Romero, who had publicly advocated human rights and aid for the poor, brought strong criticism of the political right in the Soviet media.

28. The FDR includes Marxist-led peasant, labor, and student groups; social democrats; dissident Christian Democrats; and others. Enrique Alvarez Córdova, former minister of education and president of the coalition, stated that "the junta is being sustained exclusively by the United States" (*New York Times*, June 5, 1980, p. A7). The Soviets and Cubans agree with this analysis, as did a U.S. mission to Central America headed by Congressman Robert F. Drinan, who urged President Carter on June 5, 1980, to halt military aid to the Salvadoran junta (*Christian Science Monitor*, June 6, 1980).

29. See Alan Riding, "Guatemalans Fear a Bitter Struggle," *New York Times*, June 1, 1980, p. 13. About fifty labor leaders and professors at the University of San Carlos had been murdered by June 1980 alone; some two thousand people were killed over the previous eighteen months. Riding reported that repression campaign had forced the long-passive Indian population and democratic opposition leaders closer to the Marxist guerrilla groups.

30. *Granma*, March 9, 1980, p. 11.

31. The Soviet reference was to an article in *Business Week*, behind which, the Soviets argued, lay the Central Intelligence Agency's "absurd" and "dirty fabrications" (Tass, in English, April 5, 1980; *FBIS*, April 7, 1980).

32. For an excellent analysis of "dependency" perceptions, see Richard R. Fagen, "A Funny Thing Happened on the Way to the Market: Thoughts on Extending Dependency Ideas," *International Organization* 32, no. 1 (Winter 1978): 287–300.

33. See International Monetary Fund, *International Statistics* (Washington, D.C., June 1978).

34. See World Bank, *World Development Report, 1979* (Washington, D.C.: Oxford University Press, 1979), pp. 126–27.

35. George Thomas Kurian, *Encyclopedia of the Third World* (New York: Facts on File, 1978), p. 454.

36. Wendell Bell, "Inequality in Independent Jamaica: A Preliminary Appraisal of Elite Performance," *Revista/Review Interamericana* (San Juan), Summer 1977, p. 303.

37. Statistics in this paragraph from World Bank, *World Development Report, 1979*, pp. 158–59, 164–65, 170–71.

38. Popov, Ovsyany, Nikhamin, *A Study of Soviet Foreign Policy*, p. 149.

39. Expanded Caribbean and Central American (and Latin American) trade ties with the USSR "mirror the shifts in the entire system of international relations as a result of the growth of the forces of socialism" (ibid.).

40. CIA, *Communist Aid Activities*, pp. 12–13.

41. Michael Manley's trip to the USSR on April 9–11, 1979, produced this agreement (Tass, in English, April 11, 1979). Moscow also has a fishing agreement with Guyana.

42. CIA, *Communist Aid Activities*, p. 30.

43. On Soviet attention to these matters, see A. Shulgovsky, "The Social and Political Development in Latin America," *International Affairs* (Moscow), 1979, no. 11 (November): 52–61; and Klochkovsky, "Economic Emancipation," pp. 39–47.

44. Klochkovsky, "Economic Emancipation," p. 39.

45. S. Mishin, "Latin America: Two Trends of Development," *International Affairs* (Moscow), 1976, no. 6 (June): 54.

46. For a Soviet discussion of these issues, see M. Vasilyev, "Pan-Americanism Today: Rhetoric and Politics," *International Affairs* (Moscow), 1980, no. 2 (February): 28–37.

47. *New York Times*, October 24, 1979, p. A3.

48. *Granma*, September 16, 1979, p. 11.

49. Vasilyev, "Pan-Americanism Today," pp. 31–33.

50. See Rubinstein, *Soviet and Chinese Influence*.

51. U.S., Central Intelligence Agency, National Foreign Assessment Center, *Handbook of Economic Statistics*, (Washington, D.C., 1979), p. 113.

52. The United States is the largest contributor to the Inter-American Development Bank, which extended $792 million in loans to the Latin American countries in 1978. This compares to a *total* Third World net economic aid flow from the Soviet Union of $260 million in 1977. In 1979 the World Bank approved $43.5 million in two loans to Jamaica and a $20 million loan for education in Trinidad-Tobago (*World Bank News Releases*, no. 79/100, June 4, 1979, and no. 79/100, June 11, 1979). The U.S. Congress approved a $75 million aid package for Nicaragua in May 1980. In 1980 Jamaica once again suspended negotiations with the International Monetary Fund, for a variety of reasons.

53. CIA, *Handbook of Economic Statistics*, p. 119.

54. CIA, *Communist Aid Activities*, pp. 7–10.

55. Dominguez, "Cuban Foreign Policy," p. 90.

56. See Viktor Volsky, "Relative Maturity, Absolute Dependence," *World Marxist Review*, June 1979, pp. 40–45.

57. CIA, *Communist Aid Activities*, p. 25.

58. *New York Times*, August 31, 1979, p. A3.

59. Ibid., September 6, 1979, p. A14.

60. Ibid., January 15, 1980, p. A1.

61. Roger D. Hansen, *Beyond the North-South Stalemate* (New York: McGraw-Hill, 1979), pp. 5–6.

62. See the insightful essay by Alfred Stepan, "The U.S. and Latin America: Vital Interests and Instrument of Power," *Foreign Affairs*, special edition: "America and the World, 1979," 58, no. 3 (Spring 1980): 659–92.

63. See Richard Millett, "Central American Paralysis," *Foreign Policy* 39 (Summer 1980): 99–117.

64. "Transstate" refers to interregional travel and discussion, e.g., the visits of Jamaican leaders (under the Manley government) to Grenada, the visits to Grenada by leaders from other Caribbean islands after Bishop's victory, and the travel between Cuba and leftist-leaning governments. Also at work here are the effects of Nicaragua's revolution on leftist leaders in El Salvador and Guatemala.

65. Jamaica has secured a major oil-for-bauxite contract with Mexico, and both Mexico and Venezuela played helpful roles in the Sandinista victory over Somoza. On the first event, see *Latin American Weekly Report*, February 15, 1980, p. 3; on Venezuelan solidarity with Nicaragua, see *FBIS*, April 1, 1980, quoting Managua Domestic Service in Spanish, March 29, 1980; on the current significance of earlier Mexican and Venezuelan support relative to Washington's ineffective policy responses, see Millett, "Central American Paralysis"; and on Venezuelan discussions with Caribbean leaders, see *Joint Publications Research Service, Inter-American Affairs*, April 18, 1980, quoting *Kingston Daily Gleaner*, in English, April 2, 1980, p. 12.

66. Bowdler testimony, U.S. State Department, Policy Statement no. 167, April 17, 1980.

67. See Alan Riding, "The Sword and Cross," *New York Review of Books*, May 28, 1981, pp. 3–8.

2 | CUBA

William M. LeoGrande

Located only ninety miles south of Florida and dominating the eastern approaches to the Caribbean basin, Cuba has long been of major economic and strategic interest to the United States. Despite Spanish colonial restrictions on trade outside the empire, the United States became Cuba's principal trade partner early in the nineteenth century. Over the following decades several U.S. administrations tried to purchase Cuba from Spain, but the Spanish were unwilling to part with the island.[1] At the turn of the century, when U.S. investors began to explore business opportunities beyond continental North America, the proximity of Cuba made it a logical choice for foreign investment. The collapse of the world sugar market in the 1890s and the resulting bankruptcy of the Cuban economy provided an ideal opportunity for foreign investors and marked the first large-scale acquisition of Cuban property by U.S. citizens.[2] Cuba, like Mexico, has sometimes suffered for its nearness to the United States. Cuba's second war of independence (1895–1898) aroused strong feelings in the United States, which were whipped to feverish intensity by journalistic sensationalism. Also, war damage to U.S. property on the island helped to enlist powerful private interests on the side of intervention. In 1898, the United States entered the war, quickly defeated Spain, and occupied Cuba.

The Spanish-American War revived the doctrine of Manifest Destiny, as the United States acquired its first colonies, Puerto Rico and the Philippines. President Theodore Roosevelt and Adm. Alfred Thayer

Mahan believed that a global geopolitical role for America required naval power—specifically, a Central American canal and the naval outposts necessary for its defense. Cuba's geographical position thus made it strategically important.[3]

A friendly Cuba was considered essential to American economic and military security. The U.S.-imposed Platt amendment to the Cuban Constitution of 1902 reduced Cuba to a virtual protectorate by prohibiting it from signing any foreign agreement inimical to U.S. interests and by giving the U.S. government the right to intervene in Cuban domestic affairs in case of political turmoil. Several times in the early decades of the twentieth century, the amendment was invoked to justify the landing of American troops in Cuba. The Platt amendment and subsequent U.S. interventions imparted a distinctly anti-U.S. flavor to Cuban nationalism.[4]

One of the top priorities of the revolutionary government that came to power in 1959 was to reduce Cuba's economic and political dependence on the United States. Since ousted dictator Fulgencio Batista had long been a friend of the United States, Fidel Castro and his guerrillas were wary of the U.S. reaction to their revolution. Neither Cuba nor the United States were particularly diplomatic during 1959 and 1960. Castro berated U.S. imperialism; the United States denounced Castro's radicalism. Although Cuba's transition to socialism was due largely to domestic social and political dynamics,[5] there is no doubt that the collapse of friendly relations between Cuba and the United States left moderate, pro-American domestic political forces isolated and impotent. As the rhetoric grew vitriolic, relations between the United States and Cuba rapidly deteriorated, and the spiral of hostility became irreversible.[6]

The strategic consequences of this enmity proved to be great. Faced with U.S. economic sanctions and the threat of military intervention, Cuba sought security through reliance on the Soviet Union. Soviet military assistance armed the Cuban government against both internal and external enemies. Soviet economic aid ensured Cuba's survival following the severing of Cuba's close economic ties with the United States.[7]

The Evolution of Cuban Socialism

By the end of 1960, most of the Cuban economy had been nationalized, and the nation's new leaders confronted two central tasks: the development of a planned economy and the creation of a new political system.

The radical redistributive policies of 1959–1960 stimulated demand, brought the economy's excess capacity into production, and produced two years of rapid growth. On the basis of this success, Cuban leaders adopted an ambitious strategy of industrialization and agricultural diversification away from sugar. The immense cost of industrialization, however, exceeded the financial capacity of the Cuban economy. Disruptions in production caused by the abolition of the market and the exodus of managerial personnel led to a severe recession in 1962. As sugar production fell, so did foreign exchange earnings, producing a major balance of payments crisis. The Soviet Union financed this deficit with trade credits, but was unwilling to underwrite such massive shortfalls indefinitely. In 1963, after consulting with the Soviet Union, Cuba abandoned the industrialization strategy in favor of an export-oriented strategy emphasizing Cuba's comparative advantage in sugar. The receipts from sugar exports were then to be used to develop the rest of the economy.[8] The government set ten million tons of sugar by 1970 as both an economic and a political goal.

This new development strategy was as overly optimistic as its predecessor. The previous record for the Cuban sugar industry was approximately 7.5 million tons. Meeting the 1970 goal required a 33 percent expansion—an immense investment over a very short period. The planning apparatus created during the 1960s proved too rudimentary to manage such rapid growth. In 1970, Cuba produced 8.5 million tons of sugar—a new record, but still far short of the announced goal. Even this was purchased at great cost to the rest of the economy. In a final effort to meet the goal, planners diverted resources from other economic sectors, causing major losses in virtually every other area of production. The failure was a political defeat as well. For half a decade, the 1970 sugar harvest had been the symbolic test of the revolution's progress. In the wake of the failure, Cuba's leaders not only revised economic policy but also reassessed Cuba's political structures.[9]

Cuba was the first country to have a Marxist-Leninist revolution without a communist party in the vanguard of the revolutionary struggle. The old communist party had played only a marginal role in the insurrection. After Castro's victory, it was only one of several revolutionary organizations forming the new political system. The most important group was Castro's Twenty-Sixth of July Movement. The victorious guerrilla army that defeated Batista and took effective control of the island in 1959 constituted the more radical wing of this movement— an important factor in determining the revolution's leftist course over the two years after 1959.

The creation of permanent political institutions in Cuba proceeded slowly, largely due to Fidel Castro's charismatic style of political leadership. Much of the revolution's popular support was support for Fidel;

the leaders of the revolution, Castro foremost among them, were unwilling to jeopardize this support by institutionalizing the regime too rapidly. This caution was reinforced by the first few experiments with new political institutions, virtually all of which were disappointments.[10]

The most significant of these experiments was the 1961 attempt to build a new vanguard party by merging the old communist party, the Twenty-Sixth of July Movement, and a student group (the Revolutionary Directorate) that had also fought against Batista. The new party, the Integrated Revolutionary Organizations (Organizaciones Integradas Revolucionarias; ORI), quickly fell under the control of the old Communists, whose organizational experience was superior to that of other members. In early 1962, an attempt by some old Communists to usurp control of the revolution provoked a public denunciation of the ORI from Fidel Castro. It was dismantled within months, and Cuba was once again the only Marxist state without a ruling communist party.

Although a new communist party (Partido Comunista de Cuba; PCC) was inaugurated in 1965, it did not really rule. Its committees rarely met, and its membership in 1969 was only 0.7 percent of the population (relatively only a tenth as large as the average ruling communist party).[11] Control of the political system remained in the hands of Fidel Castro and his closest advisers—the revolutionary family who had fought together in the mountains.

The event that finally led to the institutionalization of the revolution was the failure of the 1970 sugar harvest. The leadership's conclusion that the weakness of Cuba's institutional structure had been one of the key causes of the failure initiated a decade of institution building. Within five years, the PCC expanded nearly fivefold and began to play the leading role typical of ruling communist parties. But institutional changes were by no means restricted to the party. The administrative bureaucracy was completely reorganized, and a legislative branch of government was created. Begun in the mid-1960s, the Organs of People's Power provided for more direct popular participation in Cuban politics, especially at the local level, than had been possible in the early 1960s. These elected assemblies also supervised the performance of the bureaucracy, a task the PCC had performed poorly.[12]

The 1970s witnessed both a political and an economic rationalization. Rising world sugar prices at mid-decade benefited the economy, and Cuba appeared on its way as a showcase of socialism in the Third World.

The 1980s, however, brought new problems. The most dramatic indication of the crisis was the exodus of some 120,000 refugees in early 1980. The principal catalyst for this flood was an economic recession.

Crop diseases decimated both the sugar and tobacco crops, two of Cuba's largest export commodities. The consequent drop in foreign exchange earnings forced a reduction in imports, producing a decline in both economic growth and consumption.[13] The government's mismanagement of the economy aggravated the resulting shortages, and the regime now seems willing to experiment with some limited economic reforms that would give market forces a larger economic role.[14]

Various factors have intensified the political impact of Cuba's economic difficulties. As a result of agreements concluded between the Cuban government and representatives of the émigré community abroad, 110,000 exiles visited Cuba in 1979. Many brought with them consumer goods unavailable in Cuba. For the Cubans who had lived through two decades of austerity, the sharp contrast in living standards between themselves and the visitors was demoralizing. Cuba's commitments in Africa have also sparked a feeling that large-scale aid to foreign governments is a luxury for the austere Cuban economy.[15]

As the Cuban revolution enters its third decade, its political and economic problems are serious, though not yet as serious as the problems encountered in 1970. Neither the economy nor the government is on the verge of collapse.

Cuban-Soviet Relations

The Soviet Union did not rush to aid the Cuban revolution. For the first eighteen months after the guerrillas' victory, the Soviets did little more than establish normal diplomatic and trade relations with the island.[16] Even this contributed to the deterioration of U.S.-Cuban relations, however, since the United States was unaccustomed to diplomatic relations between the Soviet Union and Latin American countries.

The cautiousness of Soviet policy was intended to provide no excuse for a direct U.S. intervention against the revolutionary government. The USSR maintained this policy until the United States canceled Cuba's sugar quota in mid-1960. The Soviets thereupon moved boldly to provide large-scale economic and military assistance to the hard-pressed government.

The Bay of Pigs fiasco in April 1961 cemented the new Cuban-Soviet alliance. The installation of Soviet intermediate-range ballistic missiles in Cuba was a logical extension of the partnership. For Cuba, the missiles provided a deterrent against a U.S. invasion. For the Soviet Union, they were an opportunity to reduce U.S. nuclear superiority. The withdrawal of the missiles, however, nearly shattered the alliance. The Cubans felt betrayed at being stripped of their deterrent and insulted at being left out of the negotiations that resolved the crisis. In early 1963, Cuba signaled the United States that it was interested in rapprochement, but President Kennedy's assassination halted the dialogue. Similar initiatives in the summer of 1964 were no more productive.

During the remainder of the decade, Cuba expanded and deepened its ties with the Soviet Union despite serious ideological differences. In the late 1960s, Cuba's radical foreign and domestic policies, including an economic strategy emphasizing central planning and a near exclusive reliance on moral incentives, drew sharp Soviet criticism. Carmelo Mesa-Lago has described this period as the "Sino-Guevarist" stage of the revolution because Guevara was its chief exponent and because it closely resembled Chinese theories of development.[17] The Cubans openly disparaged the use of material incentives and market-oriented reforms in other socialist countries—most notably in the Soviet Union— hinting that they augured the restoration of capitalism.

Despite such attacks, the Soviets continued their large-scale economic aid to Cuba, in effect financing Cuba's "ultraleft" experiments. Only one incident suggests Soviet sanctions. In 1967, Soviet petroleum shipments to Cuba were delayed, ostensibly for lack of transport. Normal shipments resumed after several months, but many commentators interpret this incident as a warning to Cuba that there were limits to Soviet tolerance for Cuban deviations.[18] Cuban economic policy did not change after this incident (though it did after the failure of the 1970 sugar harvest), but Cuban-Soviet relations did begin to improve.

Cuba's foreign policy in the late 1960s was aimed at aggressively exporting revolution to Latin American participants in the Organization of American States' (OAS) embargo of Cuba. The Soviets criticized this strategy as ineffective, but Cuba generally denigrated Soviet reservations as self-serving. The Soviet Union's pursuit of détente seemed to Cuba an abdication of socialist internationalism, and the Cubans vocally demanded increased Soviet aid to revolutionary movements abroad.[19] Cuban criticism, however, did not result in any reduction in Soviet military aid. In 1968, Cuba's attacks on Soviet foreign policy waned, and Castro endorsed the Soviet intervention in Czechoslovakia.

Soviet-Cuban relations in the late 1960s were complex and multifaceted. Despite major ideological and political friction over foreign and domestic policy, the bedrock of the relationship—economic and military aid to Cuba—was virtually unaffected by the polemics. The Soviet expansion of economic aid in 1971 after the less than successful 1970 sugar harvest markedly improved Cuban-Soviet relations.

Economic and political reforms in 1971 brought the Cuban system into much closer alignment with Soviet practice, thereby eliminating one major source of discord. At the same time, Cuba abandoned its policy of exporting revolution, largely because of its ineffectiveness. For the first time, Cuba officially endorsed the Soviet doctrine of peaceful coexistence.[20]

In 1975–1976, Cuban-Soviet collaboration rose to new heights as Cuba dispatched some 36,000 combat troops to help the Popular Movement for Liberation of Angola defeat its rivals and their international allies (Zaire, South Africa) in the Angolan civil war. Although available evidence suggests that the initiative was Cuban, it was nevertheless made possible only by Soviet logistical support. In 1978, the two allies mounted another joint venture, this time to help Ethiopia's leftist government defend the Ogaden region against Somali aggression. By the late 1970s, Cuba and the Soviet Union were cooperating in several African and Middle Eastern countries.[21] These ventures, combined with Cuba's role as chief spokesman for the socialist camp within the nonaligned movement, provided the Soviet Union with the first, big tangible benefits from its two decades of aid to Cuba.[22]

Since the early 1960s, the Soviet Union has provided all the military equipment used by Cuba's armed forces. After the Angolan civil war, the technological sophistication of Soviet arms assistance increased considerably, as did the amount, which reached a level approximately twice that of the early 1970s.[23] Several thousand Soviet military advisers assist the Cuban armed forces in areas ranging from technical advice to combat training. Maneuvers conducted in 1979 by some 2,000 Soviet military personnel set off the celebrated "Soviet combat brigade" crisis.[24]

The Soviet Union has also provided economic assistance to Cuba since 1961. The largest component of the Soviet aid package during the 1960s and early 1970s was balance of payments credits. Cuban-Soviet trade perennially resulted in a Cuban trade deficit, which the Soviet Union then absorbed by granting credits on concessionary terms. By 1973, such credits totaled nearly $2 billion. Since 1973, the major means of aid has been preferential pricing. The Soviet Union pays premium prices for Cuban sugar and nickel while charging below-market prices for petroleum. In essence, this new accounting procedure simply shifts the financing of the trade imbalance from credits to grants. As the Cuban economy encountered difficulties in the late 1970s, the level of Soviet economic aid grew from approximately $600 million per year in 1971–1974 to $2 billion per year in 1975–1977 and $3 billion in 1978–1979. Soviet aid between 1961 and 1981 totals over $16 billion.[25] The floundering Cuban economy may well require even greater infusions of

Soviet aid in the years ahead, but since the investment has finally begun to pay political dividends, the Soviets will almost certainly provide whatever is necessary.

As Cuba enters the 1980s, its relationship with the Soviet Union is as close as at any time since 1959. The Reagan administration's hard line on Cuba, including threats of military action against the island, has sharply increased the Cubans' perception of a U.S. menace. In early 1981, Cuba seemed to respond to this perceived danger by drawing closer to the Soviet Union.

In an address to the PCC's Second Congress in December 1980, Castro endorsed the Soviet invasion of Afghanistan and provided what amounted to a justification before the fact of a Soviet invasion of Poland.[26] The quid pro quo was not long in coming; in an address to the Czechoslovak party congress in April 1981, Soviet party chief Leonid Brezhnev singled Cuba out as an "inseparable member of the socialist camp"—a clear warning to the United States that military action against Cuba would provoke a superpower confrontation.[27]

But despite the close coordination that now characterizes Cuban and Soviet foreign policies, it is a mistake to view Cuban policy as merely derivative. The Cubans have long had their own view on a correct revolutionary foreign policy and have pursued it consistently with or without Soviet support.

Relations with Latin America

The ideology of the Cuban revolution has always had a strong internationalist dimension. Even before Cuba adopted a socialist path of development, its new leaders offered the island as a haven to revolutionaries from around the hemisphere and in some instances supported their activities. Nor was Cuban support limited to the Western Hemisphere; assistance to anticolonial movements in Algeria and Portuguese Africa dates from the earliest years of the revolutionary government.[28]

In the 1960s, the example of the Cuban revolution spawned guerrilla movements in most Latin American nations. Cuba endorsed virtually all of them and provided material assistance to many. Since the Cuban revolution lacked the classic Leninist requirement of a vanguard party in the early 1960s, it gave rise not only to Castroist guerrillas seeking to emulate Cuba's revolutionary experience but also to a new theory of revolution. The strategy of Régis Debray, a French journalist turned Cuban revolutionary, depreciated the significance of orthodox communist parties, lauding instead the vanguard role of the guerrilla army. Debray, in a sense, inverted Mao Zedong's famous dictum: in Latin America, the gun would control the party.[29]

Cuba's support for Latin America's guerrillas and its endorsement of Debrayism brought it into conflict with the hemisphere's communist parties, most of which were pursuing united or popular front strategies emphasizing electoral competition. When Cuba sponsored the Tricontinental Conference in 1966, it invited few communist parties from Latin America to this unprecedented international assembly of revolutionaries.[30] The Soviet Union's attempt to mediate the conflict between Cuban Communists and their hemispheric colleagues was unsuccessful. Cuba's unyielding support for armed struggle and its hostility toward peaceful coexistence strained Cuban-Soviet relations in the late 1960s, though never to the point of causing an open break between them.

The insurrectionary activities of the late 1960s met with little success. Latin American guerrillas were no match for the counterinsurgency forces deployed against them under the security assistance programs of the U.S. Alliance for Progress. Che Guevara's death in Bolivia in 1967 while trying to create a *foco* for continental guerrilla war prompted a re-evaluation of the Debrayist strategy of revolution. By 1969, Cuba had for all practical purposes abandoned the policy of indiscriminate material support for guerrilla movements.[31]

For several years, no replacement for the defunct strategy of exporting revolution emerged. From 1968 to 1972, Cuba turned inward, preoccupied with the drive to produce ten million tons of sugar in 1970 and its aftermath. This retreat from foreign involvement was so startling that it led at least one commentator to describe Cuba's domestic preoccupation as "socialism in one island."[32] When Cuba re-emerged on the world scene in 1972, its foreign policy was considerably changed.

The guerrilla movements that Cuba supported in the late 1960s had failed to achieve any success through armed struggle, but in several Latin American countries, the left was making gains through unexpected methods that Cuba had always disparaged. In Chile, the Popular Unity electoral coalition of Communists and Socialists won the 1970 election; in Peru, the military government appeared to be enacting a revolution from above; and in Argentina, the Peronist left had returned from the political wilderness through the election of Héctor Cámpora. All three countries broke OAS sanctions against Cuba by re-establishing diplomatic and economic ties. In the new international climate of détente, even conservative Latin American regimes showed a willingness to normalize relations with Cuba. The newly independent nations in the English-speaking Caribbean, historically more politically independent of the United States, promoted Cuba's reintegration into hemispheric affairs. Not having been targets of Cuba's earlier efforts to export revolution, these states were less fearful of Cuban subversion. Indeed, several Caribbean nations were ruled by left-leaning populist governments.

As a result of such favorable developments in the early 1970s, Cuba adopted a hemispheric foreign policy much more conciliatory and tolerant of ideological diversity. Rather than seeking to end its isolation in the hemisphere by revolution, Cuba sought to do so by diplomacy—establishing normal state-to-state relations whenever it found willing governments. Inevitably, this new strategy required a sharp reduction in aid to guerrilla movements. Cuba continued to be a haven for Latin America's revolutionaries, but its program of arms assistance virtually halted.[33]

Cuba's conciliatory approach to its neighbors had considerable initial success. Until finally relaxed in 1975, the OAS sanctions were undermined by a continuous stream of defections during the early 1970s. Even the United States appeared willing to renew normal diplomatic and economic ties, and secret negotiations between the two states began in 1974.[34]

By the late 1970s, however, progress on the diplomatic front had halted. Cuba's military involvement in Angola and Ethiopia, both carried out in coordination with the Soviet Union, demolished prospects for normalization of relations between Cuba and the United States. These conflicts initiated a new cold war, with Cuba once again the focal point of the growing antagonism between East and West.[35]

In Latin America, the departure of Cuban troops for Africa resurrected the fears of the late 1960s—Castro once again seemed to be pursuing a militant policy of promoting revolutions abroad. Although no Latin American governments broke relations with Cuba over Angola and Ethiopia, the process of reintegrating Cuba into the inter-American community slowed perceptibly.[36]

Cuba entered the 1980s with a three-tiered policy toward the hemisphere. Its relations with its neighbors run the gamut from cordial to hostile, and Cuba has distinct policies for different categories of nations. The largest group consists of those countries that maintain normal state-to-state relations with Cuba, ranging from warm to merely "proper" (for example, Mexico, Argentina, Ecuador, Peru, Venezuela). Toward these countries, Cuba continued to pursue the conciliatory diplomatic strategy it adopted in 1970.

Cuba's relations with Mexico have improved noticeably in recent years. New commercial agreements, including one for Mexican petroleum, indicate that Mexico's increasingly activist policy in the Caribbean will not ignore the Cubans. During a trip to Cuba in 1980, Mexican President José López Portillo even promised Mexican support for Cuba should the United States become actively hostile.[37]

Cuba's relations with Venezuela and Peru, however, deteriorated after the occupation of the Peruvian Embassy compound in Havana by some ten thousand Cubans in April 1980. The incident strained Cuba's relations not only with Peru but also with Venezuela, since Venezuelan policy toward those seeking asylum in their Embassy was the same as Peru's. Shortly after the incident, Venezuela released several Cuban exiles accused of the 1976 sabotage of a Cubana airlines flight that exploded after leaving Barbados, killing everyone aboard. Cuba denounced their release in the strongest possible terms; and Venezuela, for a time, considered breaking relations with Cuba.[38] The implications of Cuba's dispute with Peru and Venezuela could be profound since the Andean Pact nations were in the forefront during the 1970s of those advocating Cuban reintegration into the inter-American system. If Cuba's relations with the Andean states do not improve, it is doubtful that Cuba's overall strategy of reducing tensions with its Latin American neighbors will progress appreciably in the near future.

Cuba's efforts at diplomatic reconciliation were not uniformly successful, and there remains a small group of countries (Chile, Uruguay, Brazil, El Salvador, Guatemala) whose relations with Cuba are as hostile today as they were in 1965. (In early 1981 Colombia and Costa Rica became the two latest members of this group when they severed relations with Cuba.) During the 1970s, the Cuban press regularly denounced their authoritarian governments, but Cuban policy essentially ignored them. Promoting insurrection against these governments would have undermined Cuba's strategy toward the rest of the hemisphere.

CENTRAL AMERICA

In Central America, Cuba modified its policy of reduced support for revolutionary movements in 1978–1979. The failure of the policy of exporting revolution during the late 1960s had convinced the Cubans that prospects for revolution in Latin America were dim, a conclusion that led to the adoption of the diplomatic strategy. But the unsuccessful September 1978 insurrection in Nicaragua persuaded the Cubans that they had underestimated the strength of the left in Central America. In late 1978 and early 1979, Cuba began once again to provide material assistance to guerrillas operating in Nicaragua, El Salvador, and Guatemala. The Sandinistas in Nicaragua were first beneficiaries of this new policy.[39]

Cuban assistance, however, was much more circumscribed than it had been in the previous decade. The Sandinistas received only a few crates of arms; Cuba's major contribution to the revolution in Nicaragua was to help mediate divisions among the three factions of the Sandinista movement. Several reasons lay behind Cuba's reluctance to become too deeply involved in supplying arms to the Nicaraguan left. Foremost was the fear that a major involvement would undo Cuba's diplomatic progress in its relations with moderate governments in the hemisphere. Another concern was that a significant Cuban presence would provoke U.S. retaliation. Although the United States did not desert Anastasio Somoza politically until the very end, neither did Washington come to his aid by supplying him with arms. Had the Cubans been more deeply involved in the Nicaraguan insurrection, the chances of U.S. intervention would have been much greater and the hemisphere's resistance to Secretary of State Cyrus Vance's 1979 suggestion for an OAS peacekeeping force might have been considerably less. Indeed, Latin Americans met Vance's attempt to justify the peacekeeping force by referring to Cuban involvement in Nicaragua with skepticism.[40] Further, the Nicaraguan revolutionaries were already receiving adequate support from other quarters, notably Costa Rica, Panama, and Venezuela.

The Sandinista victory renewed Cuba's faith in the revolutionary potential of Central America—particularly of El Salvador and Guatemala. In 1979 and 1980, Cuba provided limited quantities of arms to guerrilla forces in El Salvador. Following the pattern established in Nicaragua, Cuba acted as a consultant on strategy and helped to unify the fragmented Salvadoran left—to the Cubans a necessary condition for victory.[41]

In late 1980, the Salvadoran guerrillas began preparations for a massive offensive to achieve victory before Reagan's inauguration. According to U.S. intelligence reports, large-scale arms shipments began entering Salvador in late 1980, some of which came from Cuba through Nicaragua.[42] Although the size of the shipments was a matter of some controversy, it seemed clear that the Cubans had increased their logistical support to the Salvadoran guerrillas in late 1980 and early 1981. When the guerrillas' general offensive in January failed, the flow of arms ebbed.[43] The danger of greater internationalization of the conflict remained acute, however.

Through 1979 and 1980, guerrilla forces in Guatemala gained significant strength, and the level of internal conflict grew accordingly. While there is as yet no evidence of sizable Cuban arms shipments to the Guatemalan left, the potential for such support is obviously real, especially in light of Cuba's role in Nicaragua and El Salvador.

Cuba has maintained close and cordial relations with the new Nicaraguan government. Although the Nicaraguan government has pledged to allow political pluralism, it is dominated by the Sandinista National Liberation Front (FSLN). The FSLN's Marxism is more orthodox than that of left-wing regimes in the Caribbean; and the revolution in Nicaragua has thus far been more thoroughgoing than the populist changes in Jamaica, Guyana, or Grenada.[44] This, combined with Cuba's support for the FSLN since the late 1960s, has brought Cuba and Nicaragua very close.[45]

Within days of Somoza's downfall, Cuba pledged to help rebuild the Nicaraguan economy. Since then, Cuba and Nicaragua have signed cooperative agreements in the fields of health, education, agriculture, and construction. About 2,500 Cuban technicians and advisers were in Nicaragua in late 1979; most were involved in the literacy campaign, which was modeled after the Cuban effort of 1961. Some Cuban advisers also work with the Nicaraguan armed forces and security ministries.[46]

As Nicaraguans search for a viable political and economic structure to replace *Somocismo*, Cuba has cautioned moderation. Fidel Castro has become a close adviser of FSLN leaders, but his advice tends toward pragmatism, not militancy. Cuba paid a heavy price for its rapid transition to socialism in the early 1960s—the exodus of the technically skilled middle class, dependence on the Soviet Union, and hemispheric isolation. Castro has reportedly advised the Nicaraguans to avoid Cuba's mistakes by following a moderate economic policy that retains a substantial private sector and can gain the confidence of international financial institutions and the United States. Ironically, Cuba's influence has kept more militant leaders of the FSLN from radicalizing the Nicaraguan revolution.[47]

In early 1981, the Nicaraguan government felt itself under increasing external threat. The ongoing war in El Salvador, combined with the Reagan administration's anticommunism and its suspension of aid to Nicaragua, convinced at least some FSLN leaders that efforts to overthrow the government were in gestation. Nicaragua's enemies were by no means wholly imaginary: ex-members of Somoza's National Guard launched periodic forays into Nicaragua from training camps in Honduras and border tensions with the Hondurans were on the rise.[48]

In the event of war between Nicaragua and Honduras, the Nicaraguan government might ask Cuba for direct military aid in the form of arms, advisers, or even troops. Such a scenario would fit precisely the conditions under which Cuba has dispatched combat troops abroad in the past: a friendly government under external attack. Given the close relations between Cuba and Nicaragua, Cuba would be highly likely to respond positively.

THE CARIBBEAN

The newest aspect of Cuba's policy in the Western Hemisphere is the effort to expand its influence among the English-speaking states of the Caribbean.[49] When reconciliation with Latin America stalled in the mid-1970s, Cuba turned to the Caribbean as a region where it might cultivate new friends. Cuba had paid scant attention to this area in the 1960s because most of the territories were still colonies. Thus, relations with the region were not hindered by earlier Cuban efforts to foment revolution in these states.

The principal instrument of Cuban policy in the Caribbean has been economic assistance to those states willing to establish cordial relations. Although Cuba has few resources, the economies of the Caribbean islands are small enough for even limited aid to have a significant impact. Cuban aid consists primarily of human capital—technicians, laborers, and teachers whose salaries are paid by the Cuban government.

Cuba has been only marginally more successful in the English-speaking Caribbean than in the rest of Latin America. Barbados, Trinidad-Tobago, Jamaica, and Guyana established diplomatic relations with Cuba in 1972 in disregard of the OAS sanctions.[50] But relations with Barbados and Trinidad-Tobago never evolved much beyond "proper" state-to-state relations.[51] Indeed, as Cuba has expanded efforts to build its influence in the Caribbean, relations with conservative governments in the region have suffered. The worst setback came in mid-1980 when Cuban fighter planes attacked and sank a Bahaman naval vessel in Bahaman waters. Although Cuba eventually apologized for the attack and paid compensation, the incident shocked many governments in the region, making them newly wary of Cuban military power.[52]

The emergence of "Caribbean socialism" in Jamaica, Guyana, and Grenada seemed to provide a set of states with at least some ideological affinity with Cuba's own development model, and it was to these states that most economic aid has been channeled. Even in these cases, however, Cuba's success has been relatively limited.

Guyana's warm relations with Cuba date from the early 1970s when, in an about-face, Guyanese President Forbes Burnham declared himself a Marxist and Guyana a "cooperative republic."[53] This new course has been characterized by moderately socialistic policies domestically and fairly radical ones internationally. During the 1970s, Burnham sought an activist role for Guyana in the nonaligned movement, where it sided with the radical wing. As Cuba became chief spokesman for the radical states in the late 1970s, the two countries often found themselves ideological allies in the political battles of the Third World. The coincidence of Cuban and Guyanese international views blossomed into friendship when Burnham allowed Cuban transport planes en route to Angola to refuel in Guyana in December 1975. Over the next few years, Burnham signed several economic and technical agreements with Cuba. Some of these provide for Cuban aid to Guyana, especially in the field of sugar production; but Cuba's overall aid has been relatively small. About one hundred Cuban advisers are in Guyana.[54]

Domestically, Burnham's Marxism has always been more rhetorical than real. His conversion was largely attributable to the growing popularity of his chief rival, the communist Cheddi Jagan. The latter's credentials as a Marxist are more reputable than Burnham's, and the Cubans would probably not be upset to see Jagan replace Burnham as prime minister. In 1980, Burnham seemed to reverse course once again, returning to the conservative domestic policies he had championed before 1970. The key event in the turnabout was Guyana's willingness to accept the International Monetary Fund's economic stabilization plan in order to secure funding to develop an aluminum industry.[55]

Burnham's more conservative domestic course has been accompanied by rising tensions with Cuba, including accusations that Cuba has aided Jagan and has not observed its fishing agreement with Guyana. Cuban influence thus seems to be waning in one of the three Caribbean states that have been among Cuba's closest friends.[56]

The overwhelming victory of Edward Seaga's Jamaican Labor Party in 1980 was a much severer blow to Cuba's efforts to expand its influence in the Caribbean. Jamaica had been Cuba's most consistent friend in the Western Hemisphere since the 1972 election of Michael Manley. While Manley's radical, populist "socialism" differed considerably from Cuban Marxism-Leninism, there was nevertheless a degree of ideological closeness. As an avid participant in the nonaligned movement, Manley pursued a foreign policy that was often in agreement with Cuba's. When Cuba's intervention in Angola damaged its relations with a number of governments in the hemisphere, Manley's support was unequivocal: "We regard Cuban assistance to Angola as honorable and in the best interests of all those who care for African freedom."[57]

Cuba's economic assistance program to Manley's Jamaica was typical of such programs elsewhere. Since Cuba lacks the resources to provide financial aid to friendly governments, it concentrates on providing skilled labor in such fields as health, education, construction, transportation, and communications. Cuba and Jamaica had cooperative economic agreements in all these areas, and Jamaica was host to nearly a thousand Cuban economic advisers, by far the largest Cuban aid mission in the Caribbean.[58]

As the largest of the English-speaking islands, Jamaica has historically been a political bellwether for the Caribbean. Manley's move to establish close ties with Cuba was widely interpreted as presaging a general increase in Cuban influence in the region; Manley's defeat may well herald a decline in Cuba's regional position. Seaga waged his campaign in part against Manley's ties with Cuba, and one of his first official acts was to expel the Cuban ambassador.[59] No doubt Seaga will now join with other conservative governments in the area in a general effort to stem Cuban influence.

The new revolutionary government in Grenada is Cuba's one remaining close friend in the Caribbean. Cuba greeted the ouster of Eric Gairy by Maurice Bishop's socialist New Jewel Movement in March 1979 as a revolutionary breakthrough in the region. When Bishop requested military aid to thwart any attempt by Gairy to return to power, Cuba responded quickly by providing light arms and a few dozen military advisers.[60]

The sudden blossoming of Cuba's relationship with Grenada worried the United States, which warned Bishop that a close relationship with Cuba would prejudice relations with Washington. The Grenadian government reacted acrimoniously, and diplomatic relations with the United States have been deteriorating ever since.[61] The rhetoric of the New Jewel government has been strongly "anti-imperialist," and Grenada has ostentatiously sided with the Soviet bloc internationally; it was, for example, the only noncommunist government to vote against the January 1980 U.N. resolution on withdrawal of Soviet troops from Afghanistan.

Cuba's economic aid program to Grenada concerns the United States more than the New Jewel's diplomatic sallies against Washington. Cuba has provided construction workers and heavy equipment to help build a major airport in Grenada, which Bishop's government portrays as a means of stimulating tourism, thus diversifying the island's spice economy. Washington worries that the airport has potential military value for transport of Cuban troops abroad. The general support of Grenadan businessmen for the project as economically vital to the island's future has not allayed U.S. fears.[62]

Cuba's Challenge to the United States

What sort of challenge does Cuban activity in Central America and the Caribbean pose for the United States? Revolutionary Cuba's objectives have been remarkably consistent: (1) to ensure its own security in what has long been a hostile environment; (2) to promote domestic economic development by establishing diverse international economic linkages; (3) to increase Cuba's prestige and influence worldwide; and (4) to encourage Cuban-style revolution. The translation of these objectives into practical policy will depend on the international circumstances Cuba faces in the 1980s. The basic contours of policy, however, will probably conform to those established in the late 1970s.

For several years, Cuba's overall approach to Central America and the Caribbean has been primarily a diplomatic and economic strategy of seeking friendly relations with governments that have ideological affinity with Cuba. The principal instruments of this strategy are economic assistance and diplomatic cooperation in such international groups and organizations as the United Nations and the nonaligned movement.

The military dimension to Cuba's Western Hemisphere policy is overshadowed by the economic and diplomatic dimensions. Cuba's military involvement in the region consists of a few advisers (in Grenada since 1980 and in Nicaragua since 1979) and limited material assistance to revolutionary movements in the northern tier of Central America. There is no doubt that Cuba supports the guerrillas and hopes for their victory. But it is also true that the relatively restrained Cuban aid to revolutionary groups has not been a major factor in the internal policies of any nation in the region.

For two decades, Cuban and U.S. relations have been marked by mutual hostility. At first, U.S. policy aimed to overthrow Castro's government; later the intent was to isolate and contain it. Successive administrations in Washington have viewed Cuba as a threat to a wide range of U.S. interests in the region. Political and diplomatic interests seemed threatened by the emergence of a vocally anti-U.S. government within "our own backyard." Economic interests seemed endangered by the prospect that other countries in the region might seek to emulate Cuba's socialist transformation. But Washington's greatest concern has been the perceived security threat that Cuba poses. Rooted in the very real threat posed by the 1962 Cuban missile crisis, this anxiety was reinforced by Cuba's military involvement in Africa. These events illustrate the two distinct security concerns of U.S. policymakers: that Cuba might act as a base for Soviet military action against the United States; and that Cuba might threaten U.S. allies, thereby weakening the global geopolitical position of the United States.

The first danger is potential rather than actual. In the event of global war between East and West, Soviet forces operating out of Cuba could disrupt U.S. sea transport and thus require the deployment of U.S. forces that could otherwise be used elsewhere. But this danger must be

weighed against the probability of global conflict and against the significance that Cuba would have in such a conflict. Realistically, this
danger, though not imaginary, is not major and thus ought not deter-
mine the overall thrust of peacetime U.S. policy toward Cuba.

The second danger is more immediate but is also more difficult to
assess. Cuban aid to friendly governments and to revolutionary movements abroad is surely aimed at promoting Cuban national interest, but
to what extent does it pose a serious threat to the interests of the United
States? One of the principal challenges to the United States in the Caribbean and Central America is to forge a policy that does not allow
bilateral relations with the nations of the region to be distorted by our
preoccupation with Cuba. Many nations would prefer to maintain cordial relations with both the United States and Cuba. Cuba is striving to
build a network of friends in the Caribbean with an economic assistance
program that speaks directly to the area's social and economic needs. In
Central America, the United States has yet to devise a successful policy
for coping with the political turmoil born of poverty and repression.
Cuba may stoke the fires of Central American revolution, but Cuba did
not light them, and Cuban inaction would not lead to their dying out.

Washington's reaction to Cuban activism in Latin America has often
been to see it almost exclusively in national security terms. By responding to such activism with military assistance (in Central America) or a
higher military profile (in the Caribbean), the United States has caused
even friendly nations such as Mexico to worry more about U.S. intervention than about Cuban subversion. It is an ironic response because
the United States is well-positioned to meet the challenge on Cuba's
terms—that is, diplomatically and economically. The United States has
more to offer in this regard than Cuba will ever have, if Washington can
learn to respond to the economic needs and political demands of other
Americans without demanding ideological conformity.

Notes

1. Hugh Thomas, Cuba: The Pursuit of Freedom (New York: Harper &
Row, 1971), passim.

2. On this period of U.S.-Cuban relations, see Robert Freeman Smith, The
United States and Cuba: Business and Diplomacy (New York: Bookman Associates, 1970); and Jules Robert Benjamin, The United States and Cuba:
Hegemony and Dependent Development, 1880–1934 (Pittsburgh: University
of Pittsburgh Press, 1977).

3. Thomas, Cuba.

4. Luis E. Aguilar, *Cuba 1933: Prologue to Revolution* (New York: W. W. Norton, 1974).

5. James O'Connor, *The Origins of Socialism in Cuba* (Ithaca, N.Y.: Cornell University Press, 1970).

6. Lynn D. Bender, *The Politics of Hostility* (Hato Rey, Puerto Rico: Inter-American University Press, 1975).

7. Edward Gonzalez, "Relationship with the Soviet Union," in Carmelo Mesa-Lago, ed., *Revolutionary Change in Cuba* (Pittsburgh: University of Pittsburgh Press, 1974), pp. 81–104.

8. For a thorough study of the Cuban economy from 1959 to 1972, see Archibald R. M. Ritter, *The Economic Development of Revolutionary Cuba* (New York: Praeger, 1974).

9. On the economic and political impacts of the 1970 harvest, see Carmelo Mesa-Lago, *Cuba in the 1970s* (Albuquerque: University of New Mexico Press, 1978).

10. For a detailed discussion of these events, see William M. LeoGrande, "Party Development in Revolutionary Cuba," *Journal of Interamerican Studies and World Affairs* 21, no. 4 (November 1979): 457–80.

11. Ibid.

12. William M. LeoGrande, "The Theory and Practice of Socialist Democracy in Cuba," *Studies in Comparative Communism* 12, no. 1 (Spring 1979): 39–62.

13. Peter Winn, "Is the Cuban Revolution in Trouble?" *The Nation*, June 7, 1980, pp. 682–85.

14. *Washington Post*, April 27, 1980.

15. R. Bruce McColm and Francis X. Maier, "Fighting Castro from Exile," *New York Times Magazine*, January 4, 1981, pp. 28ff.

16. Jacques Levesque, *The USSR and the Cuban Revolution* (New York: Praeger, 1978), pp. 115ff.

17. Mesa-Lago, *Cuba in the 1970s*.

18. See for example, Jorge I. Dominguez, *Cuba: Order and Revolution* (Cambridge, Mass.: Belknap Press, 1978).

19. D. Bruce Jackson, *Castro, The Kremlin and Communism in Latin America* (Baltimore: Johns Hopkins Press, 1969).

20. Edward Gonzalez, "Complexities of Cuban Foreign Policy," *Problems of Communism* 26, no. 6 (November–December 1977): 1–15.

21. William M. LeoGrande, "Cuban-Soviet Relations and Cuban Policy in Africa," *Cuban Studies* 10, no. 1 (January 1980): 1–36.

22. William M. LeoGrande, "The Evolution of the Nonaligned Movement," *Problems of Communism* 29, no. 1 (January–February 1980): 35–52.

23. See the discussion of Cuban-Soviet military relations in U.S., Congress, House, Subcommittee on Inter-American Affairs, *Impact of Cuban-Soviet Ties*

in the Western Hemisphere: Hearings, 96th Cong., 2d sess., March 26–27, April 16–17, May 14, 1980.

24. For a review of this crisis, see *Washington Post*, October 16, 1979.

25. All economic data in this paragraph are drawn from U.S., Central Intelligence Agency, National Foreign Assessment Center, *The Cuban Economy: A Statistical Review* (Washington, D.C.: Library of Congress, DOCEX Project, 1981).

26. Fidel Castro, "Report to the Second Congress of the Communist Party of Cuba," in Foreign Broadcast Information Service, *Daily Report: Latin America*, December 22, 1980.

27. *Washington Post*, April 8, 1981.

28. William Durch, "The Cuban Military in Africa and the Middle East," Professional Paper no. 201 (Arlington: Center for Naval Analyses, 1977).

29. Régis Debray, *Revolution in the Revolution?* (New York: Penguin, 1965).

30. Jackson, *Castro*.

31. Gonzalez, "Complexities of Cuban Foreign Policy."

32. James Petras, "Socialism in One Island: A Decade of Cuban Revolutionary Government," *Politics and Society* 1, no. 2 (February 1971): 203–24.

33. Mesa-Lago, *Cuba in the 1970s*, pp. 116–45.

34. Ibid.

35. LeoGrande, "Cuban-Soviet Relations and Cuban Policy in Africa."

36. Ibid.

37. *Washington Post*, January 25, 1981.

38. Ibid., April 11, 1980.

39. William M. LeoGrande, "Cuba and Nicaragua: From the Somozas to the Sandinistas," *Caribbean Review* 9, no. 1 (Winter 1980): 11–15.

40. *New York Times* and *Washington Post*, June 23, 1979.

41. Subcommittee on Inter-American Affairs, *Impact of Cuban-Soviet Ties in the Western Hemisphere*.

42. U.S., Department of State, "Communist Interference in El Salvador," Special Report no. 80, February 23, 1980.

43. U.S. intelligence officials as quoted in the *Washington Post*, May 16, 1981.

44. Thomas W. Walker, "The Sandinist Victory in Nicaragua," *Current History*, February 1980, pp. 57ff.

45. LeoGrande, "Cuban-Soviet Relations and Cuban Policy in Africa."

46. Ibid.

47. *New York Times*, July 6, 1980; and *Washington Post*, November 9, 1980.

48. *Washington Post*, May 5, 1981.

49. Karen DeYoung, "The Caribbean: A Gathering Storm," *Washington Post*, September 28–30, 1980.

50. Ronald E. Jones, "Cuba and the English-Speaking Caribbean," in Carmelo Mesa-Lago, ed., *Cuba in the World* (Pittsburgh: University of Pittsburgh Press, 1979), pp. 131–46.

51. Anthony P. Maingot, "Cuba and the Commonwealth Caribbean," *Caribbean Review* 9, no. 1 (Winter 1980): 7–11.

52. *Washington Post*, May 12–13, 1980.

53. Jones, "Cuba and the English-Speaking Caribbean"; and W. Raymond Duncan, "Caribbean Leftism," *Problems of Communism* 27, no. 3 (May–June 1978): 33–57.

54. Jones, "Cuba and the English-Speaking Caribbean."

55. *Washington Post*, July 2, 1980.

56. Ibid.

57. Jones, "Cuba and the English-Speaking Caribbean."

58. Maingot, "Cuba and the Commonwealth Caribbean."

59. *Newsweek*, November 10, 1980.

60. Maingot, "Cuba and the Commonwealth Caribbean."

61. *Washington Post*, August 10, 1980.

62. Ibid.

3 | NICARAGUA

James Nelson Goodsell

Nicaragua, the largest nation in Central America, is also one of the area's least populated lands. With 57,143 sq. mi. (slightly larger than Wisconsin), Nicaragua has a population of 2.6 million. Largely mestizo (upwards of 70 percent), with the remainder divided among Caucasian (17 percent), Negro (9 percent), and Indian (4 percent), over half the population is under the age of fifteen. The country is roughly divided into two parts. The western, or Pacific half, is composed of rolling farm-lands, cattle pastures, scrub forests, two large lakes, and a number of dormant volcanoes that are part of two mountain chains running north to south through the country. The eastern, or Caribbean, half is largely uninhabited marshland, tropical rain forest, and flood plains. The latter area offers tremendous possibilities for future agricultural development. It is already used for cattle grazing and banana production, but its poten-tial is mostly untapped.

The most important crops are cotton, which in good years in the late 1970s brought in $350 million annually in foreign exchange, coffee, ba-nanas, sugar, rice, and tobacco. Total exports in 1978, the last normal year before civil strife engulfed the country, came to $646 million; 94 percent of which derived from agriculture. Minerals and textiles are also exported, but in limited quantities.

In pre-Hispanic times, various Indian tribes inhabited the area. With the coming of the Spanish in 1522, much of this population either died out or was assimilated by the conquerors. Independence came in 1821 and for a short time the region, along with the rest of Central America, was united with Mexico; then it merged with other area republics into the United Provinces of Central America. In 1838, Nicaragua became an independent republic.

United States influence has been strong and pervasive. In the 1850s, a freebooter, William Walker of Tennessee, made himself president of the country. In this century, U.S. Marines twice occupied Nicaragua, the last time from 1926 to 1933, in an effort to restore order following a period of civil strife.

At the end of this occupation, the United States played an unwitting role in establishing the long rule of the Somoza family, which ended in July 1979 with the triumph of the Sandinista guerrillas. In 1933, the departing U.S. Marines were replaced by the newly created Nicaraguan National Guard, headed by Gen. Anastasio Somoza García, father of Anastasio Somoza Debayle, who was overthrown in 1979. Within two years, the elder Somoza had not only strengthened his role as guard commander and beefed up the guard, but also seized power from a weak president. He is believed to have ordered the execution of a rural patriot and self-styled general, Augusto César Sandino, who had fought both the U.S. Marines and the National Guard. Using the National Guard, General Somoza launched the family dynasty that was to rule for the next 43 years. General Sandino's name was adopted by a group of Somoza opponents, many of them already claiming to be Marxists, in the 1950s.

Throughout the 1960s and well into the 1970s, the Sandinista guerrilla movement, like many similar causes throughout Latin America, lacked popular support. Spectacular raids on National Guard barracks and kidnappings of leading government officials were the prime elements in the Sandinista arsenal during these years. But these tactics were hardly enough to topple the Somoza family—the ultimate goal of the Sandinistas. Moreover, the movement itself was much splintered in these years. In 1977, Gen. Anastasio Somoza Debayle, the third Somoza, after his brother Luis, to rule, could declare that "the Sandinistas are finished—divided and conquered by me."[1] It was not until later in the same year that the various elements in the Sandinista movement began to coalesce. In September 1979, they announced "the final push against Somoza." A loose nine-member directorate was set up to exercise ultimate authority.

In January 1978, the assassination of Pedro Joaquín Chamorro Cardenal, editor and publisher of the opposition newspaper *La Prensa*, galvanized the Sandinista movement. Joined by an increasing number of middle-class businessmen, scholars, and professionals, the Sandinistas benefited from the growing nationwide disenchantment with Somoza rule and were able to lead several general strikes. Although General Somoza disclaimed responsibility for the Chamorro assassination, in the popular mind he and his National Guard were the culprits. For the next eighteen months, a civil war engulfed the country. Some 50,000 persons died, another 100,000 to 150,000 were injured or wounded, 200,000 families were left homeless, and 30,000 children were orphaned.

The magnitude of this tragedy has yet to be fully comprehended outside the tiny country. The economic loss was equally staggering. Some 33 percent of the industrial plant was destroyed, and much of the rest was damaged. Agricultural production, particularly of cotton and sugarcane, was set back at least two years; cotton planting declined 70 percent in 1979, the cane crop was partially damaged, and much of those two crops went unharvested. The lack of foreign exchange to purchase fertilizer in 1979 and early 1980 hurt production even more. Only coffee was produced in fair quantities in 1979 and early 1980, as little damage was done to coffee trees during the fighting.

To restore agricultural production, the new government hastened to provide seed and fertilizer, but foreign exchange constraints were likely to prevent such purchases through 1981 and perhaps beyond. Under a massive land reform program, the government confiscated the 25 percent of the country's arable land held by General Somoza, plus another 15 percent held by some of his associates, and a start was made at setting up cooperatives composed of previously landless peasants.

Moreover, the country was bankrupt when the Sandinistas came to power. The national treasury had no more than $3 million when the first audit was made. The war took its toll of official foreign reserves, and General Somoza and his colleagues absconded with nearly all that was left. How much was unclear, and the Sandinistas indicated it would be a year or so before some sort of accounting would be possible. But the new government did discover that General Somoza had left behind a debt of $1.6 billion. "How to service that debt," said Jaime Wheelock Román, one of the top nine Sandinistas, at the first press conference upon taking power, "is beyond us. But we will guarantee to pay the debt." Other Sandinista commanders subsequently echoed his words, although the new government will probably refuse to pay upwards of $50 million of the debt that, it is argued, went into General Somoza's personal coffers and not those of the country.[2]

When the Sandinistas came to power, they pledged to respect private property. Moreover, they had earlier, with U.S. and Latin American prompting, promised a pluralistic government, with elections at an early date, but probably not before 1983. They also indicated a preference for a mixed socialist-private economy. The goals were clear, but the means of achieving them were not.

Somoza left behind a legacy of 43 years of family dictatorship, corruption, repression, and hatred. In the months since, the Sandinistas have assembled a crazy-quilt government that is trying to construct what the official Sandinista newspaper, *Barricada*, proclaims to be "a new Nicaragua."[3] The outlines of this new Nicaragua remain vague. Moreover, the success of the effort depends in large part on the ability of the guerrillas, many of whom are self-proclaimed Marxists with ties to Cuba and the Soviet Union, to hold together their alliance with basically conservative private Nicaraguan business interests and to improve relations with the United States.

The guerrillas-turned-governors have proved—thus far—more effective than many anticipated, but the problems confronting them are clearly more serious than originally thought and doubtless tougher than their struggle with Somoza's National Guard. The Sandinistas' lack of administrative experience, their connections with Cuba and other leftist societies, the shabby governmental bureaucracy they inherited, the shattered state of the economy, and the wariness of many U.S. interests, particularly since Ronald Reagan became president, pose serious obstacles to the formation of a viable government.

Despite the facade of unity, the Sandinistas seem unable to agree on the direction they want to take Nicaragua. This uncertainty leads to confusion among Nicaraguans and foreigners eager to assist in the economic recovery. Promises of a mixed society to the contrary, the Marxist tone of the new government appears more and more prominent, proving the critics to have been correct. The growing ties of Sandinista leaders with Cuba, the role of some leaders in the shipment of Cuban and Soviet arms to Salvadoran guerrillas, and a growing number of acerbic anti-U.S. statements and actions suggest that the Marxist direction predominates.

Confusing the issue is the governmental structure. The original five-member junta of government has been cut to three members; but ultimate authority resides with the nine-member Sandinista directorate, a sort of collegiate papacy of guerrillas. On the surface, the arrangement seemed to work well at first, but strains soon developed. Yet leaders have worked at minimizing these strains; and given the staggering problems facing the Sandinistas, it is surprising that the governmental structure has worked as well as it has. Many problems have made a consolidation of victory difficult. Public services throughout the country were destroyed during the fighting. Remnants of the National Guard kept the air alive with tension even after Somoza decamped. Hundreds were killed in shoot-outs during July, August, and September 1979. But gradually, the Sandinista army brought a degree of pacification to the country, and some essential services were restored. The government machinery slowly began to gear up. The slowness, however, led to complaints by many staunch Sandinista supporters and to obvious worry from the private sector about the sincerity of Sandinista promises of a pluralistic society and a mixed economy.

Much speculation about the ultimate direction of the Sandinista-led government centered in the hybrid government structure and questions about the ranking of members of the directorate. This was particularly important since all the directorate members were longtime Sandinista guerrilla commanders and all were self-proclaimed Marxists.

It was early felt that Tomás Borge Martínez, the sole surviving founder of the Sandinista movement (the others were killed in the guerrilla struggle during the 1960s and 1970s), might well emerge as first among equals.[4] His preeminence as a founder of the movement, together with his charisma and the personal loyalty of many Sandinista field commanders, was in his favor. Moreover, Borge became interior minister, responsible for internal security and the police, an extremely important post in Latin American governments and important to any Marxist-oriented government. He also enjoyed a wide popularity, and some suggested that he might become the Fidel Castro of Nicaragua. That suggestion has yet to be borne out, although Borge clearly wields tremendous power. It is also clear that he is more of a doctrinaire Marxist than some of the other members of the directorate.

Jaime Wheelock, another influential leader, took the agrarian reform post in the government. With nearly 50 percent of Nicaragua's land in government hands, the agrarian reform ministry is extremely important. Wheelock appears much less doctrinaire than Borge. Many Nicaraguan observers see him as the bridge between the Marxists in the government and Nicaragua's important private sector.[5] Wheelock is extremely popular among some segments of the population, and his firm command of his ministry suggests to some observers that he has ambitions for more power.

It is possible that Borge and Wheelock, the former in his late forties and the latter in his mid-thirties, may someday be involved in a power struggle. For the time being, however, the oft-proclaimed Sandinista unity appears to be not merely a facade but a major underpinning of the new government.

The directorate also includes Bayardo Arce Castaño; Henry Ruiz; Carlos Núñez; Luis Carrión Cruz; Daniel Ortega Saavedra; his brother, Humberto, who heads the army; and Victor Manuel Tirado López, the only foreigner in the group, a Mexican long associated with the late Carlos Fonseca Amador, the most eminent founder of the Sandinista movement. Several of these men hold cabinet posts. Some are active in the Sandinista army, and others handle propaganda and public relations for the new government. Their meetings are secret, and little leaks out about their deliberations. Each speaks collectively for all. This approach lends itself to the idea of a unified high command—exactly what Ruiz told reporters in August 1979 did exist.

Differences among junta members have been more evident—perhaps because the junta represents the pluralistic society and mixed economy that the Sandinistas promised and continue to say is their goal. As first constituted in late June 1979, just before the Sandinista triumph, the Junta of the Government of National Reconstruction, to give its official title, included two Sandinistas, both of whom claim to be Marxists, two persons from the private sector, and a fifth person who leaned toward the left but was widely regarded as the swing vote.

Daniel Ortega Saavedra, also a member of the Sandinista directorate, and Moisés Hassán Morales were the two avowed Marxists. Businessman Alfonso Robelo Callejas, a longtime opponent of General Somoza, and Violeta Barrios de Chamorro, widow of the assassinated newspaper editor, were right of center. The fifth member, Sergio Ramírez Mercado, was initially described as a moderate, but his subsequent voting record and his public utterances have placed him much more in the leftist camp. Robelo and Chamorro frequently found themselves outvoted, and in April 1980 both resigned. Chamorro, citing legitimate health reasons, left first; Robelo followed three days later with a sharply worded denunciation of the government's leftist inclinations.

To many, this crisis appeared a deliberate effort by the new Nicaraguan leadership to purge its ranks of moderate, rightist thinking. But within two weeks, the junta had two new faces, Rafael Cordova Rivas, a conservative politician who had long opposed General Somoza, and Arturo Cruz Porras, a banker with many friends in the private sector. If anything, these two were more rightist than Robelo and Chamorro had been, and their selection temporarily dispelled some of the talk of an inexorable move toward a Marxist state. However, in March 1981 Cruz and Hassán were dropped from the junta, and Daniel Ortega emerged as the key figure.

This strange apparatus, with the directorate holding ultimate power and the junta seen by some as the directorate's puppet, has led to considerable governmental confusion and uncertainty. The cynics, of course, say that such a structure is an impossibility. They argue that historical precedent suggests that the Sandinista leaders, clearly Marxist in direction and commitment, will never allow a truly pluralistic society to develop. In a showdown, they reason, the moderates will lose out, and Sandinista Nicaragua will emerge as a full-fledged Marxist state. It was a sinister indication that in November 1980, government security forces murdered a prominent businessman and leader of the anti-Marxists, Jorge Salazar. In response to the outcry, a government spokesman accused the private sector of subversion.[6]

However, the majority of observers on the scene, including the U.S. embassy and many Nicaraguan businessmen, although worried, are less certain of the outcome and prefer to take Sandinista leaders at their word, at least until actions speak otherwise. The attitude of William Báez, a leader in the private sector, is typical: "This is my country just as much as it is the Sandinistas', and I intend to stay and make it work."[7]

The Sandinistas are clearly Marxists—and they have no intention of yielding up their victory over General Somoza by allowing immediate free elections. Nor are they willing to share governmental power between themselves and the non-Marxist opposition, whose role in the victory over General Somoza was as important as theirs. Indeed, this fact galls many non-Marxist, non-Sandinista Nicaraguans who opposed General Somoza. "We were the anchor of the opposition to Somoza; without us the Sandinistas would not have had their victories," says Robelo, who remains openly bitter about his difficulties with his fellow junta members. "In fact, I think Tacho Somoza would still be in the Bunker [General Somoza's Managua headquarters] if it were not for us."[8] Robelo's view is widespread.

The ties of the Sandinistas with Havana, Moscow, and other centers of world Marxism are evident. The Sandinistas received arms and supplies during the fighting largely from Venezuela, Panama, and Costa Rica, but some key leaders had traveled to Cuba in the years immediately before the final eighteen months, including Borge and Wheelock. The latter was in Chile during Salvador Allende's Popular Unity government between 1970 and 1973 and in Mexico, where his books have been published.

Since coming to power, all of the directorate members are thought to have gone to Cuba, and several have visited Moscow and Eastern Europe. Moreover, in July 1980 Fidel Castro was in Managua for ceremonies marking the first anniversary of the downfall of General Somoza. Although Cuba contributed little in the way of supplies to the Sandinista army during the eighteen months of fighting, it quickly dispatched some $5 million worth of relief aid in July and August 1979. In contrast, U.S. relief supplies by the end of October 1979 totaled $35 million.

But Cuba responded very quickly to Nicaraguan requests for educational and medical personnel to help reopen schools and to staff hospitals and clinics around the country. Although Borge and other leaders early said that Nicaragua would welcome such assistance from any quarter, including "our friends in the United States," it was Cuba that responded within two weeks after the new government took power. Similar assistance was not forthcoming from the United States or the Soviet Union.

Both Cuba and the Soviet Union began "staffing and stuffing" their embassies in Managua, as *La Prensa*, put it.[9] By the end of 1979, it was estimated that there were more than one hundred Cubans attached to Havana's embassy in Managua and close to three thousand Cuban teachers and medical personnel in the Nicaraguan countryside.

It is too early to tell how much impact the Cuban effort will have, much less the impact of similar U.S. actions. So far, Sandinista leaders have commented favorably on the role of the U.S. embassy under Ambassador Lawrence Pezzullo, who apparently had access to top Sandinista commanders. His task was made difficult by congressional reluctance to approve the Carter administration's $75 million aid package. All U.S. aid was suspended in early 1981 because of growing Cuban influence and the Nicaraguan role in shipping Cuban arms to the Salvadoran guerrillas.

The situation is still very much in a state of flux. In the months before General Somoza fled the country, Nicaragua had become sharply polarized. On one side was General Somoza, his National Guard, and an ever-decreasing number of civilian supporters; on the other were the Marxist-leaning Sandinistas and the non-Marxist opposition. This latter group, with the Sandinistas clearly dominant, will decide the future of the country. There are a number of minuscule Marxist groups, including a Maoist unit, and other left-leaning parties, but their numbers are extremely small. The Sandinistas' desire to monopolize the left is evident. The Maoist group, which ran the newspaper *El Pueblo* in late Somoza years and continued it during the early confusion of the government changeover, is a case in point. The government jailed its head and closed down the paper for a time. So all-pervasive is the Sandinista domination of Nicaragua that other leftist groups have been content either to join the Sandinistas or to bide their time before reasserting themselves. Some of the traditional Marxist labor union leaders have doubts about the young Sandinista leaders. Government labor administrators are aware of this and have made overtures, so far only lukewarmly received, to the unions.

The Marxist underpinnings of the new government are unmistakable.

But just where the Sandinistas plan to take Nicaragua remains to be seen. They may not be certain themselves; indeed, there may well be sharper divisions among them than is apparent. But the Sandinista leaders, grappling with the country's economic and social malaise, have discarded Nicaragua's traditional alliance with the United States and are forging very different international links. Many of these are with the socialist camp, which gives pause to the optimists who claim that a pluralistic political structure and a mixed economy are plausible goals. It will be some time, however, before a definitive reading of events in Nicaragua can accurately tell which direction the country is moving. Moreover, events in Washington, Havana, and Moscow may well have as much impact as events in Managua. If Washington gives substantial aid to the new government, a mixed economy may emerge. On the other hand, Cuban pressure on Managua to be more radical and supportive of Cuban adventures in the Caribbean and Central America may well jeopardize the pluralistic society.

In sum, the verdict on Nicaragua is not in. But the possibility of a major contest in Nicaragua between the United States and the socialist bloc cannot be ruled out. The danger signals are up.

Notes

1. *Christian Science Monitor*, May 15, 1977.
2. Ibid., August 3, 1979.
3. *Barricada*, August 4, 1979.
4. *Christian Science Monitor*, May 18, 1979.
5. Ibid., August 3, 1979.
6. *New York Times*, November 19, 1980.
7. *Excelsior* (Mexico City), February 15, 1980.
8. *Barricada*, February 18, 1980.
9. *La Prensa*, October 20, 1979.

4 | EL SALVADOR

Thomas P. Anderson

By 1980, El Salvador was in a virtual state of civil war, a war lacking battle lines or major engagements but claiming more than one hundred lives a week. Many of these were noncombatants, caught in the struggle between ultra right-wing terrorists and security forces on one side and left-wing guerrilla bands on the other. This struggle for control of the scarce resources of this desperately poor and overcrowded country was of great significance to the future of Central America, given El Salvador's strategic location between Guatemala, ruled for decades by conservative military men, and Marxist-dominated Nicaragua.

The stage for this struggle is small. El Salvador's population of five million is compressed into 8,000 square miles, making it, with over 600 persons per square mile, the most densely populated nation in the Western Hemisphere. It is a land of large crater lakes and volcanic peaks, the highest rising to over 6,000 feet; there are broad valleys suitable for farming and a fertile littoral plain along its eastern Pacific shore. Unlike the other Central American states, it has no Atlantic coastline. Since the late nineteenth century, the principal cash crop has been coffee; in recent decades, sugar and cotton have also assumed importance. What little industry there is has been concentrated in the capital city, San Salvador (population 450,000), and consists largely of textile mills and small factories.

The large Indian population of early colonial times blended with the Hispanic conquerors, producing a mestizo population. Until 1932 some isolated Indian communities existed in the western part of the country, but they were exterminated or dispersed following the unsuccessful Marxist-inspired uprising that year.[1]

The United States and West Germany have traditionally been El Salvador's best customers, buying a large part of the coffee crop. Japan was, until the recent political turmoil, the leader in investment, with textile mills and other plants. Although little investment comes from the United States, its presence has always been considerable and it has been the primary source of the foreign military training and equipment of the Salvadoran army and security forces.

Badly frightened by the uprising of Marxist-led *campesinos* (peasants) in 1932, the great landowners, who had traditionally dominated politics, were content to turn over political power to the army, and Gen. Maximiliano Hernández Martínez established a dictatorship that lasted until 1944. There followed a period of coups and countercoups, with military men generally in control and only brief periods of civilian government. Early in 1961, however, Col. Julio Adalberto Rivera came to power in still another barracks revolt and established a system that endured eighteen years. Every five years, the Party of National Conciliation (Partido de Conciliación Nacional; PCN), which was dominated by senior army officers, would win the presidential election, using whatever means were necessary.

The most prominent of the opposition parties came to be the Christian Democratic Party (Partido Demócrata Cristiano; PDC), under the leadership of engineer José Napoleón Duarte.[2] The social democratic National Revolutionary Movement (Movimiento Nacional Revolucionario; MNR), founded in 1965, is led by Guillermo Manuel Ungo. Since the revolt of 1932, the Communist Party of El Salvador (Partido Comunista de El Salvador; PCES) has been illegal; it functions through a legal front organization known as the National Democratic Union (Unión Democrática Nacionalista; UDN). The PDC, the MNR, and the UDN banded together in 1971 as the National Opposition Union (Unión Nacional Opositaria; UNO) to contest the presidential election of 1972. Their candidate, Duarte, probably won the election, but fraud allowed the PCN candidate to claim a plurality, and he was chosen president by a PCN-dominated National Assembly.[3]

Elections in following years were marked by increasingly blatant manipulation. Despite this, the UNO participated in the 1977 presidential election. Again it appears that the UNO candidate would have beaten Gen. Carlos Humberto Romero, had there not been massive fraud. So patent was the fakery that there was widespread unrest; and on February 28, 1977, the defeated candidate and his supporters staged a massive protest in the capital. Members of the security forces and of ORDEN, a paramilitary group acting on behalf of the government, attacked the demonstrators and killed an estimated 200 persons.

A significant factor in the 1970s was the growth of "popular forces." Peasant organizations have been banned since 1932, but two came into existence in the early 1970s: the Union of Farm Workers (Unión de Trabajadores del Campo; UTC) and the Catholic-sponsored Federation of Christian Peasants of El Salvador (Federación Cristiana de Campesinos Salvadoreños; FECCAS). Both groups worked for better wages and working conditions and for land reform. In 1974 the formation of the Front of Popular United Action (Frente de Acción Popular Unificada; FAPU) brought together some small peasant groups; FENASTRAS, the second largest labor organization; and a teachers' group. The next year FECCAS and UTC in imitation founded the powerful Popular Revolutionary Bloc (Bloque Popular Revolucionario; BPR), which also included several labor unions and the National Association of Salvadoran Educators (Asociación Nacional de Educadores Salvadoreños), the country's most important teachers' organization. By 1980, FECCAS-UTC had an estimated 80,000 members in the rural sector. Although not ideological in the beginning, both FAPU and BPR moved to the point where BPR Secretary General Facundo Guardado could label his group "Marxist-Leninist" in May 1979.[4]

Recent Political Developments

The response of the Romero government to the challenge of the left was heavy-handed repression, using the regular army, the Guardia Nacional (an elite rural police force), the Policía Nacional, and several smaller organizations. In addition to these regular units, the several thousand members of ORDEN functioned as part-time police and were allowed to carry weapons without a permit. Further, a group of conservative Salvadorans formed a right-wing terrorist organization known as the White Warrior Union (Unión Guerrera Blanca; UGB) to assassinate reputed left-wingers.

FECCAS and UTC were frequent targets; sometimes whole villages were seized and many of the inhabitants killed. Notable examples are Aguilares (May 1977) and San Pedro Perulapán (March 1978). Many individuals seized by the security forces simply "disappeared."[5] The Catholic clergy also became targets. Rightists killed seven priests between 1977 and 1979. One major effect of this was a change in the outlook of Msgr. Oscar Arnulfo Romero y Galdámez, a supposed conservative who had been appointed archbishop of San Salvador at about the same time as Carlos Humberto Romero (no relation) became president. From the spring of 1977 until his assassination in March 1980, the archbishop was the spokesman of the masses.

Far from squelching the leftist "popular forces," the activities of the security forces, ORDEN, and the UGB caused an unprecedented growth in membership and contributed considerably to their Marxist radicalization. FAPU, BPR, and the Popular Leagues–February 28 (Ligas Populares 28 de Febrero; LP-28), an organization founded after the massacre of that date in 1977, began a new tactic in 1979: the dramatic seizure of buildings, such as the Red Cross headquarters, ministries of the government, embassies, and churches. Early in May 1979, BPR supporters took over the cathedral of San Salvador after the police seized Facundo Guardado. On May 8, the Policía Nacional fired on a BPR demonstration, killing 24. That same month, the French, Costa Rican, and Venezuelan embassies were seized; on May 22 a group of marchers bringing food to BPR forces holding the Venezuelan Embassy was cut down in the streets, leaving more than 20 killed.

The May massacres precipitated a renewed wave of violence, culminating in a series of bombings and killings in September, which convinced many that the government of Gen. Carlos Humberto Romero was incapable of functioning. Many younger officers began to regard a coup as the only way to avoid a civil war. They received encouragement from the U.S. Embassy, from Jesuit fathers, and from the Jesuit-run Catholic University, the locus of intellectual dissent since the government's seizure of the National University following an abortive 1972 coup.

On October 15, 1979, Col. Adolfo Majano and Col. Jaime Abdul Gutiérrez easily seized control of the major tactical positions around the capital. Romero was exiled the next day, and a junta was established two days later. Archbishop Romero, most church leaders, the U.S. Embassy, and the opposition parties welcomed the "coup of the Jesuits," as it was popularly known. Leftist forces remained suspicious, however, and the composition of the junta did not lessen their suspicions. In addition to Colonels Majano and Gutiérrez, it included a San Salvador businessman and two moderate civilians, Guillermo Manuel Ungo of the MNR and Román Mayorga Quirós, rector of the Catholic University. The cabinet contained no representatives from the leftist movements, although a UDN-PCES member was labor minister. Colonel José Guillermo García, a right-wing military hard-liner, was defense minister.

Despite the junta's promises of reform and democracy, the struggle between security forces and popular groups continued, with acts of terrorism by the UGB and leftist guerrillas increasing. In mid-December the army surrounded and seized the villages of El Congo and Opico, killing, according to FAPU, 125 villagers.[6]

As PCES leader Jorge Shafick Handal commented in November 1979, "What we have here are two governments."[7] The army and security forces, both under Colonel García, constituted one; the junta was the other. Increasingly alarmed over this situation, a number of ministers threatened to resign in late December if the junta could not bring the army under control. Junta members Guillermo Ungo and Román Mayorga drafted a set of demands to the Superior Military Council (the group that made military policy), including junta control of all military appointments. When the army refused to compromise, the junta resigned on January 2, 1980.

Unknown to most members of the government, the two military members of the junta had been secretly negotiating with the PDC to form a new government in which the Christian Democrats would play the preponderant role. Within two days of the government's collapse, a new junta was announced with two PDC leaders in it: Héctor Dada and Antonio Morales Erlich. The two officers remained, as did Colonel García. Many Christian Democrats soon became disgusted with the new government's policies and defected to the opposition, including Héctor Dada, who declared that the junta was "without popular support."[8] Dada was replaced by José Napoleón Duarte.

The second junta was soon the target of leftist forces. A massive demonstration on January 22, 1980, led to a massacre by government forces. Other acts of repression by the military, ORDEN, and the UGB followed. There was mounting evidence of an impending coup by the right, but strong pressure from the U.S. Embassy, which still believed that the junta represented a moderate middle position, staved off one coup on February 24.[9] On May 2, a second plot also failed.

The unpopular junta, realizing that it must take action, decided to implement a long anticipated land reform program on March 6. Three hundred seventy-six estates, totaling 224,000 hectares or 25 percent of the arable land, were seized. Eventually no one was to own more than 100 hectares (about 250 acres). From the beginning the land reform encountered severe problems. No proper inventories were prepared, nor was there a clear notion of which peasants would receive land. Nevertheless, the reform achieved a measure of success. Ten days after its inauguration, there was a massive general strike and a series of land seizures by the BPR. They were repressed by the army, with some sixty deaths. On March 23, Archbishop Romero was shot and killed, probably by the UGB.[10] The extreme right sought by his death to plunge the country into civil war; although no battle lines appeared, the tempo of killings indeed increased.

By November 1980, over six thousand persons had lost their lives in civil strife since the formation of the second junta. Within the junta, it was apparent that the faction of Colonel Majano, who favored compromise with the leftist forces, was losing out to that of Gutiérrez and Defense Minister García, who favored greater repression. On September 1, all the leading officers believed to favor Majano were transferred to diplomatic posts abroad. The civilians on the junta were not consulted in this transfer, which plainly signaled the ascendancy of the military hardliners.[11] Finally, on December 8, 1980, Majano was forced out of the junta.

Social and Economic Structure

A major reason for the bitter struggle in El Salvador is the great disparity of wealth. The small oligarchy, which, prior to the land reform of March 1980 owned 60 percent of the land, was often called "the fourteen families," and although the exact number was uncertain, the expression indicated the extent of the concentration of wealth. Per capita income in the late 1970s was around $600, but many peasant families subsisted on no more than $150 a year. Per capita income barely kept pace with the rapidly expanding population, which grows at the rate of 3 percent a year (that is, doubles every 25 years). Since the overutilized farmland could no longer support the population, a great drift to the capital occurred. Most of the peasants migrating to San Salvador found little or no work and settled in wretched slums.[12] Both the peasantry and the proletariat were ready material for radical movements.

Radical Movements

Following the unsuccessful uprising of 1932, the outlawed PCES went underground, becoming a small, Moscow-oriented group that preferred to remain relatively passive. It participated in politics through its legal arm, the UDN. In a 1970 ideological split, Secretary General Salvador Cayetano Carpio, seeking a more active position, broke with his own party and formed the Popular Liberation Forces (Fuerzas Populares de Liberación; FPL), based on the ideas of Che Guevara. Following the fraudulent elections of 1972, the FPL became an active terrorist movement. The PCES then decided to form its own guerrilla-terrorist organization, the People's Revolutionary Army (Ejército Revolucionario del

Pueblo; ERP), led by the revolutionary poet Roque Dalton García; but in May 1975, Dalton was assassinated by his own followers, who subsequently broke with the PCES and assumed a Trotskyite position. In 1975, a third guerrilla movement, the Armed Forces of National Resistance (Fuerzas Armadas de Resistencia Nacional; FARN), with Maoist principles, came into existence. The activities of the guerrilla movements included bank robberies, bombings, seizures of radio stations to broadcast propaganda, kidnappings for ransom to buy arms, the takeovers of embassies and other buildings, and assassinations.

When, in the late 1970s, the leftist forces adopted a militant Marxist-Leninist stand, each linked itself to one of the guerrilla movements: the BPR to the FPL, FAPU to FARN, and LP-28 to the ERP. On January 11, 1980, following the breakdown of the first junta and the establishment of the more conservative second, the three popular organizations announced the formation of the Revolutionary Coordination of the Masses (Coordinadora Revolucionaria de las Masas; CRM [Masas]). The UDN also joined this group, and the PCES suddenly declared itself the guerrilla arm of the UDN.

The abrupt change in the policy of the PCES caught many observers by surprise. As late as 1978, the BPR had attacked the communist party as "revisionist" and accused it of betraying the Salvadoran people.[13] The Communists, for their part, had accused the other leftist forces of "adventurism." But at the Seventh National Congress of the PCES, held in May 1979, Secretary General Handal declared that revolt was both necessary and possible and that it was a heresy to believe otherwise. As he later admitted in a candid interview, "our decision was a bit late, but still in time."[14]

The CRM (Masas) announced a ten-point "pragmatic program": overthrow of the military dictatorship, liquidation of U.S. domination, destruction of the power of the oligarchy, assurance of democratic rights, distribution of the means of production to the people, raising of the living standard of Salvadorans, creation of a new people's army, encouragement of popular organizations, pursuit of an independent foreign policy, and assurance of peace and freedom.[15]

The CRM (Masas) demonstrated its strength in the massive march of January 22, 1980, which brought some 80,000 persons onto the streets. Both this demonstration and a similar outpouring on March 30 for the funeral of Archbishop Romero resulted in clashes with right-wing terrorists and the police; after March the tactic was abandoned. Embassy seizures and other acts also declined in frequency, a notable exception being the seizure of the Costa Rican Embassy on July 11, in which LP-28 deposited some hundred peasant "refugees" and then departed.

The focus shifted to rural areas, where ambushes of government patrols and the assassination of officials and ORDEN members became common.

In April, 49 trade unions, professional groups, and political movements not linked to the CRM (Masas) formed the Salvadoran Democratic Front (Frente Democrático Salvadoreño; FDS). The most prominent groups in this organization were the socialist MNR under Guillermo Ungo, the dissident faction of the Christian Democrats, and independent socialists led by Enrique Alvarez Córdova, minister of education under the first junta. The FDS then joined with the CRM (Masas) to form the Revolutionary Democratic Front (Frente Democrático Revolucionario; FDR), nominally led by Enrique Alvarez, but in reality controlled by the Marxist CRM (Masas).

To strengthen their unity, the CRM (Masas) parties formed a United Revolutionary Directorate (Dirección Revolucionaria Unificada; UDR) on June 25, 1980. The UDR consisted of the secretary generals of the member-parties: Juan Angel Chacón Vasquez, a 24-year-old student who had replaced Facundo Guardado as leader of the BPR in September 1979; José Leoncio Pinchinte of LP-28; Alberto Ramos of FAPU; Mario Aguiñada of the UDN; and Luis Díaz of the small Marxist-oriented People's Liberation Movement (Movimiento de Liberación Popular). On June 10, in another unity move, the guerrilla groups formed the Revolutionary Military Coordination (Coordinadora Revolucionaria Militar; CRM [Militar]), consisting of the secretary generals of their movements: Handal of the PCES, Joaquín Villalobos of ERP, Salvador Cayetano Carpio of the FPL, and, until his accidental death in September 1980, Ernesto Jovel of FARN. This unity on the military front was short-lived, the ERP breaking with the CRM (Militar) almost immediately and the FARN announcing its withdrawal in September 1980. FARN had favored an immediate popular uprising with the aid of non-Marxist elements, a tactic to which other elements in the CRM (Militar) would not agree.[16]

During the summer and fall of 1980, fighting centered in the northern department of Chalatenango, long a BPR stronghold, and spilled over into the neighboring departments of Santa Ana, Cabañas, and Morazán. All these border Honduras, and the rugged border area, officially declared a demilitarized zone after the 1969 war between the two states, became a staging area for guerrilla activities. The Salvadoran army declared parts of the region a "free-fire zone" and conducted sweeps, reminiscent of Vietnam, into the area. Despite the existence of an official state of war between Honduras and El Salvador until October 1, 1980, the Honduran army often cooperated. On June 14, an estimated six hundred peasants were allegedly killed along the Rio Sumpul when they tried to flee the war zone into Honduras. The army admitted heavy losses at Perquín, Morazán province, on July 30, 1980;[17] but in general the military appeared to have the best of the guerrillas.

Another CRM (Masas) and FDR tactic was the general strike. One such strike on March 17, 1980, achieved some success. A subsequent effort on June 24–25 was only partially successful, however, and the general strike of August 13–15, billed by the FDR as the forerunner of a major offensive, failed completely, as the government took measures to patrol the streets and protect public transportation in the urban centers.

These failures and the continuing inability of the Marxists to win the guerrilla war tended to demoralize the left. A crushing blow struck them on November 27, 1980, when right-wing terrorists seized Enrique Alvarez Córdova, Juan Chacón, and four other leaders of the FDR during a supposedly secret meeting at the Jesuit high school in San Salvador. Their tortured bodies were discovered the next day. On November 29, the FDR announced a new directorate composed of Carlos Gómez, Juan José Martell, and Saul Villata, among others.

In January 1981, the FDR created a new body, the Political Commission. In all but name this was a government in exile (since it had to operate from Mexico City, it could not use that title officially without risking expulsion from Mexico). The president of this body was Guillermo Manuel Ungo of the MNR; other members were Mario Aguiñada of the UDN (the communist front party); Salvador Samayoa, an independent socialist; Angel Guadalupe Martínez, the young BPR firebrand; José Napoleón Rodríguez Ruiz of FAPU; Fabio Castillo, another member of the socialist MNR; and Rubén Zamorra of the Social Christians, a PDC splinter movement. The group announced a "final offensive," begun on January 10, 1981, to bring them to power, but the offensive petered out. The resulting military stalemate dragged on through 1981, the principal efforts of the guerrillas being directed to sabotaging the economy by blowing up bridges, power lines, and so forth.

Foreign Infiltration

In March 1980, both Deputy Assistant Secretary of Defense Franklin Kramer and Deputy Assistant Secretary of State for Latin American Affairs John A. Bushnell declared to the U.S. Congress that Cubans were actively infiltrating into El Salvador across the Honduran border.[18] It appears improbable, however, that much in the way of advisers or aid could come from Cuba by this route, which would require crossing hostile Honduras, avoiding the Honduran army posted along the border, and traversing a tangled and rugged terrain. More plausible were reports of aid for the FDR coming through Nicaragua. The Salvadoran government charged in May 1980 that 3,000 Marxist mercenaries from Cuba and other countries were training in Nicaragua and that a number of infiltrators had already been killed coming across the Gulf of Fonseca.[19] Although the Nicaraguan government denied the report, it made no secret of its sympathies with the FDR and broke relations with the junta. In mid-April 1980 it declared a solidarity week with the Salvadoran people. The PCES maintains its traditional ties to the Soviet Union; delegations from the FDR have visited twenty European countries and much of Latin America seeking support but studiously avoided going to the USSR or Soviet bloc countries. Any direct Soviet intervention appeared unlikely at the close of 1980, although the USSR, like Cuba and Nicaragua, clearly favored the leftist forces.

On February 23, 1981, the U.S. Department of State released a white paper on El Salvador, which dealt with two topics: the travels of Shafik Handal to Eastern Europe and Nicaraguan-Cuban aid to the Salvadoran rebels. The report stated that the information came from captured Nicaraguan documents. Although some have cast doubt on the authenticity of the documents, the picture they give of Nicaragua's position in the struggle is probably accurate. After January 1981 Nicaragua appears to have reduced the level of arms shipments.

Prospects

In El Salvador the moderate middle has virtually ceased to exist. Even moderates like Guillermo Ungo of the MNR have thrown in their lot with the leftist forces. The Christian Democrats were long thought to represent a "third force" between right and left that might bring change without revolution, but the PDC leaders lost contact with the mass organizations in the mid-1970s. Many Christian Democrats have joined the left. The United States, however, had little choice but to support the junta, which it saw as a stabilizing influence, especially since the leftist forces had become conditioned by Marxist rhetoric to see the United States as the enemy. The right was also becoming anti-American, barricading Ambassador Robert White in his residence for three days in May 1980. Rightist terrorists or the security forces killed three American nuns and a lay worker on December 5, 1980.

A key factor in the weakness of the junta is the lack of civilian control over the army. The military is confident that out of repression will come order and out of order will come reform. The immediate prospects for peace and stability in El Salvador are not good. Perhaps the problem is that the right has long viewed stability in itself as a goal without reflecting that genuine stability must arise from a recognition of the legitimacy of the social, economic, and political aspirations of the vast majority of the people.

On the other hand, the factionalism of the guerrilla movements, the diminutive size of the country, and its isolation from direct contact with Cuba appeared to make a guerrilla victory unlikely in the near future. Another complicating factor was the increased activity of the United States in the struggle. More than $5 million in military aid went to the junta in 1980; and, despite initial denials from the Carter administration, a large-scale U.S. effort to train Salvadoran security forces was under way. Juan Chacón, in a June 15, 1980 interview with *Granma* in Havana, bitterly complained that "the people have won the political battle. But ... the Salvadoran masses are unable to withstand multinational armed intervention, prepared and directed by the U.S. government."

The Reagan administration increased the level of aid considerably. Some $26 million worth of military equipment was to be sent to the country, along with massive aid for the ruined economy. Fifty-two military advisers were dispatched to train the Salvadoran army. It appeared that the new administration was willing to achieve a military solution to the civil war. Increasingly, the U.S. government appeared to disregard the question of whether Duarte and his associates represented a "moderate" position and to concentrate on the military as a bastion of strength against the menace of communism. El Salvador was seen as the next link in the chain of communist aggression after Cuba and Nicaragua.

It is quite possible that the military can win the civil war. The guerrillas have no friendly border behind them as did the Sandinistas and must rely on air shipments from Nicaragua and other friendly sources. El Salvador, despite its rugged terrain, is too small to lend itself readily to guerrilla warfare.

But the very tactic used by the military in their antiguerrilla campaign makes it very likely that the majority of the people will continue to see the leftist forces as their allies and the government as their enemy. Even the ambitious land reform program, although a partial success, did not appear to win substantial numbers of peasants over to the junta. For most Salvadorans the chief problem remained the military power that has dominated the country since 1930.

Notes

1. For an account of these events, see Thomas P. Anderson, *Matanza: El Salvador's Communist Revolt of 1932* (Lincoln: University of Nebraska Press, 1971).

2. Stephen Webre, *José Napoleón Duarte and the Christian Democratic Party in Salvadoran Politics: 1960-1972* (Baton Rouge, Louisiana: Louisiana State University Press, 1979), p. 82.

3. Ibid., pp. 179-81.

4. Interview in *Jornal do Brasil*, May 21, 1979; in *Foreign Broadcast Information Service (FBIS)*, May 25, 1979.

5. Robert Drinan, John McAward, and Thomas P. Anderson, *Human Rights in El Salvador, 1978: Report of the Findings of an Investigatory Mission* (Boston: Unitarian Universalist Service Committee, 1978), pp. 43-50.

6. Author's interview with FAPU leaders in San Salvador, January 1980.

7. *Vancouver Sun*, November 14, 1979.

8. *Latin America* (London), March 14, 1980.

9. *New York Times*, February 25, 1980.

10. Ibid., March 26, 1980.

11. *This Week Central America and Panama*, September 8, 1980.

12. Alastair White, *El Salvador* (New York: Praeger, 1973), pp. 146-48.

13. *El Salvador Reports* (New York), August 1978.

14. Tass, May 7, 1979; and *Granma*, June 1, 1980.

15. *Intercontinental Press*, April 7, 1980.

16. Ibid., July 7, 1980; and *New York Times*, September 28, 1980.

17. Telivisora Nacional (Panama City), July 30, 1980; in *FBIS*, July 31, 1980.

18. *Washington Post*, March 26, 1980.

19. *La Prensa Gráfica* (San Salvador), May 19, 1980.

5 | GUATEMALA

Daniel L. Premo

With a total area of 42,042 square miles (roughly the size of Tennessee), Guatemala is smaller than Nicaragua and Honduras, but its population of 7.2 million (1981) makes it the most populous nation in Central America. Of the country's four distinct geographic regions, the dominant highlands extending southeast from Mexico contain over 80 percent of the total population and approximately one-fifth of the national territory. Guatemala City, the capital, displays the characteristics typical of the "primate city" of Central American countries.[1] To the north lies the dense Petén forest region, which occupies one-third of the country's land area but is inhabited by less than 2 percent of its population. The sugar and cotton plantations of the Pacific coastal lowlands, along with the coffee trees of the highlands, provide Guatemala with its principal sources of foreign exchange. The Caribbean lowlands are sparsely inhabited, although the ports of Puerto Barrios and Livingston should increase in importance as development of the Northern Transversal Strip (see below) opens the region.

Ethnicity is an important structural and cultural feature of national life. The 1964 census separates Guatemalans into two social categories: Spanish and Hispanicized indigenous groups, commonly known as *ladinos*; and the numerous subordinate Indian groups descended from the Maya. "*Ladino*" has no exact definition; the term refers more to cultural characteristics than to physical features.[2] The Maya comprise an estimated 40–45 percent of the population; no other country of Central America is so predominantly Indian in its ethnic composition. Two-thirds of the country's Indian population resides in the western and central highlands, occupying less than one-quarter of the total area of the country.[3] Although in the country as a whole the Indian population has declined relatively as a result of gradual cultural and social assimilation to the dominant *ladino* group, the ethnic ratio has remained stable in the predominantly Indian regions.

Guatemala had an average annual growth rate of 2.9 percent in the 1970s.[4] Assuming a constant growth rate, Guatemala's population will double every 21 years.[5] More than half the population is under twenty years of age. The country's crude birthrate of 41.5 per 1,000 inhabitants is comparable to that found in El Salvador, Honduras, and Nicaragua. However, Guatemala's death rate of 10.9 per 1,000 inhabitants is exceeded in Central America and the Caribbean only by those of Haiti and Nicaragua. Infant mortality is high, 82.9 per 1,000 live births officially, and perhaps double that unofficially. An estimated 81 percent of rural children suffer from malnutrition. Debilitated by an inadequate diet, the country's largely rural population is susceptible to recurrent epidemics of childhood diseases.[6] The average life expectancy in 1970 was 53.2 for the population as a whole. However, the average for *ladinos* was approximately 60.5, while that for Indians was only 44.5.[7] This difference of sixteen years illustrates vividly the disparity in the standard of living between rural and urban sectors.

Educational data also confirm the depressed state of the traditional Indian communities. The overall illiteracy level of approximately 70 percent is second in Latin America only to that of Haiti. In 1977 slightly over one-third of the school-age population (5–20 years) was attending school, despite a 100 percent increase between 1960 and 1970 in school attendance.[8] The dropout rate is one of the most serious problems in primary education, particularly in densely populated rural areas, where, because of seasonal migrations to farms on the southern coast and the shortage of schools, only 4 percent of the enrollees complete primary school.[9] In sum, Guatemala is a country that, by virtually any statistical index, suffers from low socioeconomic and cultural levels, especially in rural areas, where 70 percent of the population resides. The problem of integrating the traditional Indian communities into national life has been one of the underlying structural factors contributing to the country's turbulent political history.

At present, agricultural products constitute Guatemala's principal exports. Prior to 1950, the country was commonly called a "banana republic." The United Fruit Company (now part of United Brands) acquired concessions to develop banana plantations in 1906, and by

1948 bananas made up more than 40 percent of total exports. A combination of political and natural disasters, beginning with the company's implication in the 1954 overthrow of the Arbenz government, led in 1968 to the company's withdrawal from its once extensive operations. As a result, bananas now occupy a relatively minor position in the national economy. In 1976 they accounted for only 5.9 percent of total exports.[10]

In the 1950s coffee made up 70 to 80 percent of the value of all exports, and Guatemala appeared destined to become a one-crop country. However, exports of coffee gradually declined to about 30 percent of the total as the production of sugar, cotton, and beef for export increased. As in other countries dependent on agricultural exports, climatic changes and the vagaries of the world market dramatically affect the annual growth rate and export value of Guatemala's major crops.

Guatemala has few natural resources. However, the government is optimistic that petroleum will become a major export product. In September 1976 the Shenandoah Oil Corporation of Texas confirmed the discovery of marketable quantities of petroleum at the Alta Verapaz field near the Mexican border. The government subsequently marked out five prospecting zones covering over 20,000 kilometers (the Northern Transversal Strip) and opened bidding for exploration and exploitation contracts to some fifty oil companies in 1978. At present the amount of oil in Guatemala is the subject of debate. The wells discovered by Shenandoah in Rubelsanto and Chinajá have an estimated production potential of 8,000 barrels per day, considerably less than the minimum of 18,000 needed to make the construction of a 200-kilometer pipeline to the Caribbean economically viable.[11] Current production of 7,000 barrels per day represents one-sixth of the nation's daily usage. Annual production increased from 97,000 barrels in 1976 to 1.4 million in 1980.

Guatemala hopes to become a major producer of nickel within a few years. In 1960 the International Nickel Company and the Hanna Mining Company of Cleveland formed Exploraciones y Explotaciones Mineras Izabal (EXIMBAL). However, the Niquegua nickel plant, which expects to produce 25 million pounds of nickel annually, did not begin operations until July 1977. Production costs currently exceed the world nickel price, and profits are unlikely before the mid-1980s unless the price of nickel rises sharply or EXIMBAL can reduce its costs.[12]

The largest portion of the govennment's 1980 budget, roughly 28 percent, went to the energy and mining sectors. In early 1980 President Romeo Lucas García expressed optimism about Guatemala's oil potential. He pronounced the country "in a good economic position," after considerable increase in production, with a record $700 million in international monetary reserves.[13] The country's economic condition, attributable largely to the 70 percent increase in coffee prices since 1977, must be viewed against its large external public debt ($790 million at year-end 1978).[14]

Class Structure

Guatemala's basic socioeconomic class structure resulted from relationships established during the colonial period. Since Guatemala lacked the precious metals of Mexico and Peru, the Spaniards who settled Guatemala devoted themselves largely to agricultural pursuits, developing large estates in the traditional Spanish manner. The latifundium system concentrated landownership in the hands of a few colonists who formed the genesis of a wealthy upper class.[15] A class structure that relegated nonwhites to sharply inferior social and economic positions reinforced the privileged position of the landed elite.

Political and economic power in Guatemala is still concentrated in the hands of a small group, with shared interests, of large landowners, industrialists, and their relatives. Historically, this group has been allied with the military and backed by the representatives of foreign corporations and the Catholic hierarchy. According to the 1964 census, 2 percent of the landowners hold title to 63 percent of the cultivated area. In contrast, 87 percent of the total number of farms occupy only 19 percent of the country's arable land area and average less than 2.5 acres in size.[16]

In recent decades population pressures and the inability or unwillingness of the elite to bring about a more equitable distribution of land have aggravated the problem of "minifundia." The large-scale agrarian reform program initiated under the government of Jacobo Arbenz in June 1952 proposed to give land to agricultural workers by expropriating and redistributing private and nationally owned estates. From January 1953 to June 1954, a thousand farms covering 2.7 million acres were apportioned among an estimated 100,000 campesinos.[17] The government expropriated almost 400,000 acres from Guatemala's largest landowner, the United Fruit Company (no more than 15 percent of the company's 550,000 acres were under cultivation).[18] In June 1954 an exile movement supported by the CIA overthrew the Arbenz regime. Colonel Carlos Castillo Armas became president on July 8, 1954, and immediately suspended the agrarian reform law. Subsequent governmental actions permitted the large landowners, including the United Fruit Company, to recover most of their property.

Approximately six out of every ten Guatemalans continue to work in some phase of agriculture; yet the country must rely on imports to meet demand for basic foodstuffs. In the highlands, 50 percent of the plots are smaller than three acres. The majority of minifundistas are illiterate Indians divorced from national life who subsist on corn.[19] A recent report of the Agency for International Development estimated that 60 percent of the rural population has a per capita income of less than $80 a year.[20] As a result, some 200,000 landless peasants and an estimated 400,000 Indian smallholders are forced by poverty and tenancy agreements to migrate to southern coastal areas to pick cotton or cut cane on the latifundia for an average $.80 a day.[21]

In the mid-1970s, President Kjell Laugerud García discreetly supported a movement originally founded by Catholic priests to establish cooperatives among poor Indian farmers in the highland region. Large landowners strongly opposed the policy, as did the two right-wing parties providing the main civilian backing for the regime, the Institutional Democratic Party (PID) and the National Liberation Movement (MLN). The latter's outspoken leader and the country's vice-president at the time, Mario Sandoval Alarcón, likened cooperativism to communism.[22] However, the disastrous earthquake of February 4, 1976, which claimed an estimated 25,000 lives, aborted this potential rural movement. The greatest damage and loss of life occurred precisely in the highland areas where cooperatives were being developed.[23]

The present government of General Lucas García has turned its attention away from cooperatives to a modest program of land redistribution in the jungle areas of El Petén. However, a conflict over landownership, much like that long common in the highland region, has erupted in the Northern Transversal Strip. Stimulated by the discovery of oil, the construction of roads and pipelines and the exploitation of nickel deposits, land speculators established title to much of the land before the resettlement program was even under way. Would-be colonizers have ended up working as peons on the large farms now appearing in the area.[24] President Lucas, who in 1977 was in charge of development of the strip, reportedly owns three estates totaling 130,000 acres. Other military officials, including former Defense Minister Otto Spiegler, have also been provided with land to "colonize." One district near Sebol is known as "the area of the generals."[25]

Richard Adams wrote in 1970 that the economic change occurring in Guatemala, if anything, was "reinforcing the existing power structure, not substantially modifying it."[26] Nothing has happened in the following decade to challenge Adams's assessment. A succession of governmental failures since 1954 to meet the demands of a rapidly expanding population has resulted in the aggravation of social and economic tensions.

These, in turn, have led to a rapid polarization of political forces. Since the mid-1960s these forces have not hesitated to make calculated use of repression and violence to achieve their objectives.

Recent Political Developments

Contemporary political developments, particularly the question of communist influence and the alarming level of institutionalized violence, must be placed in historical perspective.

Long periods of personalist dictatorships alternating with much shorter periods of political instability characterize Guatemalan political history. In the 105 years preceding the overthrow of Jorge Ubico in 1944, four men had occupied the presidency for a total of 73 years. Six of the country's last seven presidents have been career military officers, supported by an array of reactionary, moderate, and centrist political parties, none of which existed prior to 1955.[27] Beginning with Carlos Arana Osorio in 1970, Guatemala's military presidents have been supported by precarious electoral minorities sharing only a liking for the status quo and a staunch anticommunism.[28]

The issue of communism in Guatemala dates back to the reformist governments of Juan José Arévalo (1945–1950) and Jacobo Arbenz Guzmán (1950–1954). Although Arévalo was widely denounced in the United States as a communist, his actions in office suggest, rather, a nationalist-oriented government.[29] The case of Arbenz is more complex, beginning with his government's granting of legal recognition to the Guatemalan Communist Party in 1951.[30] In the atmosphere of militant anticommunism in the early 1950s, the Eisenhower administration concluded that the Arbenz regime represented a "communist threat" and conspired for its overthrow. Many observers date the beginning of Guatemala's current violence to the ouster of the Arbenz government in June 1954.[31] A counterrevolution carried out by the self-proclaimed group of "liberationists" swiftly negated the reforms introduced by Arévalo and Arbenz. Castillo Armas and his supporters also established the principle that political opposition to governmental policy was tantamount to "communist" subversion.

Although street demonstrations led by students and trade unionists occurred sporadically under the governments of Castillo Armas and Miguel Ydígoras Fuentes, no sustained, violent opposition arose until the appearance of several left-wing guerrilla groups during the regime of Colonel Enrique Peralta Azurdia (1963–1966).[32] The military's inability to eradicate guerrilla groups operating in Zacapa and Izabal departments in 1966 led to the adoption of a policy of systematic repression of groups thought to be supporting them. One such group was the the communist Guatemalan Party of Labor (PGT), which had been forced to operate underground since 1954.[33]

Following Méndez Montenegro's election in 1966, Colonel Arana Osorio was appointed military commander of Zacapa and soon integrated anticommunist civilians drawn from among participants in the 1954 coup into the military's security apparatus, forming the first in a series of right-wing paramilitary associations. Initially, such groups as the National Organized Anticommunist Movement (MANO), the New Anticommunist Organization (NOA), and the "Eye for an Eye" (OJO) chose their victims from individuals associated with the Arévalo-Arbenz years or more recent guerrilla insurgency.[34] Soon, however, right-wing terrorists began seeking out and eliminating noncommunist leftists. Leaflets threatened not only prominent members of the PGT and rebel groups, but also students, professors, trade unionists, and professionals protesting social injustice. In December 1966, legislation authorizing large landowners to serve as law enforcement agents was passed. Between October 1966 and March 1968 an estimated 3,000–8,000 Guatemalans were reportedly killed in the Zacapa-Izabal campaign. The use of "counterterror" by civilian paramilitary groups is credited for much of the success of the campaign against rural guerrillas and their suspected supporters.[35]

Following the destruction of rural guerrilla movements in the late 1960s, left-wing opposition moved into urban areas. Arana Osorio was elected president in 1970 on a campaign of "law and order" and a promise to destroy the urban guerrilla movement. During the first three years of his presidency, the incidence of murders and "disappearances" reached unprecedented levels. Depending on the source, the number of victims, many mutilated beyond recognition, ranges from 3,500 to 15,000.

Although political violence lessened before the 1974 elections, the inauguration of General Laugerud García was followed by a rash of killings by paramilitary groups. Acts of violence by leftist organizations and clandestine movements of the right occurred with alarming frequency in 1975, spreading fear among residents in both urban and rural areas. MANO, NOA, and OJO gave way to self-styled "death squads" whose avowed purpose was to eliminate "antisocial elements" and anyone who cooperated with subversive organizations. Between 1972 and 1976, Amnesty International documented a total of 1,105 cases of executions and disappearances.[36] Most of the victims were probably petty criminals from the peasantry or the urban poor. The second largest group were clearly peasants. Others included members and leaders of opposition parties, among them all seven members of the PGT's Executive Committee, who "disappeared" in September 1972; trade unionists; journalists; university professors and students; and assorted professionals. During the same period, Guatemalan newspapers reported a high incidence of left-wing political violence, including 149 murders of members of security forces, other government personnel, businessmen, and large landowners and their agents.

Political killings involving leftist groups and right-wing paramilitary organizations remained a disturbingly common feature of Guatemalan daily life from 1974 to 1978. Although President Laugerud attempted to dissociate his administration from extreme right-wing violence, the government's inability to account for the disappearance and assassination of individuals with leftist sympathies led to continued criticism of the state of human rights. The principal instrument of right-wing assassination since 1977 has been the Secret Anticommunist Army (Ejército Secreto Anticomunista; ESA). The ESA's first communiqué announced its intention to "protect social classes attacked by communist gangs." The new organization stated that it would wage a "bitter struggle" against extreme leftist groups such as the PGT and the Guerrilla Army of the Poor (Ejército Guerrillero de los Pobres; EGP), warning that it had already begun to judge "the most prominent communists who promote terror in the country."[37] The emergence of the ESA reintroduced an element of counterterror reminiscent of the extremist operations of the MANO, NOA, and the OJO in the early 1970s.

Political Violence Since 1978

Political life has become increasingly polarized since the inauguration of President Lucas García on July 1, 1978. The new administration immediately announced "a harsh campaign against guerrilla groups." By the end of Lucas's first six months in office, more than 500 victims of violence were reported. Amnesty International claimed in September 1979 that political murder and repression had taken 2,000 lives in the previous sixteen months, many of them government opponents murdered by "semiclandestine death squads."[38] The group published a chronological list of abductions and killings since May 1978, with more than 1,000 bodies found in the first four months of 1979.[39] While the information provided through the Guatemalan press is not always accurate or necessarily complete, it reported 546 identifiably political murders during a period of less than two months at the beginning of 1979.[40] By the end of 1980, an average of ten bodies was being found daily in or near Guatemala City. In addition, mass graves discovered in rural areas contained as many as thirty bodies.[41] Amnesty International reported that between January and November 1980 some 3,364 people described by government officials as "subversives" and "criminals" either were assassinated or have disappeared.[42] Estimates of political murders committed during the Lucas García regime range from 5,000 to 6,000.

Top leaders of the moderate political left have been assassinated in an attempt to prevent the organization and legal representation of opposition parties.[43] A dozen national and regional leaders of the opposition United Revolutionary Front (FUR) were killed in 1980. In addition, local party leaders belonging to the Christian Democratic Party (PDC) and the Social Democratic Party (PSD) have been systematically murdered in recent years. On May 14, 1981, the PDC's secretary general informed U.S. officials that 76 party members had been killed in the previous ten months.[44] Indications are that neither the PDC nor the PSD will participate in the 1982 elections, signifying at least a temporary absence of the political center.

The growth of trade unionism in Guatemala has also been a factor in the resurgence of right-wing paramilitary and death squad activity. At least 25 labor leaders have been murdered since 1978. Another 150 trade unionists have either been killed, disappeared, or been forced into exile. Agricultural union leaders have also been the victims of systematic violence. According to the Democratic Front Against Repression (FDCR), 311 peasant leaders were murdered in 1980 by government security forces and civilian paramilitary groups.[45] Attacks have been directed especially against suspected members of the Peasant Unity Committee (Comité de Unidad Campesino), an Indian-dominated union founded in 1978.

The academic sector's continued involvement with opposition groups has made it a prime target for kidnappings and murder. The University of San Carlos and its regional affiliates have long been considered centers of "leftist subversion." Academics have played a leading role in advising trade unions and *campesino* organizations concerning legal registration and questions of land rights. During 1980, over fifty professors and officials associated with San Carlos and more than one hundred students were assassinated. Others, including the university's rector, have fled into exile.

While right-wing assassination of popular leaders has clearly escalated, left-wing extremist groups, especially the EGP's urban unit, have also intensified the level of violence against the government. The present wave of terror is generally believed to exceed that of the early 1970s. Although leftist groups also employ the tactic of political murder, right-wing death squads and paramilitary organizations such as the ESA have become a Guatemalan tradition. In recent years the kill ratio between right and left has been roughly 15:1.

The PGT and Guerrilla Movements

The largest and most active of the guerrilla organizations is the EGP, which began operations in November 1975. Its membership is believed to contain remnants of leftist guerrilla groups that succumbed to the counterinsurgency tactics of Arana Osorio in the late 1960s.

The EGP guerrillas have increased in number from about 300 in 1975 to an estimated 1,200 at the end of 1980. They are divided into four independent commands, three in the countryside and one in Guatemala City. The EGP has been most active in propagandizing and organizing in El Quiché; near Escuintla, along the tropical Pacific coast; and to a lesser extent in Zacapa.

There is no firm evidence of significant communist leadership in the guerrilla movement, although a large percentage of the EGP's urban guerrillas are believed to be party members.[46] The movement's leaders appear to have concluded that no armed struggle can succeed in Guatemala without the participation of the Indians. The EGP intensified its efforts at indoctrination in 1979–1980, briefly occupying over one hundred villages to deliver political lectures, distribute Marxist propaganda, and secure arms and supplies. According to news reports, Indians, including women, have joined the guerrilla movement in increasing numbers, especially in the northwest.[47] The EGP has abandoned its early policy of avoiding armed confrontation and now attacks army outposts and patrols over wide areas of western Guatemala. Simultaneously, the EGP's urban front selectively assassinates military and civilian officials.[48]

A second guerrilla group, the self-styled Armed People's Organization (ORPA), undertook its first military action in September 1979. ORPA's political affiliation, strength, and leadership hierarchy are undetermined. However, guerrilla units of up to 150 members have occupied villages and carried out propaganda activities in the departments of Huehuetenango, San Marcos, Quezaltenango, Chimaltenango, Solalá, and Suchitepéquez.

The pro-Soviet PGT has an estimated membership of 750, many of whom date back to the Arbenz regime. The party has not yet recovered from the loss of its political directorates in 1966 and 1972. Little information on the party's present leadership or structure is available. The PGT has expressed support for a broad alliance of forces to create the conditions for revolution. However, factionalism between those who seek to regain legal status and those who advocate the primacy of armed struggle has undermined the party's internal cohesion. Judging from statements attributed to the party's general secretary, the PGT is not eager to endorse an immediate appeal to arms, despite its belief that a further escalation of repression and terror is "inevitable."[49] In 1980 the "military coordinating" committee denounced the party's Central Committee for disavowing responsibility for recent acts of violence attributed to the PGT by the government.[50] The Central Committee was accused of "distorting the true nature of the Communist Party" and developing a "defeatist, timid and opportunist tendency."[51] The militant faction of the PGT has protested the party's most recent platform, which supports elections and seeks to unify the "antidictatorship" movement.

In 1980 the EGP and ORPA agreed in principle to begin political and military cooperation. In a message sent to Fidel Castro in May, guerrilla leaders proclaimed their support for unity "to organize a popular and democratic broad front to overthrow Lucas García's criminal regime."[52] On January 27, 1981, Guatemala's major guerrilla organizations issued their first joint communiqué, which strongly criticized the Lucas government and confirmed their unification. While the consensus is greater than in the past, no organizational merger of the groups has yet occurred. Initial links have been established, but there is no indication that activities are being coordinated by a single leadership. Despite presumed differences in ideology and tactics, Guatemala's guerrilla forces are believed to be working toward an alliance with the major non-Marxist mass organizations of popular resistance associated with the FDCR, which comprises labor, peasant, and student organizations, along with remnants of the democratic opposition groups.

By the spring of 1981, guerrilla fighting had intensified throughout El Quiché, Alta Verapaz, and in a large area of the country's southern coast. Government forces maintain control of the towns, but guerrillas entrenched in the mountains present the Guatemalan government with its most serious threat since the late 1960s.

Cuban and Soviet Influence

Government officials in Guatemala, including military spokesmen, have maintained for some years that Guatemala is the target of an international communist plan to destroy the country's image and unleash a guerrilla struggle to seize power. In 1976 President Laugerud García accused international communism of "dragging the country into a bloodbath." In commenting on the general increase in violence, the president charged that it was the work of "communists who are being directed, financed, and incited by the Cuban government."[53] In an unusually candid interview, however, Government Minister General Vassaux Martínez declared that the resurgence of violence resulted from social and economic problems "that cannot be eradicated simply by means of coercive measures." He added that the major cause of violence lies in "the failure for many years to extend an effective system of social justice to all the people."[54]

According to a presidential communiqué in 1980, the step preceding the guerrillas' frontal attack is a campaign aimed at discrediting the country internationally. Amnesty International is said to be participating in this campaign by spreading the idea of "a Guatemala marked by violence and social injustice."[55] Without doubt, Amnesty International has made the most serious attempt to document the Guatemalan government's involvement in right-wing terrorism. A report released in February 1981 categorically charges that "routine assassinations, secret detentions and summary executions are part of a clearly defined program of government in Guatemala ... carried out by a specialized agency under the direct supervision of President Lucas García."[56] A representative for the president called the report "biased, ridiculous and childish," and referred to Amnesty International as "the spokesman of international communism."[57]

The Guatemalan Defense Ministry has stated that Cuban mercenaries have been detected with the guerrillas operating in El Quiché. The minister also charged that Guatemalan guerrillas are receiving training in Cuba, Nicaragua, and the Soviet Union, which, he said, accounts for the increase in subversive activity since the beginning of 1980.[58] A U.S. intelligence report issued in July 1979 partially substantiated these allegations. The report concluded that Cuba had intensified its attempts to unify insurgent groups in Guatemala and was accelerating its program of training guerrillas from various Central American countries.[59] The U.S. ambassador to Guatemala informed the State Department in June 1980 that "unmistakable signals of increased Cuban (and perhaps ultimately Soviet) support" had emboldened the far left in Guatemala, which, he added, was probably "no longer willing to dialogue, to accept concessions, or even to share power in the constituted institutional framework."[60]

An unattributed article published in the Guatemalan daily Prensa Libre alleges that since 1975 the Soviet Union has operated through the "American Department" of the Cuban Communist Party to pursue its Central American and Caribbean policy. According to Soviet strategy, a softening-up process is to be applied through labor unions, student groups, the press, and political organizations in order to create favorable conditions for the final stage of armed struggle. While these groups carry out their "spontaneous" activities, the strategy calls for "making charges about missing people, tortures, and repression against the nation's civilian population." El Salvador is expected to follow the course of Nicaragua's armed struggle. Belize would go next, while Guatemala would be the last to experience armed struggle, in order not to provoke a reaction from Mexico.[61]

The recent increase in generalized violence in Guatemala is to some degree a result of the uncertain political situation in Central America. The Sandinista victory in Nicaragua and the conflict in neighboring El Salvador have exacerbated political divisions in Guatemala. While the State Department under President Carter maintained that Castroites and Marxists were not the cause of instability in Central America, the Reagan administration firmly believes that Guatemala is faced with "externally supported subversion." In testimony before the House Subcommittee on Inter-American Affairs, John Bushnell, acting assistant secretary of state for inter-American affairs, attributed the escalation of violence in Guatemala to "Communist exploitation of traditional social and political inequities." He accused the Soviet Union and Cuba of "seeking to advance their own interests in the region at its and our expense." Cuba, in particular, is singled out, as it has been in El Salvador, for promoting the unification of Guatemala's diverse Marxist guerrilla groups and in assisting them to obtain arms and training.[62]

For his part, President Lucas García vows to "defend the freedom of Guatemala" against the Soviet Union's goal of expanding its penetration of the area and further weakening the U.S. presence in the Caribbean. The Guatemalan military's response to increasing criticism has been to close ranks with the private sector to fight the "communist plague." In a 1980 report on the state of the nation, President Lucas reiterated the charge that there is an international plot, abetted by Cuban guerrillas, to establish "a communist regime" in Guatemala. He pledged that his government will continue to deal harshly with "communist subversion."[63]

Prospects

The official position of the Guatemalan government has been to deny any complicity in the organization or activities of any paramilitary group or death squad. Exactly who is behind such groups is still a matter of some speculation. The tendency has been to blame the MLN and its passionately anticommunist leader, Sandoval Alarcón, as the most likely protagonists.[64] However, labor and student movements whose leaders have received death threats from the ESA are more inclined to accuse officials closer to the center of power, namely the national police chief, the minister of government, and the defense minister. University sources have pointed out that numerous murders have occurred in the presence of police or persons driving vehicles with official license plates. From this they have concluded that the government, acting at times on information provided by the business sector, is primarily responsible for the systematic elimination of opposition. Their view is supported by a number of human rights and church-related organizations. Amnesty International, for example, unequivocally states that "people who oppose or are imagined to oppose the Guatemalan government are systematically seized without warrant, tortured and murdered as part of a deliberate and long-standing program of the Guatemalan Government."[65]

While it is difficult to single out responsibility for Guatemala's political violence, it has not been coincidence that the overwhelming majority of its victims have been student, peasant, and trade union leaders, professors and intellectuals, and politicians who attempted to organize parties of the moderate left. Increasing numbers of Guatemalans are subject to classification as "communists" and so eligible for "death lists." Among them are undoubtedly some who have concluded that the most appealing alternative awaiting them is to support a form of armed struggle similar to those in Nicaragua and El Salvador.

At a time of increasing domestic pressure, the Lucas García government is also the focus of growing international attention. The old Central American order of the Somoza era has broken down. The current leaders of Guatemala blame former President Carter's human rights policy for destabilizing the region. For emphasizing the need for economic and social change, U.S. spokesmen have been accused in the past of encouraging opposition groups and abetting subversion in the area.[66] Guatemalan officials and businessmen are unguardedly optimistic that President Reagan will re-establish the containment of communism as the cornerstone of U.S. policy in Central America. Such a policy will presumably include the resumption of military assistance and increased economic aid to "moderately repressive autocratic governments" friendly to the United States.[67]

President Reagan has yet to define a clear policy for dealing with what his administration perceives as Soviet-backed subversion in Central America and the Caribbean. Secretary Haig has implied that military aid for Guatemala will be proposed in the 1981 foreign aid bill in the name of anticommunism. Retired General Vernon Walters visited the country in May as Haig's special emissary to investigate the possibility of renewing military assistance. In dismissing much of the human rights situation in Guatemala, Walters said that the United States hopes to help the Guatemalan government defend "peace and liberty" and "the constitutional institutions of this country against the ideologies that want to finish off those institutions."[68]

Meanwhile, Guatemala continues to experience the highest levels of political violence and abuse of personal rights in its history.[69] A review of that history suggests that the root of the country's political crisis remains the unjust distribution of wealth stemming from an archaic economic and social structure. Apart from President Lucas García's projected literacy campaign and colonization program, there is little evidence that either the military or the private sector is willing to consider broadening the political process and undertaking the social and economic reforms that might conceivably alleviate existing tensions.[70]

In few countries of the world is it as dangerous to struggle for the simplest democratic rights as it is today in Guatemala. If the situation in Guatemala continues to deteriorate, the Reagan administration will be increasingly tempted to intervene directly in order to maintain stability. Although Secretary Haig's attempt to transform El Salvador into an East-West battleground appears to have been lowered, at least temporarily, events in Guatemala may rekindle support for a more vigorous policy of confrontation and containment of radicalism in Central America.

The disintegration of the established order is not likely to occur as rapidly in Guatemala as in Nicaragua or apparently in El Salvador. For one thing, there is no symbol to unify the diverse opposition groups. For another, apart from the capital the population is still predominantly Indian, illiterate and politically unaware. Moreover, the extreme left has yet to demonstrate conclusively that Guatemala's Indians are not as susceptible to mobilization in support of the status quo as they are in opposition.[71] Finally, the Guatemalan military has developed a corporate tradition of independent conservatism, supported by an equally conservative private sector that is disposed to assist in the repression of popular movements in order to retain its monopoly of the benefits of economic growth. The result is a continuing accentuation of social antagonisms and polarization of political forces without likely victory for either side. The country is presently engulfed in a politics of attrition, intimidation, and violence in which there are no clear winners in the short term, only victims.

Notes

1. Guatemala City is the political, economic, educational, and social center for the entire country. Its population grew from 287,000 in 1950 to over 1 mil-

lion in 1980. In contrast, Quezaltenango, the second city of the country, has an estimated population of only 60,000. For an early study of the impact of urbanization on Guatemala's social structure, see Michael Micklin, "Urbanization, Technology, and Traditional Values in Guatemala: Some Consequences of a Changing Social Structure," *Social Forces* 47 (June 1969): 440.

2. For a discussion of the distinction between Indian and *ladino* status, see Pierre I. van den Berghe, "Ethnic Membership and Cultural Change in Guatemala," *Social Forces* 46 (June 1968): 514–22.

3. Although some degree of geographical mobility is in evidence, available data indicate that little change occurred in ethnic composition in the heavily (75–94 percent) Indian departments of Totonicapán, Sololá, Alta Verapaz, Quiché, Chimaltenango, San Marcos, and Huehuetenango during the period between 1940 and 1964 (see John D. Early, "Revision of Ladino and Maya Census Populations of Guatemala, 1950 and 1964," *Demography* 11 [February 1974]: 105–17).

4. *Economic and Social Progress in Latin America, 1979* (Washington, D.C.: Inter-American Development Bank, n.d.), p. 258; based on data from Banco de Guatemala.

5. John D. Early, "Population Increase and Family Planning in Guatemala," *Human Organization* 34 (Fall 1975): 276.

6. In a study of a Guatemalan highland community, Oscar Horst determined that 43 percent of all deaths recorded in 1960 occurred among infants under two years of age ("The Specter of Death in a Guatemalan Highland Community," *Geographical Review* 57 [April 1967]: 159).

7. Elena Ruíz de Barrios Klee, 7 *Días en la USAC* (Guatemala City), no. 19 (February 26, 1979): 8.

8. Ibid.; estimates based on 1974–75 data taken from *Anuarios Estadísticos de OPIE* of the Guatemalan Ministry of Education. A 1980 survey showed that of an estimated 1.5 million potential elementary school students age 7–14, only 52 percent were actually enrolled—still one of the lowest levels in Latin America (*Voice of Guatemala* [New York], no. 1 [February 1981]: 3).

9. Inter-American Development Bank, *Economic and Social Progress*, p. 266.

10. United Nations, Economic Commission for Latin America, *Economic Survey of Latin America, 1976* (Santiago: Editorial Universitaria, 1977), p. 209.

11. *Latin America Economic Report* 6 (March 3, 1978): 70.

12. Ibid., 5 (July 29, 1977): 116. According to Economy Minister Valentín Solórzano, nickel exports should reach U.S. $75 million in 1980 (*El Imparcial*, June 19, 1980).

13. *El Imparcial*, January 6, 1980.

14. Inter-American Development Bank, *Economic and Social Progress*, p. 266.

15. For an incisive interpretation of the evolution of Guatemala's social and economic structure during the colonial era, see Severo Martínez Peláez, *La Patria del Criollo*, 4th ed. (San José: Editorial Universitaria Centroamericana, 1976).

16. Susanne Jonas and David Tobis, eds., *Guatemala* (Berkeley: North American Congress on Latin America, 1974), p. 14. Alan Riding reported in 1979 that "2 percent of the farmers own 53 percent of the cultivable land, while 77 percent of the farmers own only 36 percent" (*New York Times*, April 5, 1979, p. 5).

17. Solon Barraclough, *Agrarian Structure in Latin America* (Lexington, Mass.: D.C. Heath, 1973), pp. 242–43.

18. Susanne Jonas, "Guatemala: Land of Eternal Struggle," in Ronald H. Chilcote and Joel C. Edelstein, eds., *Latin America: The Struggle with Dependency and Beyond* (New York: Halstead Press, 1974), p. 160.

19. Barraclough, *Agrarian Structure*, p. 238.

20. *New York Times*, April 5, 1979, p. 5.

21. In March 1980 the minimum daily wage for farm workers on the southern coast was raised to $3.20 following work stoppages and prolonged strikes. The previous official minimum daily wage of $1.12 had remained virtually constant since 1973, despite an annual inflation rate averaging 14 percent (*7 Días en la USAC*, March 17, 1980, p. 10).

22. *New York Times*, September 14, 1975, p. 6.

23. *Latin America Political Report*, March 5, 1976, p. 78.

24. The dispossession of Indians from their ancestral lands underlies several recent tragic confrontations; namely, the Panzós "massacre" in Alta Verapaz on May 29, 1978, in which troops killed over one hundred Indians; and the government's precipitous assault on the Spanish Embassy on January 31, 1980, after its occupation by a delegation of Indians from El Quiché. At least three instances of mass violence involving Indians and special army forces were reported between January and May 1981. Confrontations are likely to recur as long as landowners and would-be landowners attempt to gain control over known or suspected oil and nickel deposits.

25. Alan Riding, "Guatemala Opening New Lands, but Best Goes to the Rich," *New York Times*, April 5, 1979, p. 5. In 1980 the National Institute for Agricultural Reform (INTA) reportedly distributed 8,838 land titles covering 153,000 acres. According to President Lucas, INTA eventually plans to colonize 5,500 square miles of the Northern Transversal Strip in an effort to decongest the densely populated highlands (*Voice of Guatemala*, p. 1).

26. Richard N. Adams, *Crucifixion by Power* (Austin: University of Texas Press, 1970), p. 125.

27. For an excellent study of the political party system in Guatemala since 1944, see the special issue of *Política y Sociedad* (Guatemala), April 1978.

28. The military does not have its own political party, but since 1970 it has run its own presidential candidates. To ensure their election it has been sufficient to secure a temporary alliance with one or a coalition of rightist parties. In 1970 Col. Carlos Arana Osorio drew his support from the MLN, the most reactionary of the three major right-wing parties. In 1974 an MLN-PID coalition threw its support behind General Laugerud García in elections that are generally considered the most fraudulent in Guatemala's modern history. In 1978 the PID and the Revolutionary Party (PR) formed an electoral alliance to support General Lucas García. In 1970 the PR appeared in the "opposition," after providing the country with its only civilian president in over twenty years, Julio César Méndez Montenegro (1966–1970). Since 1978 the opposition role has been carried out by the MLN. From the military's point of view, any one or combination of the three parties serves the purpose equally well.

29. Although new Marxist groups appeared in the trade union and student movements in 1946–47, Arévalo did not hesitate to exile communist agitators. Moreover, he refused to legalize the Communist Party of Guatemala (PCG) in 1949.

30. In 1952 the party adopted the name Guatemalan Party of Labor (Partido Guatemalteco del Trabajo; PGT), which it has continued to use. Under Arbenz, the PGT held 4 of the 56 seats in Congress and established close ties with labor and peasant confederations. Several Marxists occupied important government positions, particularly in agrarian reform.

31. The classic attempt to document the charges of communism directed at the Arbenz government is Ronald M. Schneider, *Communism in Guatemala, 1944–1954* (New York: Praeger, 1958).

32. For a thorough account of the origin and activities of guerrilla movements in the early 1960s, see Richard Gott, *Guerrilla Movements in Latin America* (New York: Doubleday, 1970), pp. 39–118.

33. On March 6, 1966, 28 PGT leaders and trade unionists "disappeared" following their arrests.

34. For an early study of the tactics designed to institutionalize terror through the repression of subversive groups, see Kenneth F. Johnson, "On the Guatemalan Political Violence," *Politics and Society*, Fall 1973, pp. 55–82. For a more recent, empirically oriented study of the same period, see John A. Booth, "A Guatemalan Nightmare: Levels of Political Violence, 1966–1972," *Journal of Inter-American Studies and World Affairs* 22 (May 1980): 195–223.

35. *Guatemala* (London: Amnesty International, 1976), p. 3.

36. *7 Días en la USAC*, May 7, 1979, p. 8.

37. *El Imparcial*, June 23, 1977.

38. *New York Times*, December 6, 1979.

39. *Los Angeles Times*, September 14, 1979.

40. Edelberto Torres Rivas, "Vida y muerte en Guatemala: Reflexiones sobre la violencia," *7 Días en la USAC*, October 20, 1979, p. 6.

41. *7 Días en la USAC*, April 14, 1980, p. 5.

42. *Guatemala: A Government Program of Political Murder* (London: Amnesty International, 1981).

43. The most prominent victims were Alberto Fuentes Mohr, former foreign minister and leader of the small Social Democratic Party (PSD) who was murdered on January 25, 1979; and Manuel Colóm Argueta, head of the opposition United Revolutionary Front (FUR), who was assassinated in the capital on March 22, 1979. A popular former mayor of Guatemala City, Colóm Argueta was considered by many to be the best hope of the combined opposition to lead a future government.

44. Christopher Dickey, "Haig's Emissary in Guatemala Discounts Charges of Rights Abuse," *Washington Post*, May 14, 1981, p. 16.

45. *Update Latin America* 6 (March/April 1981), p. 5.

46. The EGP's principal leader, César Montes, is a onetime member of the PGT's Central Committee. He reportedly resigned in 1968 to protest the party's failure to support the guerrilla movement fully.

47. *Prensa Libre* (Guatemala City), May 5, 1979; *New York Times*, January 28, 1980, p. 4; and *Washington Report on the Hemisphere*, November 11, 1980, p. 8.

48. Guatemala's third-ranking army chief and the head of the IV Corps of the National Police were murdered in 1980; the interior minister and chief of national police survived assassination attempts.

49. Carlos Gonzales, *World Marxist Review*, October 1979, pp. 57–60.

50. Specifically, the PGT denied responsibility for the March 22 assassination of Col. Máximo Zepeda Martínez, who fought against leftist guerrillas in the 1960s, or the murder of Alberto Habie Mishaan, business leader and president of the influential Association of Agricultural, Trade, Industrial, and Financial Chambers.

51. Foreign Broadcast Information Service, *Daily Report, Latin America*, June 3, 1980, p. P10.

52. Havana, International Service, May 26, 1980.

53. *El Imparcial*, May 18, 1976, p. 1.

54. Ibid., May 22, 1976, p. 6.

55. Ibid., January 17, 1980, p. 1.

56. *Guatemala: A Government Program*, p. 7.

57. *El Imparcial*, February 20, 1981, p. 1.

58. *Prensa Libre*, March 7, 1980, p. 2. Almost identical allegations appear in the issue of May 11, 1981, p. 2. At a luncheon hosted for the diplomatic corps, President Lucas García said in January 1980 that "just like the coffee rust disease, communism appeared for the first time in Central America in Nicaragua, and it is now creeping into neighboring El Salvador" (*El Imparcial*, January 6, 1980).

59. *New York Times,* July 22, 1979, p. 13.

60. Quoted by Graham Hovey in the *New York Times,* June 28, 1980, pp. 1, 4. The ambassador, Frank V. Ortiz, Jr., was relieved of his duties in early August 1980.

61. *Prensa Libre,* April 10–11, 1980.

62. U.S., Department of State, Bureau of Public Affairs, "Central American Review," Current Policy Document no. 261 (Washington, D.C., March 5, 1981).

63. On January 26, 1981, President Lucas García inaugurated a nationwide literacy campaign intended to reach more than one million Guatemalans. On April 3, the government announced that state-owned farms will be turned over to Guatemalan peasants. The program is expected to affect "no fewer than 25,000 peasant families." While such programs may be a case of "too little, too late," they suggest that in attempting to deal with growing guerrilla insurgency, the government has become sensitive to the social reforms taking place in Nicaragua and El Salvador.

64. See, for example, Marlise Simon's article on Sandoval in the *Washington Post,* April 6, 1980, p. 14.

65. *Guatemala: A Government Program,* p. 3.

66. See the editorial in *El Imparcial* criticizing the end of the United States' "traditional anticommunist policy," January 26, 1980, p. 13.

67. The phrase was used by Jeane Kirkpatrick, ambassador-designate to the United Nations at the time, who considered such governments preferable to "Cuban-sponsored insurgency" (John M. Goshko, "Castro's Trojan Horses vs. Reagan's Crusaders," *Washington Post,* December 28, 1980, p. 2).

68. Dickey, "Haig's Emissary," p. 16. The United States is expected to increase economic aid from $6 million to about $11 million in fiscal year 1981–82.

69. One does not get this impression from reading the Department of State's country report on Guatemala for 1979 (*Country Reports on Human Rights Practices* [Washington, D.C.: Government Printing Office, 1980], pp. 327–33). In November 1979 Ambassador Ortiz wrote the State Department that in his opinion, government-condoned violence in Guatemala was abating. The ambassador's evaluation of the situation changed perceptibly during the ensuing six months. In a classified cable to Secretary of State Muskie dated June 19, 1980, Ortiz sharply criticized the Lucas García government for engaging in "heavy-handed repression in dealing with political dissidents" (see Nicholas Lemann's analysis in the *Washington Post,* July 6, 1980, p. 8). Ortiz further stated that his "greatest immediate fear" was not so much that the far left would take over Guatemala soon, but that the most retrograde elements on the right would "unleash an even greater wave of terror" (reported by Graham Hovey in the *New York Times,* June 28, 1980). The State Department's 1980 report is still tentative, but, on the whole, more critical of the Guatemalan government for its failure to halt abuses or carry out serious investigations

(*Country Reports on Human Rights Practices* [Washington, D.C.: Government Printing Office, February 2, 1981], pp. 441–49).

70. The likelihood of the government's seeking an understanding with even moderate elements of the left was reduced by the resignation of Vice-President Francisco Villagrán Kramer on September 1, 1980. Villagrán, a member of the PR's first directorate in 1957, had become increasingly critical of the government's failure to fulfill its political program and of the escalation of political violence.

71. For example, the Northeast Anticommunist Front, which encompasses the country's seven northeastern departments, claimed in May 1980 to have 150,000 men ready "to smash the communist guerrillas" as they did in 1962–1970 (*El Imparcial*, May 8, 1980). On June 22, a reported 100,000 persons participated in an anticommunist demonstration in Quezaltenango organized by ex-President Arana Osorio (*Prensa Libre*, June 24, 1980). Through carefully orchestrated rallies and visits to rural areas in 1981, President Lucas García has initiated an anticommunist campaign intended to retain Indian peasants' confidence and to generate support for the government's modest social reforms.

6 | COSTA RICA, HONDURAS, AND PANAMA

Neale J. Pearson

Costa Rica, Honduras, and Panama together are about the size of Oregon or Wyoming. Like the rest of Central America, they were ruled by Spain from the sixteenth century until independence in 1821. After a brief period of Mexican rule, the region formed the Federation of Central America in 1825. All but Panama became separate states in 1838 and remained relatively unimportant in Western Hemisphere affairs until World War II. Of the three, Panama has received the most headlines in recent years because of the controversy surrounding the new Panama Canal treaty and Panamanian positions that paralleled those of Cuba. However, relations between the two nations cooled in 1981, while Honduras attracted more attention because of its use as a conduit for weapons and guerrillas in the Salvadoran civil war and the tension with Nicaragua over the alleged use of Honduran territory as a staging ground for counterrevolutionary attacks by pro-Somoza forces.

Unlike Costa Rica, Honduras and Panama display political and social characteristics similar to those of their Central American neighbors that contribute to internal conflict—and a potential for outside meddling:

1. Inequitable distribution of income and land;
2. Inadequate and frequently stagnant agricultural productivity, especially in food for domestic consumption;
3. Oligarchical political systems marked by fraud and political violence employed to oppose political, economic, and social change;

4. Failure of commitment to economic development (in Honduras) to lead to significant reforms; and
5. Political cultures lacking institutions for resolving disputes while managing the difficult processes of national development.

Although communist parties, trade unions, and student groups are active in all three countries, their structures, leadership, and tactics vary considerably despite the similarities in the countries' problems.

Socioeconomic Characteristics

The bulk of the population in Honduras and Panama is mestizo, while that of Costa Rica is largely descended from early Spanish settlers and more recent immigrants from Europe and the United States. Panama has a large minority of English-speaking blacks whose ancestors did not return to Jamaica or the other Caribbean islands after helping construct the Panama Canal. Blacks in Honduras and Costa Rica were brought in to build railroads and develop banana plantations. While the economies of Costa Rica and Honduras are largely based on agriculture, they—like Panama and other Latin American countries—are experiencing problems of rural-urban migration and the lack of jobs in urban areas. Table 6.1 shows basic population data; figures for Nicaragua are given for comparison.

Most Costa Ricans and Hondurans live in the central highlands, where coffee is the major export product and corn and beans the chief subsistence crops. Sugarcane is another important cash crop in the Costa Rican highlands. Banana and sugar plantations dominate the Caribbean and Pacific coastal lowlands of all three nations; cotton is grown on the Pacific coast of Honduras. The export of beef to the United States has been important in all three states since the early 1960s.

The capital cities of San José (estimated population 500,000 in 1980) and Panama City (750,000) are called primate cities by demographers and economists because they dominate the political, economic, and cultural lives of their countries. The Honduran capital, Tegucigalpa (400,000), is an exception; San Pedro Sula (238,000) on the northern coast is the foremost economic center.

Although agriculture remains a primary source of employment and foreign exchange (see Table 6.2), all three countries are working to diversify their economies by replacing some imports with domestically produced manufactures. Costa Rica has been the most successful, especially since it joined the Central American Common Market in 1963.

In all Central American countries, landownership is concentrated in

TABLE 6.1
POPULATION AND AREA

	Population (1979)	Area (sq. mi)	Urban Population (percentage)	
			1960	1975
Costa Rica	2,168,000	19,575	34	40
Honduras	3,639,000	43,277	23	32
Nicaragua	2,485,000	50,193	40	50
Panama	1,862,000	29,209	41	51

SOURCES: *The Europa Yearbook, 1979*; World Bank, *World Development Report, 1979*.

the hands of *latifundistas* or *terratenientes*; most peasants, or *campesinos*, hold very small plots. In Honduras, 2 percent of the farms accounted for 46.7 percent of the land under cultivation in 1952, while 75 percent of the farms covered only 16 percent.[1] In 1974, 0.7 percent of Honduran farms controlled 33.9 percent of the land, while farms under 10 hectares (24.7 acreas) represented 88.2 percent of the total number of farms but only 16.7 percent of cultivated land.[2] In Costa Rica, less than 1 percent of the country's 64,621 farms occupied 31 percent of the farmland in 1963.[3] The 1973 agricultural census data reveal that the 2.1 percent of farms over 500 hectares in size controlled 42.2 percent of the cultivated land. At the other end of the spectrum, farms under 20 hectares in size—or 55.7 percent of the total—accounted for only 5.8 percent.[4] De-

TABLE 6.2
AGRICULTURE

	Percentage of Population Engaged in Agriculture			Primary Commodities as Percentage of Exports	
	1960	1970	1977	1960	1975
Costa Rica	51	42	30	95	74
Honduras	70	67	63	98	89
Nicaragua	62	51	44	98	83
Panama	51	42	30	100	na
51 Middle Income Countries	60	51	46	95	82

SOURCES: *World Development Report, 1978, 1979*.

TABLE 6.3
PER CAPITA INCOME AND EDUCATION

	Per Capita GNP		Elementary Age Population in School–1975 (percentage)	Secondary Age Population in School–1975 (percentage)	Adult Literacy 1975
	1960	1976			
Costa Rica	$540	$1,040	109	52	83
Honduras	260	390	89	13	57
Nicaragua	325	750	85	21	57
Panama	437	1,310	124	52	78
Cuba	na	860	126	35	96
58 Middle Income Countries	na	750	97	35	69

SOURCES: *World Development Report, 1978* and *1979.*

spite Costa Rica's successful political system, its rural proletariat could become the focus of social and political tension in the near future.

Panama has not faced peasant demands for land or pressures to expropriate large landholdings since over 90 percent of the land is state-owned; only about 3.1 percent of the land was cultivated in the late 1960s, with an additional 7.3 percent devoted to grazing.[5] In the words of one observer, "in Panama, many campesinos do not want title to a particular parcel of land. The majority ... have been practicing slash-and-burn agriculture on state land for years and feel that the only 'benefit' of landownership would be the payment of survey fees and taxes to the government."[6]

All Central American countries are poor compared with Canada, the United States, and Western Europe. Table 6.3 shows that Costa Rica and Panama are not as poor as their neighbors; indeed, the purchase of imported manufactured goods by the small urban and rural middle class in both countries contributes to their balance of payments problems.

In other measures of social progress, Honduras is the most backward of the three. Costa Rica and Panama far surpass their neighbors in the percentage of the school-age population enrolled in elementary, secondary, and higher education, and in overall adult literacy. Despite improvements in health care since World War II, the death rate is still high. Tropical diseases are endemic in many coastal and other areas with poor water and sanitation systems. Life expectancy is still low in Honduras and Nicaragua, and the ratio of physicians to population is generally low. While Costa Rica and Panama have made substantial progress in sanitation, more than half the population of Honduras does

TABLE 6.4
SELECTED HEALTH INDICATORS

	Death Rate per 1,000 (1975)	Life Expectancy at Birth (1975)	Population per Physician (1974)	Population with Access to Safe Water (1975, percentage)
Costa Rica	6	68	1,580	72
Honduras	14	54	3,360	41
Nicaragua	13	53	1,720	46
Panama	7	67	1,240	77
Cuba	6	70	1,200	na
58 Middle Income Countries	12	58	2,430	52

SOURCE: *World Development Report, 1978*

not have access to safe drinking water, a factor in the prevalence of intestinal parasites and water-borne diseases.

None of the three countries is rich in resources, especially petroleum and natural gas, although small gold and silver deposits are mined in Costa Rica and Honduras. Offshore oil wells are being drilled on the Caribbean coast of all three countries. Large hydroelectric projects are under way in all three countries to provide more electricity for industry and agriculture and to avoid the increasing costs of imported fuel. A government corporation is to develop large bauxite deposits found in Costa Rica; American, Canadian, and Japanese firms are extracting copper in Panama. A $600 million project in Olancho, Honduras, involving the construction of sawmills, a pulp factory, and paper plant should greatly increase Honduran exports and supply much of domestic demand for such products by 1983–1984.

All the Central American nations have faced trade deficits due to increasing costs of imported petroleum products, machinery, and consumer goods at a time when prices for their primary agricultural and mineral products have not risen as fast. Honduran agricultural production and exports were especially hard hit by Hurricane Fifi, which struck the north coast of that country in September 1974.

Recent Political Developments

As in many other Latin American nations, international forces contributed to political trends in Costa Rica, Honduras, and Panama immediately after World War II that have continued to the present. In Costa Rica, José Figueres Ferrer, leader of the Social Democratic Party

TABLE 6.5
FOREIGN TRADE INDICATORS

	1976		Average Annual Growth, 1970–1976	
	Exports	Imports	Exports	Imports
	(U.S. $ millions)		(percentage)	
Costa Rica	$584	$714	4.0	1.5
Honduras	392	453	−1.4	−2.0
Nicaragua	543	532	5.2	4.5
Panama	227	838	3.8	−3.7
58 Middle Income Countries	—	—	3.8	6.3

SOURCES: *World Development Report, 1978,* and *1979.*

(later transformed into the Party of National Liberation [PLN]), led a successful 1948 revolt when the ruling party of Rafael Calderón Guardia refused to recognize the election of Otilio Ulate as president. Figueres—aided by the governments of Juan José Arévalo in Guatemala, Carlos Prío Socarras in Cuba, and Dominican exiles—defeated Calderón Guardia, who had the support of the local communist party and the governments of Anastasio Somoza in Nicaragua and Tiburcio Carías Andino in Honduras. An interim junta headed by Figueres drafted a new constitution, abolished the army, outlawed the communist party, nationalized the banks, and established a career civil service system based on merit. When Ulate assumed the presidency on November 8, 1949, Costa Rica resumed its tradition of peaceful transfer of power from one president to another, and usually from one party to another.

In Panama, the National Guard became the decisive force in politics after World War II. After easily winning election in May 1952, its chief, José Antonio Remón, instituted various administrative reforms and economic development of the hinterlands. He negotiated a new canal treaty with the United States that increased U.S. payments to $1.93 million per year. However, in 1955, Remón was assassinated. In October 1968, the guard, led by Lt. Col. Omar Torrijos Herrera, overthrew the civilian government of Arnulfo Arias Madrid after a hotly disputed election. In October 1972, the National Assembly of Community Representatives delegated Torrijos extraordinary powers as chief of government for six years, even though a civilian president was nominal head of state. During this six-year period—frequently referred to as "the Revolution"—land was distributed to the peasants, and two new Canal Zone treaties were negotiated and finally signed in September 1977—although not without violent clashes between students and police. In October 1978, Torrijos (now a general) resigned as head of the government although not as head of the guard, and the National Assembly elected Minister of Education Arístides Royo president. The ruling Democratic Revolutionary Party (PRD) of Torrijos won eleven of the nineteen elected seats in the 57-member National Council on Legislation on September 28, 1980; the other 38 seats were already filled by appointment. The Liberal Party won five seats, the Christian Democrats two, and a member of the communist People's Party of Panama (PPP) was one of two independents elected. The Panamenista Party of aging former President Arnulfo Arias refused to participate and claimed a victory because of the high rate of abstention (35–40 percent of the 800,000 eligible voters) and the opposition's combined total of 60 percent of the vote. Arias was charged in 1980 and 1981 with organizing guerrilla-training bases in Costa Rica to topple the Royo-Torrijos regime. On August 1, 1981, Torrijos was killed in the crash of a small plane. Colonel Florencio Flórez Aguilar succeeded him as commander of the National Guard.

In Honduras, Tiburcio Carías Andino of the National Party dominated politics from 1932 to January 1949, when he relinquished the presidency to a handpicked successor, Juan Manuel Gálvez. Gálvez established a military school that became the basis for a professional officer corps and created the Central Bank and the National Development Bank to improve the nation's financial structures and to stimulate agricultural and livestock production. A banana strike in May–June 1954 established a noncommunist labor movement as a politically potent force. Gálvez's successor, Liberal Party leader Ramón Villeda Morales, implemented a 1958 labor code. A 1962 agrarian reform law, however, was not enforced for many years because Col. Oswaldo López Arrellano, chief of the Air Force, seized power just before the 1963 elections to prevent the likely victory of Liberal Modesto Rodas Alvarado, who favored reducing the military's role in politics. Under López Arrellano, an important factor in politics for the next fifteen years, the country experienced economic difficulties in the Central American Common Market, a short-lived war with El Salvador in 1969, and the birth and demise of López's Pact of National Unity, a coalition of the military, the traditional Liberal and National Parties, and business, labor, and peasant groups.

After eighteen months in office, civilian President Ramón Ernesto Cruz was overthrown by the military under López on December 4, 1972, because of widespread popular discontent over government fiscal ineptitude, a scandal in the national lottery involving the president's wife and the minister of government, and the threat of a peasant march through the capital city over the failure to distribute land under the 1962 agrarian reform law. López's second term in office was weakened by charges of inept response to the enormous destruction caused by Hurricane Fifi in September 1974. On March 31, 1975, López was replaced as military commander by Col. Juan Alberto Melgar Castro after dissatisfied junior officers seized control of the Supreme Council of the Armed Forces. On April 22, 1975, Melgar Castro succeeded López as chief of state in a bloodless coup following revelations in the *Wall Street Journal* that López had accepted a $1.25 million bribe from United Brands to reduce export taxes on bananas in 1974.

Melgar Castro—much more conservative than López, who had implemented agrarian reform in January 1975—was in turn ousted on August 7, 1978, by a three-man junta headed by Gen. Policarpo Paz Garcia after high government officials were implicated in drug-smuggling between Colombia and the United States. On April 20, 1980, the Liberal Party (PL), in an upset, won 52 percent of the valid votes cast for the 71-member Constituent Assembly, which began meeting July 20 to draft a new constitution and to transfer power to an elected president and legislature in early 1982.[7] In the Assembly, the Liberals won 35 seats, the Nationalists (PN) 33 seats, and the Party of Innovation and Unity (PINU) 3 seats. While a majority of peasants and older persons voted along traditional lines, a growing number of independents—especially among young and urban voters—rejected the PN and its links with the military to vote for the PL or PINU. With 82 percent of the registered voters going to the polls, the electorate overwhelmingly rejected calls for abstention from the Christian Democrats, the Honduran Communist Party (PCH), and some Liberals disenchanted with the PL slate of candidates. The vote can be interpreted as a rejection of violence in favor of moderate change.

In 1981, it was difficult for observers to guess if either the PL or the PN would move beyond patronage questions to address the serious questions facing the nation. Perhaps the three most serious problems were the large number of landless peasants (an estimated 46,000 families), many of whom seized agricultural land between December 1980 and March 1981—as in previous year-end "invasions"—in an effort to pressure the government to revive an agrarian reform program stalled since 1977; the large number of high school and National University (UNAH) graduates unable to find work, a ready source of support for leftist groups; and the inability of civilian politicians to control the military, many of whose senior officers have built expensive mansions and drive Mercedes-Benzes on salaries of $1,500 per month while at the same time permitting or ordering the indiscriminate roundup of young men on the streets for military service.

Marxist Parties, Trade Unions, and Pressure Groups

Central American Marxist parties vary greatly in size and strength, although generally appealing to only a small segment of the population. The most successful groups, in terms of survival and impact on policy decisions, have sought, in the words of one writer in 1971:

> (1) to maintain good, or at least working relations with the ruling governments, whether of the left, center, or right; (2) to manipulate to their advantage the "progressive" theme of the day, chiefly demands for political, economic, and cultural independence, especially from the United States, and calls for the restructuring of domestic social, economic, and political relationships; and (3) to exploit inter-American or international events.[8]

Setbacks have resulted principally from failure to maintain any or all three of these objectives, whether from internal party decisions or as a consequence of following decisions of the Soviet Union. Marxist groups have exercised influence far beyond their numbers because of good party organization, strong discipline, clearly defined domestic objectives, and generally adequate financing.

Pro-Soviet parties began in Central America in the late 1920s and early 1930s. In the three countries studied here, the local parties developed organizational bases among urban workers and university intellectuals—and among banana plantation workers in the Costa Rican case. None has attempted to seize power through an armed uprising or through protracted rural or urban guerrilla warfare. In the 1960s, these Marxist-Leninist parties split into several factions—many of which subsequently disappeared—over the Sino-Soviet disagreement over achieving power and the role of parties in the international environment, and differences in attitudes about relations with Cuba and the Castroist route to power through rural guerrilla warfare. For example, in 1961, in Honduras:

> A small group claiming to be "scientifically Marxist" split off to become the Honduran Revolutionary Party . . . believed to be Castroite in orientation. Since 1967, when a major dispute over tactics and strategy arose within the PCH, there have been two groups calling themselves the PCH, referred to here as the PCH (Traditional) and the PCH (Revolutionary). The former . . . is unequivocally pro-Soviet and advocates the use of peaceful means of struggle. The latter is Castroite in ideology and advocates armed struggle as the road to power . . .
>
> There is also a small Castroite group known as the Francisco Morazán Movement (MFM). In 1960, the appearance of yet another revolutionary group was reported, the Ernesto "Che" Guevara Revolutionary Front.[9]

Although the 1967 split was healed, some leaders of each faction left the party. Both the Guevara Front and the MFM disappeared after 1970. In February and August 1980, a group calling itself the Morazanista Front announced plans to initiate "armed action to assume power"—during the front's news conferences, the members' faces were covered with red and black cloths reminiscent of the colors of the Sandinista Liberation Front in Nicaragua and anarchist groups at the time of the Spanish Civil War. In 1980–1981, other left-wing groups engaged in kidnappings, hijackings, or an occasional bombing in Tegucigalpa and San Pedro Sula. The variety of names used by these groups, which seldom commit subsequent acts of violence, suggests that the individuals involved invent new names to lend themselves greater stature and notoriety.

The same leaders have dominated most pro-Soviet parties for decades, although there appears to be a shift in the top leadership of the Costa Rican and Honduran parties towards a somewhat younger group of veterans who favor a much more militant course of action involving strikes, kidnappings, and media-oriented acts of violence. Periodically, the leaders enjoy what appear to be all-expense-paid trips to Eastern Europe, the Soviet Union, and Cuba. However, no Central American leader has received the acclaim accorded Colombian or Venezuelan guerrilla leaders in Havana or Moscow. And General Torrijos and President Royo of Panama have been given much more coverage in *Granma*, the Cuban party newspaper, than PPP Secretary General Ruben Darío Souza.

The pro-Chinese groups that developed in Central America in the mid-1970s have had their greatest success among university student groups. Despite frequent espousal of a "people's war," pro-Chinese groups in Central America have engaged in little fighting other than an occasional scuffle with police during demonstrations at the U.S. Embassy or the Ministry of Education, depending on the "progressive" cause of the moment.

Alejandra Calderón, youngest daughter of former Costa Rican President Calderón Guardia, helped organize the Socialist Workers' Organization (OST), which was sympathetic to the Trotskyite Fourth International in the 1970s, but her death in late 1979 resulted in the disappearance of the OST. Other far-left groups in Costa Rica include the pro-Cuban Socialist Party (PS), which is not affiliated with the Socialist International, and the Revolutionary Movement of the People (MRP), which joined with the communist Popular Vanguard Party (PVP) to form the United People's Party (PPU) coalition. In 1978, Dr. Rodrigo Gutiérrez—a PS member—received only 2.7 percent of the total presidential vote while PPU nominees received 7 percent of the vote; three PPU members were elected to the 57-member unicameral Legislative Assembly. By February 1981, Dr. Gutiérrez was once again campaigning around the country with the aid of PVP leaders.

There is no significant Trotskyite group in Panama. Honduran police announced in April 1980 that they had broken up a plot by the Trotskyite Revolutionary Party of Central American Workers to disrupt the April 20 Constituent Assembly elections.

THE COSTA RICAN COMMUNIST PARTY

The Communist Party of Costa Rica was founded in 1929 by a nine-teen-year-old university student, Manuel Mora Valverde, its first and only secretary general. As Harry Kantor has noted,

> the Communist Party was practically the only outspoken supporter of the rights of the workers and poor peasants. In addition, Mora won the sup-port of many of the more socially-conscious university students. In 1933, Mora was elected to the national legislature, and in 1935 he led a strike of about 15,000 workers against the United Fruit Company and won con-cessions for the workers. In 1936, the Communist Party received 4,500 of the 85,500 votes cast in a national election.[10]

The party reorganized itself into the Popular Vanguard Party (PVP) in 1943 in accordance with the Comintern's wartime policy of seeking alliances with progressive groups. Since the 1930s, the party has had a strong base in the Federation of Agricultural and Plantation Workers (FENTRAP) and the General Confederation of Workers (CGT), which have grown from a membership of 2,500 of an estimated 24,000 unionized Costa Rican workers in 1969–1970 to an estimated 21,000–25,000 workers in 45 *sindicatos* in 1980. On November 21, 1980, FENTRAP and CGT leaders, joined by delegates of the National Federation of Workers in Public Administration, the Federation of Mu-nicipal Workers and [white-collar] Employees, the National Peasant Federation,—all of which are led by PVP members—and representa-tives of small dockworker, university, and railroad groups, formed the Unitary Confederation of Workers (CUT), which the PVP claims rep-resents more than 50,000 workers. The CGT and CUT have been su-perior in financial and organizational strength outside of San José in comparison with the noncommunist Confederation of Democratic Workers, which is affiliated with the Inter-American Regional Organi-zation of Workers (ORIT), to which the AFL-CIO and most demo-cratic, socialist–oriented trade union federations in the hemisphere belong. In 1978, the CGT was said to have an annual income of more than $90,000, a sum that permitted it to maintain a staff of 32 well-trained activists and thirteen lawyers, many of whom played an active role in the PVP and PS.[11] Most of these activists and lawyers provided "bread and butter" union services to banana plantation workers, dockworkers, and municipal government employees in the outlying provinces of Guanacaste, Heredia, and Puntarenas.

Communist abilities to upset the economy and roil the political atmosphere of Costa Rica were demonstrated twice during 1980. A troublesome 28-day strike by banana workers started on Standard Fruit plantations on the Caribbean coast but spread to United Brands plantations on the Pacific coast. Ultimately, up to 20,000 workers struck to support demands for a seven-hour workday instead of the existing eight-hour day. During the strike, five communist labor leaders were arrested for erecting barricades and distributing leaflets.[12] The strike had international repercussions and reduced government revenues from export taxes on bananas. On January 11, Vice-President José Miguel Alfaro announced the expulsion of three Cubans, one Russian, one Yugoslav, and a Bulgarian trade union official who had arrived one or two days earlier and immediately established contact with PVP and CGT leaders.[13] In the latter stages of the strike, President Rodrigo Carazo denounced the PVP's role as being "at the service of the Soviet Union . . . with clearcut objectives of carrying out national subversion." Implicitly referring to noncommunist workers' peaceful demonstrations of solidarity for the strikers, Carazo stated that many Costa Ricans "do not realize they are harming Costa Rica. In this way, many people . . . become partners of the Communists without realizing it."[14] The strike was finally settled through the efforts of Labor Minister Serrano Pinto. The workers obtained a seven-hour workday, the reinstatement of fired workers, and company loans to offset expenses incurred through the loss of wages during the strike. According to Serrano, Standard Fruit would not repay wages lost by the workers.[15]

During the strike, many Costa Rican business groups pressured the Carazo government to break diplomatic relations with the Soviet Union and consular relations with Cuba. Costa Rica established relations with East Germany and Albania in 1973 after Manuel Mora visited Eastern Europe and the Soviet Union in the late 1960s to urge them to buy Costa Rican coffee at a time of international surpluses. Although pressured to sever relations with Cuba and the Soviet Union, the Carazo government resisted until May 8, 1981. It renounced a technical and economic cooperation agreement with the Soviet Union signed in October 1977 on the grounds that labor training by Soviet technicians in Costa Rica was no longer advisable because it represented a "profound contradiction" with the restriction and repression of the labor movement and individual expression in the Soviet Union itself. On May 11, 1981, Costa Rica suspended consular relations with Cuba. It had closed its consulate in Havana "temporarily" in March because of revelations that Ministry of Public Security officials had been indicted for "embezzlement, bribery, and illegal enrichment" for issuing visas to permit Cubans to enter Costa Rica en route to the United States. The final break in diplomatic relations with Cuba most likely resulted from reports in late April that groups of Costa Ricans were receiving training in Cuba alongside Salvadoran guerrillas as well as hints of Cuban involvement in the bazooka attack on a U.S. Embassy vehicle and the explosion of a bomb at the Honduran Embassy in San José on March 17, 1981. In late April, the Costa Rican government arrested four persons who claimed membership in the Organización de Avanzada Popular (People's Avant-Garde Organization)—a group previously unknown in Costa Rican politics. The so-called Carlos Echeverriá Command—a group named after a Costa Rican who fought in Nicaragua with the Sandinistas—also claimed credit for the attack. The Carazo government was also embarrassed in 1980–1981 by charges that it had stockpiled arms shipped from Cuba and Panama to the Sandinistas—but withheld for Costa Rican police use "in case the National Guard of Somoza should invade Costa Rica in retaliation for the ... granting of safe havens to the Sandinistas."[16]

Costa Rica was unhappy with Cuban and Nicaraguan opposition to Costa Rica's candidacy for election to a two-year term on the U.N. Security Council in October–November 1980—a seat ultimately won by Panama. Costa Ricans have seen no reason for the large military buildup and increasing press restrictions in Nicaragua. They have been supportive generally of El Salvador's Napoleón Duarte, although concerned about his inability to control right-wing military and paramilitary forces in that divided country. Cuba's standing with the Carazo government was not helped either by the March 1981 rupture of diplomatic relations by Colombia, which accused the Castro regime of financing and arming guerrillas trying to topple the Turbay Ayala government in Bogotá. In 1981, labor-management problems, especially those of multinational corporations, were a principal item in the pages of Libertad, the weekly PVP newspaper, and El Trabajador, the MRP weekly, both of which are openly sold on the streets of San José for one colon (11.7 cents U.S. in 1980).

The Juventud Vanguardista Costaricense (JVC) is one of several Marxist-Leninist groups active among university students. The JVC is probably the best organized, with some fourteen regional organizations, and is headed by César Solano, a voting member of the PVP Central Committee. In 1980, the JVC was active among student groups demanding that the Legislative Assembly create a permanent fund for higher education amounting to 12 percent of the national budget.

One consequence of diplomatic relations between Costa Rica and the Soviet Union is the existence of the Costa Rican–Soviet Cultural Institute, which administers a program of scholarships for study in the Soviet Union. In 1980, *Libertad* listed the names of 70 students who were eligible for fellowships.[17]

Costa Rica's relatively free society was the setting from late 1979 to March 1981 of a controversy over the broadcasting activities of the 50,000-watt clear-channel station Radio Noticias del Continente, which seldom carried commercials but which reportedly aimed "subversive programs" at the governments of El Salvador, Guatemala, Uruguay, Argentina, and Chile. The transmitter was attacked three times in 1980. The station's woes came to a head in February 1981 when Costa Rican police found a cache of automatic weapons, two pistols, ammunition, uniforms, and other items at the station and a nearby house. In late March, a local judge—responding to complaints from nearby citizens— was surprised to discover that all the equipment and transmitters had been removed.[18]

THE HONDURAN COMMUNIST PARTY

The Honduran Communist Party (PCH) has actively recruited and organized university and secondary students as well as workers. Two PCH-sponsored youth groups, the Socialist Student Front and the Federation of Secondary Students, were active after late 1979 in organizing street parades and demonstrations on the campuses of the National Autonomous University of Honduras (UNAH) in Tegucigalpa, San Pedro Sula, and La Ceiba supporting revolutionary groups in other Central American countries and calling on Hondurans to abstain from the April 20, 1980 elections for a Constituent Assembly.

The PCH has been active in selected urban industrial sectors, especially the subsidiaries of American multinational corporations such as United Fruit, Standard Fruit/Castle and Cooke, and Coca-Cola. Its influence in the trade union movement was heightened by a series of strikes in early 1980, whose probable aim was as much the disruption or blocking of the Constituent Assembly elections as economic or political benefits. On January 15, some 10,000 workers at a sugar mill in western Honduras and 1,000 canecutters at a mill on the south coast went on strike over the dismissal of nine union leaders.[19] On February 14, 6,500 Standard Fruit Company workers went on a five-day strike. Following mediation by Labor Minister Adalberto Discua—as in Costa Rica, government revenues were affected by the interruption in banana exports—the workers received a 66 percent increase in wages. Shortly thereafter, workers at a Coca-Cola subsidiary went on strike over the dismissal of several workers. This strike lasted twelve days and ended only after the intervention of Labor Minister Discua and the commander of the Third Infantry Battalion in San Pedro Sula.[20] In March, banana workers belonging to the Tela Railroad Company, a United Fruit subsidiary, also went on strike and won a 66 percent pay raise. General Policarpo Paz García, president of the governing junta, said that the strikes, along with the occupation of schools by student groups (which continued into 1981) were part of a "preconceived plan" to block the April 20 elections, a plan that the junta would not tolerate.[21]

In 1980–1981, Honduras became more and more embroiled in the Salvadoran civil war, both through the efforts of Honduran leftists in transporting arms from Cuba to the guerrillas and through incidents involving Honduran army units aiding the Salvadoran military in preventing guerrillas and sympathizers from escaping into Honduras. In August 1980, eight members of the newly organized People's Revolutionary Union (Unión Revolucionaria del Pueblo; URP) held thirteen persons hostage for two days after occupying offices of the Organization of American States in Tegucigalpa. Subsequently, Tomas Nativi, a well-known PCH faculty member at UNAH, announced that he was leading the URP in a new armed struggle to change the nation's political structure as well as to prevent further Honduran collaboration with the Salvadoran National Guard in "the genocide against the people of that country."[22] In December 1980, the president of the Banco Atlantida, a Chase-Manhattan subsidiary, was abducted; reportedly this was a collaborative effort between Salvadoran guerrillas and Honduran extremists. In March 1981, members of a group calling itself the Movimiento Popular de Liberacion Cinchonero hijacked a Honduran airliner en route to Florida, freeing the aircraft and its passengers in Managua, Nicaragua, in return for the release of fifteen Salvadorans and Hondurans in police custody in Honduras, including Facundo Guardado, ex–secretary general of the Salvadoran Popular Revolutionary Bloc.[23]

In 1981, the Honduran government denounced as untrue reports that, on at least three occasions, Honduran troops tortured and killed unarmed Salvadoran civilians among the 25,000 fleeing the violence of their native country.

THE COMMUNIST ROLE IN PANAMA

Panama has become important in Third World politics since 1968, especially in the Central American and Caribbean region. Panamanian foreign policy initiatives supported by the communist People's Party of Panama (PPP) and the communist Federation of Workers of the Republic of Panama (FSTRP) and the Federation of Students (FEP) are similar to those of many nonaligned or Third World nations. These positions favorable to Cuba and the Soviet bloc neutralize leftist and nationalist criticism of the civilian-military regime that has dominated the country since 1968. On the other hand, Panama has followed economic policies that have attracted U.S. and other multinational corporations. In return for general support of General Torrijos and his foreign policy, communist leaders have enjoyed considerable freedom of action—knowing there is an ever-present possibility of exile or a cutoff of government funds needed for PPP operations. Panamanian Communists have been vocal on the Canal Zone, Iran, independence for Puerto Rico, and Afghanistan, and they have asserted the preeminent role of the Soviet Union in bloc relationships. On the other hand, the domestic role of the PPP, FSTRP, and FEP has been more restrained.

In the trade union movement, which is divided over the issue of representation of Canal Zone workers by U.S.-affiliated or Panamanian-affiliated unions, the FSTRP joined the ORIT-affiliated Confederation of Workers of the Republic of Panama (CTRP) in seeking modification of the Labor Code of December 31, 1976 and 1977, which (1) stipulated compulsory arbitration of worker-management differences, (2) prohibited changes in existing contracts for two years, (3) eliminated seniority rights, and (4) permitted dismissal of "unproductive workers"—which many interpret as "uncooperative" union leaders.

Panamanian support for Cuban and Soviet policies is recent. In May 1969, 80 Cubans led by Maj. César Vega landed at Nombre de Dios on the Caribbean coast in an effort to regain power for the families of Arnulfo and Roberto Arias, toppled for the second time by the National Guard in October 1968.[24] Fidel Castro claimed that he had nothing to do with the invasion and said that the Panamanian regime was not a dictatorship like Nicaragua. However, diplomatic relations had been severed in December 1961 after Castro referred to Panama as a government of "traitors" and "accomplices of the imperialist Yankees." Panama did not object when Cuban exiles trained for the 1961 Bay of Pigs invasion at Fort Sherman in the Canal Zone. The break continued until April 1972 when Cuban Foreign Minister Raul Roa backed Panama's demand for a new canal treaty. Panama reciprocated by arguing for an end to Cuba's diplomatic and economic isolation in the hemisphere. Since 1975, Cuba has purchased goods in the Colon Free Trade Zone that were not directly available elsewhere in the hemisphere. Cuban and Panamanian support for the Sandinista Liberation Front in Nicaragua and opposition to Anastasio Somoza resulted from a convoluted series of events. Both Castro and Torrijos disliked the Somoza dynasty, which supported the Bay of Pigs invasion. Congressman John Murphy of New York—a long-term friend of Somoza and member of the House Panama Canal Subcommittee—tried to convince Howard Hughes and Daniel Ludwig to finance construction of a sea-level canal through Nicaragua. The Nixon administration, through E. Howard Hunt and his Cuban "plumbers," contemplated the assassination of Torrijos. Even though a 1970 U.S. government study favored construction of a second canal through Panama, not Nicaragua, Murphy and other conservatives argued that the political safety of a Nicaraguan route made it more acceptable than the politically vulnerable Panamanian route. The Panamanian government supplied Sandinista guerrillas with Cuban arms and arms purchased in Miami and provided training facilities on the island of Coiba for a group of 40–45 Panamanians who fought in Nicaragua.[25] In June 1979, PPP Secretary General Ruben Darío Souza joined senior communists from Brazil, Chile, the Dominican Republic, El Salvador, Paraguay, and Uruguay in signing a statement of support "for the Nicaraguan people to overthrow the hated Somoza tyranny."[26]

Street demonstrations by the PPP and FEP against the refuge given the former shah of Iran served as a domestic counterweight to President Royo's statements of support for the Latin American concept of the right to asylum. On December 18, 1979, the PPP Politburo issued a communiqué denouncing the presence of the former Iranian monarch: "We do not believe Panama should take charge of the former emperor to help him escape from the justice of the fraternal Iranian people."[27] The next day, the General Executive Council of the FEP said that the "act of giving asylum to Reza Pahlavi is no more than that of a banana republic, with the United States imposing the rules of the game. [While there was] a direct connection between the national government's decision to take a humanitarian step and the pre-electoral situation in the United States in which Mr. Carter is running for re-election . . . no argument could ever justify the measure or excuse such a mistake."[28] Torrijos's admission of the shah was a masterful political stroke. At the same time that it lessened opposition to him in the United States over the Canal treaties, it also undercut Representative Murphy, who not only opposed Panama on the treaties but also supported the shah.

In December 1979, FEP students at both the secondary Instituto Nacional and the Instituto Comercial and the National University demonstrated outside the U.S. Embassy and stoned Panamanian government vehicles and buildings for five days before quitting for Christmas and

New Year's holidays.[29] In January 1980, following an anti-American demonstration by 200 students from the Instituto Comercial, FEP leaders announced a suspension of protests so that students would not lose any more days from a schoolyear already reduced by a long teachers' strike in the fall. Instead, Secretary General Mario Panther and two other FEP leaders accepted an invitation to visit Teheran from the Iranian militants holding the 53 American hostages.[30]

Differences between the Panamanian government and the PPP over Afghanistan were noticeable, however. PPP communiqués in January 1980 supported "the revolution being carried out in Afghanistan" and agreed "with the moral and military aid that the USSR has given to that country." The party found it strange that the Panamanian representative to the United Nations "has run up to the forefront of those who hypocritically accuse the USSR of intervention." In June, the PPP criticized the government's decision to boycott the Moscow Olympics in response to the invasion.[31]

In February 1980, the PPP held its Sixth Congress, acknowledging the receipt of "fraternal greetings" from the Bulgarian and Soviet parties. During the congress, Secretary General Darío Souza said Panama "is not ready for socialism or communism, but it should advance toward a progressive democracy"—a statement with which General Torrijos probably would agree.[32]

Seizure of public buildings and street demonstrations are common tactics of Panamanian student and trade union groups, as well as of communist groups. In late February 1980, a group calling itself the Federation of Revolutionary Students (FER-29) seized the Salvadoran Embassy in Panama City, demanding that the Salvadoran government release Juan Chacón, a leader of the Salvadoran Popular Revolutionary Bloc. The FER-29 action was accompanied by cables to the Salvadoran government from the PPP and the National Committee for the Defense of Sovereignty and Peace asking for Chacón's release.[33]

The ability of communist youth groups to mobilize a small core of disciplined members on behalf of "progressive" or pro-Soviet causes was illustrated in two May 1980 incidents. On May 6, several hundred FEP members occupied the Education Ministry and several schools in Panama City to protest problems in the schools, including the ministry's failure to give jobs to some two thousand teachers.[34] The students left the ministry later in the afternoon after presenting their concerns and demands to Education Minister Gustavo Garcia de Paredes. One week later, hundreds of FEP students blocked traffic and held marches to protest the presence in Panama of Harold Parfitt, the last governor of the U.S. Canal Zone. Mario Panther said that the protest occurred in part because Parfitt, as vice-governor of the Canal Zone in 1964, had ordered U.S. troops to fire on student demonstrators inside the zone, resulting in the deaths of twenty youths and causing Panama to break diplomatic relations with the United States for a short time.[35]

In January 1980, several thousand banana workers joined the ORIT-affiliated CTRP after democratic elements defeated communist organizers in elections. The PPP's acceptance or need of a pluralistic political climate and its co-optation by Torrijos are reflected in the presentation by PPP leaders Carlos Changmarin and Cesar de Leon of the party's programs and its view of national problems to National Guard garrison and zone commanders in April 1980. Changmarin told the officers that the PPP was not going to "seize power" because Panama had not progressed to a stage of development where that was possible. He further asserted that "we communists were the first to go to the Canal Zone to fight Yankee imperialists, for which reasons we are patriots. We are not exotic . . . because our ideas are universal." He went on to state that the "oligarchs do not accept the military although they deal with them and even invite them to meet with them because they do not consider them as being within their social class." Representatives of the Agrarian Labor, Liberal, Christian Democratic, and National Liberation parties participated in the seminars, but the Panameñista Party of Arnulfo Arias and the Popular Action Party did not.[36]

The PPP's continued lack of electoral appeal was reflected in its inability to obtain the 30,000 signatures needed to nominate candidates under its banner for the September 1980 elections. The government, fearing abstentions because of its own unpopularity and not wishing to further antagonize the PPP, formulated a special electoral law that made it possible for communist candidates to run as "independents"— who needed only 771 signatures from supporters.

Between 1968 and 1978, the PPP benefited from its status as a key component in Torrijos's political coalition and his isolation from the business community. However, in contrast to the other Central American parties discussed here, the leaders of the PPP and the communist trade union movement have been unable to cope with the complex, competitive situation that has developed since 1978 with the appointment of civilian Royo as president, the establishment of the PRD as the official government party, and the regime's shift toward conservative economic policies designed to attract foreign investment.

Between January and March 1981, according to an unnamed high-ranking Panamanian official, relations with Cuba reached "their lowest level in recent years." Panama was unhappy with "Castro's insistence on stimulating armed struggle in the continent," especially "the excessive Cuban presence in Nicaragua," Cuba's preference for "military conflict" in El Salvador rather than mediation, its supplying of weapons to the Colombian April 19th Movement to topple the Turbay Ayala government, and its failure to protect the extraterritoriality of foreign embassies and consulates in Havana, especially those of Ecuador and Peru. The official went on to note that "Cuba's war-oriented policy is the best justification for Reagan's interventionist intentions in Latin America."[37]

Pospects of Revolution and Turmoil

Poverty and maldistribution of wealth might appear to make Costa Rica, Honduras, and Panama fertile ground for Castroite or communist appeals. Yet only the workers of multinational corporations—principally in the banana industry—and some secondary and university students appear capable of and interested in disrupting their societies to an extent that would favor Cuban or Soviet goals. In Honduras a combination of rural poverty, lack of access to land, and a history of organized peasant groups offers conditions in which the countryside might support turmoil similar to that of El Salvador or Guatemala; but Honduras is not dominated by a small group of "fourteen families" as is El Salvador or by a group of right-wing military officers opposed to social change and trade unions as is Guatemala. Lack of land and rural unemployment are serious problems in Costa Rica, but the political system has responded in many ways to both rural and urban residents. Prospects are that it will continue to be responsive.

Communist parties have survived in the region because they have tried to maintain good relations with existing governments despite differences in ideology. Notwithstanding the turnover in leadership of the Costa Rican and Honduran parties, the new chieftains are unlikely to challenge the ruling civilian-military regimes. Communist parties will continue to manipulate existing domestic and international grievances to embarrass local regimes and the United States. But the communist parties and their affiliated worker and student groups have not developed any ideas or solutions to social problems that are not also advocated by democratically oriented parties, trade unions, peasant, and schoolteacher groups—including those affiliated with the Christian Democratic movement.

The Soviet Union is paying a high price for its occupation of Afghanistan that will take several years to overcome. The Costa Rican and Honduran communist parties have not taken a public position, although the Costa Rican party published one Soviet news dispatch on the June 1980 troop withdrawals from Kabul. Cuban experiments in eradicating illiteracy and the delivery of health care appeal to intellectuals and students in many countries. Nevertheless, the exodus of 120,-000 Cuban "boat people" in May–June 1980—plus many others who were flown to Costa Rica after seeking refuge at the Peruvian Embassy in Havana—reduced the appeal of the Cuban model. The Peruvian model of "military socialism" appealed to many in Honduras and Panama, but the difficulties experienced by the Peruvian military in implementing reforms and promoting economic growth, as well as the return to power of the civilian Belaunde Terry regime through elections, contributed to a drive for elections, constitutionally elected governments, and political solutions.

Marxist and communist parties are relatively well-organized in Costa Rica, Honduras, and Panama, but they appeal only to a small percentage of the population. The leaders of these parties—plus other intellectuals, military officers, and peasant leaders—have not become so disenchanted with existing political systems that they seriously contemplate "going to the hills" to fight, Cuban-, Nicaraguan-, or Salvadoran-style. There is still sufficient stability in these societies that polarization can be avoided by agrarian and tax reforms, by eliminating corruption among civilian and military leaders, by permitting free trade unions to exist and bargain collectively on behalf of their members, and by responding to popular demands for increased government services.

Notes

1. Harry Kantor, *Patterns of Politics and Political Systems in Latin America* (Chicago: Rand-McNally, 1969), p. 133.

2. Calculated from data contained in *Censo Nacional Agropecuario* (Tegucigalpa: Dirección General de Estadística y Censos, 1978), 2: 12.

3. Kantor, *Patterns*, p. 193.

4. Calculated from data in Table 11, "Land Distribution in Costa Rica, 1963 and 1975," in Mitchell A. Seligson, *Peasants of Costa Rica and the Development of Agrarian Capitalism* (Madison: University of Wisconsin Press, 1980), p. 147.

5. Kantor, *Patterns*, p. 230.

6. Steve C. Ropp, "Panama's Domestic Structure and the Canal: History and Future," in Howard J. Wiarda and Harvey F. Kline, eds., *Latin American Politics and Development* (Boston: Houghton-Mifflin, 1979), p. 488.

7. Calculated from mimeographed final report of the Tribunal Nacional de Elecciones, May 17, 1980. Vote totals for each of the parties may also be found

in Foreign Broadcast Information Service, *Daily Report, Latin America* (hereafter *DR*), May 22, 1980, pp. 8–9.

8. William E. Ratliff, "Introduction," *Yearbook on Latin American Communist Affairs, 1971* (Stanford: Hoover Institution Press, 1971), p. 4.

9. Lynn Ratliff, "Honduras," in ibid., p. 109.

10. Kantor, *Patterns*, p. 194.

11. Rodrigo Carreras Jimenez, "Costa Rica," in Richard F. Staar, ed., *Yearbook on International Communist Affairs, 1979* (Stanford: Hoover Institution Press, 1979), p. 334.

12. *DR*, January 14, 1980, p. P1; and *Granma*, January 27, 1980, p. 5.

13. *DR*, January 16, 1980, pp. P1–2.

14. Ibid.

15. Ibid.

16. "Cuban Refugee Scheme Revealed," *Tico Times* (San José), February 27, 1981, pp. 1, 12; *DR*, April 29, 1981, p. P1; May 11, 1981, p. P2; and May 18, 1981, p. P1.

17. *Libertad* (San José), June 27–July 3, 1980, p. 11.

18. *La Nación* (San José), March 4, 1980; *DR*, February 21, 1980, p. P2, March 8, 1981, p. P2, March 27, 1981, p. P4. *DR*, March 7, 1981, p. P2, carried a broadcast of Radio Reloj of San José that noted that Radio Noticias issued a communiqué stating that a "network of solidarity" was being established by radio stations in different countries, such as International Radio of Sweden, Radio Mexico, Radio Canada International, Radio Cuzco, and others to transmit its programs while a judicial investigation was being carried out. In April 1981, Radio Managua, which is supported by the Sandinista-dominated government, broadcast programs under the auspices of the former Costa Rican station.

19. *DR*, January 17, 1980, p. P9.

20. Ibid., March 12, 1980, p. P12; March 14, 1980, p. P8.

21. Ibid., March 12, 1980, p. P11.

22. Ibid., August 18, 1980, p. P12; January 21, 1981, p. P12; March 12, 1981, p. P11; March 19, 1981, p. P9; March 26, 1981, p. P4; and *Facts on File*, April 1980, p. 314.

23. *DR*, March 4, 1981, pp. 7–8; March 20, 1981, p. P16; and *Latin America Weekly Report* (London), April 3, 1981, p. 2.

24. Steve C. Ropp, "Cuba and Panama, Signaling Left and Going Right?" *Caribbean Review*, 9, no. 1 (Winter 1980): 15–16.

25. Ibid., p. 16.

26. *World Marxist Review, Information Bulletin* 1979, no. 15, pp. 27–28.

27. *DR*, December 19, 1979, p. N1.

28. Ibid.

29. Ibid., pp. N1–2; and "Estudiantes deciden suspender manifestaciones contra el Sha," *El Tiempo* (San Pedro Sula), January 7, 1980.

30. *DR*, January 7, 1980, pp. N3–5.

31. Ibid., January 15, 1980, P. N2; and *Crítica* (Panama City), January 14, June 5, and July 5, 1980.

32. *DR*, February 11, 1980, p. N1.

33. Ibid., February 29, 1980, P. N1.

34. Ibid., May 7, 1980, p. N1.

35. Ibid., May 14, 1980, p. N1.

36. Ibid., May 2, 1980, pp. N1–3; March 20, 1981, p. N2.

37. Ibid., March 26, 1981, pp. N1–3; and March 27, 1981, pp. N1–3.

7 | JAMAICA

W. Raymond Duncan

A relatively new movement in the English-speaking Caribbean,[1] communism was a major issue in Jamaica's violence-ridden elections of late 1980 when anticommunist Edward Seaga's Jamaica Labor Party (JLP) defeated prosocialist Michael Manley's People's National Party (PNP).[2] Communism shapes foreign policy: Manley courted close Cuban ties; Seaga is determined to rid the island of Cuban influence. It also conditions Jamaica's role in the international relations of the Caribbean. Kingston supported an expanded Cuban presence in the Caribbean and within the Third World nonaligned movement during the 1970s. This action attracted considerable Soviet interest in this strategically important region and alarmed Washington about growing Cuban and Soviet influence. In response, the new government of Prime Minister Seaga promised to return Jamaica to a pro-American course, using opposition to the communist threat as one means to attract international aid and private U.S. investment.

Communism's place within the Jamaican political landscape depends on its underlying ideological power and long-term political impact, factors conditioned by the perceptions of Jamaica's competing political leaders. Manley, who polled more than 40 percent of the vote in the October 1980 elections and retains wide support despite his defeat, is convinced that "democratic socialism" is the correct path to development. Manley's vision involves alignment with Cuba, extended Soviet contacts, and widened links with other leftist Caribbean and Third

World governments. These competing views of communism make the issue a continuing source of conflict between radical Manley supporters and strongly conservative followers of Seaga.

Communism remains an issue because Jamaica is wracked by economic and social tensions, strained by an increasingly polarized political system, and clearly influenced by Fidel Castro's model 90 miles to the north.[3] Between 1975 and 1980, the country experienced food riots, strikes, and an economic crisis that left approximately 20 percent of the island's industrial plant shut down and another 40 percent working at only marginal capacity.[4] Inflation, spawned by petroleum price rises since 1973, is rampant; raw materials are in short supply; 50 percent of the island's young people face unemployment; and educated Jamaicans are departing the island in exceptionally large numbers.[5] It was Seaga's promise to deal effectively with these conditions that gave his JLP 51 of the 60 seats in Parliament in the October 1980 elections.

The violence of the 1980 election campaign, however, adds to the difficulty of assessing the long-run ideological appeal and political impact of communism or the extent of its presence. During the nine months preceding the 1980 elections, hundreds of urban residents were killed by feuding groups. Seaga characterized Manley's supporters as "communists," and Manley described Seaga as a "fascist." This legacy remains. Immediately after assuming office, Seaga expelled the Cuban ambassador, requested that the incoming Reagan administration form a U.S.-backed anticommunist alliance in the Caribbean, and appealed for a new Marshall Plan to combat the economic conditions that make communism seem attractive.[6] Meanwhile, some Jamaicans were concerned that radical Manley supporters, many of them trained in Cuba, were preparing to wage a guerrilla war.

The domestic elements in communism's appeal include a long and melancholy history of colonialism and slavery; a psychology of dependence on outside powers; grinding poverty, hunger, and unemployment; discontent with the status quo; and, consequently, political instability. Another factor is the presence of left-wing intellectuals within the PNP, many of whom are attracted to the Cuban model. Two communist parties, moreover, have been formed since 1975: the Jamaican Communist Party (JCP) and the Jamaican Workers' Party (JWP). Given the heightened Soviet attention and influx of Cuban personnel during 1972–1980, a perception of a drift toward communism was understandable.[7] The close relations between former Prime Minister Manley and Fidel Castro strengthened that conclusion.

Yet caution is in order regarding communist strength in Jamaica. It is not simply that leftist tendencies in the PNP are offset by the more conservative JLP now in power. Manley's political beliefs are also a factor. Although friends with Castro, Manley values democracy, social justice, and equality, not Marxism-Leninism. As the 1980s began, he remained committed to furthering the public interest through mixed forms of economic ownership, which translated into a determined effort to prevent foreign domination, but a continued interest in foreign investment and tourism. Manley did not overlook the financial strength of the West, despite his flirtation with Cuba and the Soviet Union. Moreover, not all sectors of the PNP supported Jamaica's affair with Cuba; ideological divisions within the party were strong.

Communism in Jamaica is one of several competing political ideologies, which adds to the complexity of the situation and to Jamaican instability. Jamaica's history and its current economic and social problems form the backdrop to leftism on the island, as well as to the conflict between most leftists and the JLP's more conservative position and ascendancy after October 1980.

The Legacy of the Past

Jamaica's national self-image is based on its location, ethnic-racial background, resources, production, and historic ties. The essential leitmotiv in Jamaica's legacy is one of perceived and real *dependency* that makes the island both sensitive and vulnerable to external economic and political pressures.[8] Jamaica became a British colony in 1655, gaining independence only in 1962, whereas most of Latin America's Spanish-speaking states had acquired political independence by the early nineteenth century. This colonial past, vividly imprinted in leadership perceptions, corresponds to a largely black population; about 90 to 95 percent of Jamaicans descend from African slaves brought in during the eighteenth century. The historical forces of colonialism and slavery created a psychological dependency in the Jamaican population against which many leaders—communist and Fabian socialists alike—wage a continuing struggle.

Sensitivity to dependence forces Jamaican leaders into economic nationalism and the urge to carve their own way in the world, to steer clear of cold war antagonisms, and to shake off past indignities of outside control.[9] This objective—the concerted effort to find a Jamaican way—inspires the moderate and radical leaders inside the PNP as much as the Marxist-Leninists outside the party. It results in an egalitarian ethic—in Marxist and non-Marxist form—within Jamaica's left wing (replicated elsewhere in the Caribbean).[10] The colonial and slave heritage also fosters a "neocolonialist" view of Jamaica's contemporary economic status among Marxist and non-Marxist politicians, but given the extensiveness of foreign ownership and control over Jamaica's economy despite political independence, this is not surprising.[11]

Owing largely to physical and economic conditions, the realities of dependence continue to plague the country. Its small size, restricted consumer markets, limited resources, diseconomies of scale, constrained domestic productivity, and insular setting force Jamaican leaders to seek outside financial, technical, and other types of support. Sources of support range from other Caribbean nations, Western lending institutions, such as the International Monetary Fund (IMF) and the World Bank, and Cuba and the Soviet Union. This continuing economic dependency, evolving out of an essentially single-commodity export system (from sugar in the earlier periods, to bananas, to bauxite after 1952) has created enormous development problems. Manley's attempt to reverse patterns of dependency—largely through increased government control of bauxite operations and by joining other Third World countries in the call for a New International Economic Order (NIEO) to share resources, money, and power more equitably between the developed and the developing countries—still assumed that the impetus for growth must come from outside.[12]

Economic and Social Strains

Despite government efforts, dependency will not go away, and Jamaica finds itself increasingly in an economic crisis. The oil price rises of 1973–1974 adversely affected Jamaica, as did a decline in sugar prices and droughts that cut sugar and coffee production.[13] Bauxite production, which earns 35 percent of the country's foreign exchange, fell 32 percent between 1974 and 1976 for a variety of reasons. The result is a persistent balance of payments deficit.[14] The country's foreign debt reached a staggering $1.7 billion by early 1980.[15] External borrowing unfortunately did not improve the island's economic growth rate in the 1970s, as demonstrated by declines in the gross national product, registering −2.6 percent in 1973, −6.9 in 1976, −4.0 in 1977, and −2.0 in 1978.[16] By early 1980, Jamaica's economy had worsened to the point where U.S. and European banks were refusing to make new loans. Meanwhile, the Manley government had decided to end its negotiations with the IMF, given the country's inability to meet IMF conditions for new loans.[17] As might be expected, the deteriorating economy led to a flight of domestic capital and professionals as well as a sharp slowdown in foreign investment—problems that the Seaga government began to address by November 1980.

Jamaica is plagued by high unemployment, escalating inflation, rapid urbanization, low agricultural productivity, and violent crime that further weakens the economy and political system. Unemployment, officially estimated at 24 percent, is probably over 50 percent in the 14–24 age group, in a country where 60 percent of the population is under 21 years old. Inflation exceeds 20 percent, following a period in 1978 when it reached 50 percent. Urban growth has greatly increased the need for public services in an already overextended economic and political system. By 1970, for example, only 14 percent of all dwellings in central Kingston had running water, 80 percent of all households shared toilet facilities with others, and 43 percent of all dwellings consisted of one room.[18] The average black in Kingston could expect inadequate water and sewage systems and poor police protection and recreational opportunities. Breakdowns in public transportation, public health systems, and postal facilities were a regular occurrence. Maldistribution of income is clear: per capita income is over $1,000, but 85 percent of the population exists on less than $200 a year.[19]

Herein lies the origin of the violent crime and gang warfare that rocked Kingston before the 1980 elections.[20] Victims of Kingston's high crime rate are generally middle and upper-middle class individuals who tend to be fairer skinned. They live in the suburban homes on the hills outside Kingston, where security measures have recently been increased. By 1974 violent crimes were up 50 percent over the 1960–61 crime rate, with robberies rising from 43 to 418 cases reported per 100,-000 population.[21] Accompanying the crime rate have been high rates of labor unrest and strikes, which formerly were rare in Jamaica.

Recent Political Developments

Jamaica has a functioning two-party system, which draws strongly on the liberal ideas, parliamentary institutions, and rule of law inherited from Great Britain. The political system provides representation for diverse class and sectional interests, and elections are held at least every five years. During the 1950s and 1960s neither the JLP nor the PNP seemed willing or able to address key economic issues or stimulate any radical economic transformation of the country. Manley's program of "democratic socialism," however, began to move in this direction following his election in 1972 and his re-election in 1976. Both parties today appeal to all sectors of the population, although neither has gained the support of the politically alienated, chronically frustrated, and volatile sector of unskilled laborers.

Manley's version of socialism is decidedly Fabian in origin and concept, drawing on the ideas of British socialist theoretician Harold Laski, understandably so given Manley's training at the London School of Economics in the 1940s during Laski's tenure there and his subsequent political career as a union organizer. Manley's father was a union leader and founded the PNP in 1938. The PNP is not a Marxist-Leninist association, either in ideological origins or in organization. There is no official government or party newspaper, no massive youth organization, and certainly no systematic propaganda tactics.[22] Manley has been the essential carrier of the message of democratic socialism since the early 1970s, emphasizing government control of the economy and stressing equality and social justice. And it was Manley who decided to open new avenues of diplomacy to Cuba and the Soviet Union, albeit with considerable encouragement from others within the PNP, in an effort to escape traditional U.S. and British Commonwealth ties—a direction widespread in Latin America from the 1960s.

By the late 1970s, Manley's democratic socialism was in trouble. Discernible frictions existed within the ruling PNP, with Marxist radicals opposing moderates on a number of matters, including relations with the IMF.[23] This situation was not eased by Manley's commitment to allowing opposing viewpoints within the PNP and his appointment of antagonistic ministers to party positions. These decisions not only stimulated public PNP disunity, but led Jamaica's businessmen and the JLP to see the specter of communism within the government itself and the possibility of the government's eliminating private enterprise and establishing Jamaica as a second communist country in the Caribbean.[24] By late 1978 Manley's popularity had sunk to a new low. An opinion poll conducted by Carl Stone, a Jamaican social scientist, indicated that 29 percent of the Jamaican people supported the JLP and only 15 percent the PNP.[25]

As Manley's popularity waned and the economy stagnated, political violence began to rise. A number of people were killed in clashes between Manley's and Seaga's supporters. On April 13, 1980, gunmen fired on a party of 500 people accompanying Manley on a tour of a decaying section of downtown Kingston. One week later 25 uniformed gunmen attacked a dance being held in the area by the opposition JLP, killing four people and wounding ten others. By May 1980 rival JLP and PNP gangs maintained roadblocks at the boundaries of their territories.[26] As elections approached in late 1980, tension arising from deepseated economic and social frustrations continued to increase.

A number of distinct, frequently conflicting, political trends operate in Jamaica. Prime Minister Seaga and the JLP seem determined to diversify the economy and produce for North American and European markets by using Jamaican labor and foreign capital, management, and technology.[27] During the 1980 election compaign, the JLP constantly hammered away at the theme of growing communist tendencies and "Marxist takeover" of the PNP. Manley, on the other hand, continued to flirt with Cuba, the Soviet Union, and the United States. His government invited Cuban technicians and medical personnel into Jamaica; Manley and Fidel Castro were on the best of terms and exchanged visits; and a number of agreements with the Soviet Union were signed. At the same time, Manley welcomed foreign investment. As he stated in Miami in January 1980, he encouraged the United States not to look on Jamaica as a hotbed of communism or of "some mysterious conspiracy or adventurist plot"; rather the United States should realize that the Caribbean

> contains a lot of very poor people who are struggling to find answers to their poverty. It has the energy to try new things when old things seem to fail . . . I think that the United States of America will contribute toward its own stature as a great power to the extent it recognizes and respects these small, vigorous and sometimes fractious neighbors to its south and holds out the hand of cooperation on a basis of respect offered and respect returned regardless of the size of those who shake hands.[28]

In the search for Jamaica's own special way at home and abroad, however, some policies of Manley and the PNP suggested increased radical perceptions within the government. Following a trip to Cuba in March 1980, Manley named a new, more radical finance minister after the PNP Executive Committee voted 103–45 against further negotiations with the IMF. To what extent Manley's relations with Cuba and with Grenada's new, pro-Cuban radical-leftist government under Maurice Bishop may have helped to shape these decisions is difficult to judge, especially since the IMF conditions for further loans were notably unpopular among many leading Jamaican politicians. But the decision to stop the negotiations continued to polarize the Jamaican political system among conservatives, moderates, and Marxists.[29] Ironically, the lack of foreign support could exacerbate this tension and threaten the democratic character of Jamaica's political system, thus undermining the possibilities for future loans. Prime Minister Seaga, clearly aware of this situation, began to seek new IMF loans after his election victory.

Another recent trend in Jamaica is the emergence of two communist parties: the Jamaican Workers' Party (JWP), formed in 1978 under the leadership of Trevor Monroe, and the Jamaican Communist Party (JCP), founded in 1975 and headed by its general secretary, Chris Lawrence.[30] These parties fully supported Manley's suspension of negotiations with the IMF in 1980 and the seeking of close ties with Cuba and the Soviet Union, as do left-wing members of the PNP itself. Both parties strongly support the PNP over Seaga's "fascist" JLP and reject the notion that Cubans are subverting the country.

Although communist parties exert some influence on students, teachers, intellectuals, and workers, there is no probability of a cataclysmic slide toward a Marxist-Leninist Jamaica. Neither party has a large grassroots base, and opposition to them is strong. The presence of two competing Marxist parties, moreover, suggests further division in the movement, despite their pro-Soviet orientation. Jamaica lies in a geographical and cultural region where most parties lack strong organizational unity and broad-based links that tie leaders with the led through a party program. The views of intellectual leaders themselves shape party goals independent of tight party discipline and a large following. Still, the presence of Marxist parties and Marxist intellectuals inside and outside the PNP tends to polarize the Jamaican political system, making the creation of a national consensus and the mobilization of the society to carry out an agreed developmental strategy difficult. This problem troubles the new Seaga government just as it plagued Manley's.

Cuban and Soviet Ties

The steady buildup of diplomatic relations between Jamaica and the Cubans and the Soviets since the mid-1970s produced a number of cultural, diplomatic, economic, and technical links. Approximately 400–450 Cubans—doctors, nurses, school-building teams, and mini-dam construction workers—came to Jamaica.[31] Jamaican youths in turn went to Cuba for cultural, educational, and athletic training. Cuban activities thus were less financial and political than technical in content, although the obvious side effects of ideology and propaganda cannot be discounted. Manley maintained that relations were based on noninterference in domestic policies, a judgment that appears to be accurate. Cuban aid and relations did not come even close to producing a centralized political system and party organization like those found in Cuba.

Manley paid his first visit to the Soviet Union in April 1979, after relations were established between the two countries. Among the economic agreements signed during Manley's trip was a contract specifying the export of 50,000 tons of alumina per year to the USSR between 1980 and 1983 and 250,000 tons thereafter. Jamaica and the USSR also established a joint fisheries company; and Moscow, unlike Cuba, granted a long-term loan to Jamaica to finance imports of Soviet goods.[32] Jamaica also had trade agreements with Hungary and Yugoslavia and was working toward closer ties with Bulgaria, Czechoslovakia, East Germany, Poland, and Romania. These moves were undoubtedly designed to reduce Jamaica's dependence on the IMF, but nevertheless they point up the country's enormous reliance on external support wherever it can find it. As expected, Seaga and the JLP soundly criticized Manley's visit to the USSR, his visit to Cuba in March 1980, and Castro's trip to Jamaica in 1977.

Although these events did not propel Jamaica into communism, they clearly aroused suspicions inside the United States. Cuba's geographic proximity did nothing to ease concern, for it has facilitated increased travel to Havana by left-wing members of the PNP and other Jamaican Marxists. Nor is the perception of communist influence in Jamaica produced strictly by Cuban-Jamaican relations. Cuba's expanded presence elsewhere in the Caribbean and Central America (Grenada, Nicaragua, El Salvador), the general rise of Soviet influence in the area, and domestic leftist trends in many other Caribbean and Central American countries also affect U.S. perceptions. These perceptions resulted in reduced aid for Jamaica, support for tariffs on Jamaican imports, such as rum and sugar, and a tendency for Congress and some members of the executive branch to couple Jamaican events with the Cuban problem. Seaga's victory in late 1980 greatly modified Washington's perceptions.

Recent events, however, could decrease Manley's willingness to associate closely with Cuba and the Soviet Union. Jamaica voted with the majority of Third World countries to condemn the Soviet move into Afghanistan. Like other developing countries, Jamaica is pressing the Kremlin for greater financial aid and not allowing it to continue to dismiss the needs of these states as the responsibility of the "imperialists."[33] Cuba's image as a Third World model, meanwhile, has been tarnished by its unabashed pressure for increased support from developing countries for the USSR at the September 1979 meeting of nonaligned countries in Havana and especially by Cuban support for Moscow's invasion of Afghanistan. Cuba's recent economic difficulties, made so visible by Castro's public acknowledgment and the flight of refugees from April 1980 onward, do not improve its attractiveness as a role model.[34]

Stability or Instability

Jamaican prospects turn essentially on economic development. The essential question is whether, and to what extent, the Seaga government can build a consensus on dealing with poverty and chronic unemployment, or barring consensus, whether the political system can handle the conflicting relations produced by economic stagnation.

Jamaica's capacity to cope with these issues will be conditioned by both internal and external forces. Key external elements are aid and investment responses by the United States and other developed countries and of the IMF and World Bank to Jamaica's development needs. Key internal factors are government successes and failures in agriculture, the mix of labor- versus capital-intensive investment to ease unemployment, the stimulation of capital formation, bauxite production, and a more equitable distribution of national income. Complex economic problems will challenge Prime Minister Seaga's best political skills.

The future of Jamaican communism depends directly on economic development. Certainly its organized presence makes the building of consensus on development strategy difficult. Major questions for the future include the type of opposition mounted by ex–Prime Minister Manley, his ability to control his radical procommunist supporters during the Seaga administration, and the types of contact between Manley and Castro in the 1980s. Also important is the manner in which the United States and other developed countries react to the Seaga victory by either enhancing or decreasing his capacity to ease Jamaica's poverty. Should Seaga fail, either communism will become more appealing or at least radical nationalism will be forthcoming. Both would destabilize the Jamaican political system.

Communism would affect Jamaican stability and instability by affecting U.S. perceptions. Given the visibility of Cuban and Soviet activities in the Caribbean and the proximity of Jamaica to Cuba, Washington during the 1970s began to see Jamaica as part of a strategically important region in a state of dislocation and increasing leftist tendencies. As the 1980s began, U.S. foreign policy responses were of a dual nature.[35] First, Washington displayed new attention to the economic problems of the Caribbean, emphasizing foreign aid and economic development. But the rise of Soviet and Cuban power projection in the area, such as the Soviet-troops-in-Cuba issue of summer 1979, produced a military response to counter a perceived Cuban-Soviet threat.[36] While the Carter administration sought to keep its dual policies separated, it nevertheless created confusion in the minds of Caribbean leaders, including the Jamaicans.[37] Moderate and Marxist leftists in Jamaica much preferred the first response; the second had the effect of giving them a common cause against U.S. military action. The second response may also have tended, in combination with the erosion of Jamaica's economic and political situation, to undermine congressional approval of economic aid.

Seaga's victory of 1980, given his procapitalist and anticommunist position, may ease U.S. fears of communism in the Caribbean, especially in light of other conservative electoral victories in Puerto Rico and the Turks and Caicos islands and in view of Jamaica's diplomatic break with Cuba. If so, increased economic aid may accompany a downplaying of military responses in the region.[38] Yet events in Central America may encourage U.S. military responses, fueling Seaga's leftist opposition in Jamaica and encouraging political instability. That scenario could in turn reduce U.S. willingness to aid or invest in Jamaica.

We are left, then, with a complicated picture. The instability is rooted in economic dislocation, which the Manley government was unable to address satisfactorily. Indeed, that government's efforts produced deep political antagonisms. What is needed is an economic breakthrough to help mute the social and political turmoil. The 1980 election of Seaga restored the Jamaican commitment to capitalism, with a distinctly pro-American edge. Whether it will fare better than Manley's experiment with "democratic socialism" remains to be seen.

Notes

1. For a discussion of Caribbean communism, with an emphasis on Jamaica, see Trevor Monroe, "Winds of Change in the Caribbean," *World Marxist Review* 23, no. 11 (November 1980): 28–35.

2. The 50-year-old Seaga took office on November 1, 1980, as Jamaica's fifth prime minister. He is a Harvard graduate and a financial specialist. (See *Jamaica Newsletter* 11, no. 4 [October 1980]: 1).

3. For a general description of Jamaica's economic, political, and social setting, see *Area Handbook for Jamaica* (Washington, D.C.: Government Printing Office, 1976); and Adam Kuper, *Changing Jamaica* (Kingston: Kingston Publishers, 1976).

4. Reports of these events may be found in radio broadcasts monitored by the Foreign Broadcast Information Service (FBIS). For example, see the report on antigovernment demonstrations, FBIS, *Latin America and the Caribbean*, January 10, 1980; and on workers' strikes that disrupted health services, water supplies, transportation, and food supplies, ibid., January 22, 1980.

5. Gasoline sold at $2.65 a gallon in March 1980, bread was often unavailable, and wheat had to be imported (see James Nelson Goodsell, "Sunny Jamaica Losing Its Gloss," *Christian Science Monitor*, March 26, 1980, p. 16; and Tad Szulc, "Radical Winds in the Caribbean," *New York Times*, May 25, 1980, "Magazine Section," pp. 16ff.

6. See *Latin America Weekly Report*, December 12, 1980, p. 4. Seaga's keynote address at the November 1980 conference of the Caribbean Central American Action left no doubt about his determination to struggle against

Cuban and Soviet influence in the Caribbean (*Caribbean Contact* 8, no. 4 [December 1980]: 9).

7. Soviet scholarly journals pay increasing attention to the Caribbean, an area depicted as hastening the weakening of imperialism and neocolonialism. See L. Klochkovsky, "The Struggle for Economic Emancipation in Latin America," *International Affairs* (Moscow), 1979, no. 4 (April): 39–47; and V. Yakubov, "Behind the Screen of the 'New Approach,'" *Pravda*, March 2, 1978, in FBIS, *USSR International Affairs*, March 7, 1978. At the same time Moscow accused the United States of fomenting violence in Jamaica in late 1980 (*Pravda*, October 15, 1980).

8. For Michael Manley's sharp perception of Jamaica's dependency legacy, see his *The Politics of Change: A Jamaica Testament* (London: Tonbridge Printers, 1974), chap. 1; and *The Search for Solutions* (Ontario, Canada: Maple House Publishing Co., 1976), introduction.

9. See Wendell Bell and J. William Gibson, "Independent Jamaica Faces the Outside World," *International Studies Quarterly* 22, no. 1 (March 1978): 5–45; and Wendell Bell, "Independent Jamaica Enters World Politics: Foreign Policy in a New State," *Political Science Quarterly* 92, no. 4 (Winter 1977–78): 683–703.

10. See W. Raymond Duncan, "Caribbean Leftism," *Problems of Communism* 27 (May–June 1978): 33–57.

11. "Neocolonialism" refers to the high prices Caribbean countries pay for foreign goods, the lesser amounts they receive for their products, the high interest rates they frequently have to pay for loans, the profits that foreign investors expect to make, and the tendency for foreign investment to be capital- rather than labor-intensive (see *The Economic Crisis, Broadcast by the Prime Minister, Honorable Michael Manley, January 5, 1977* [Kingston: Government of Jamaica, n.d.]).

12. Manley sees Jamaica as distinctly within the Third World. He advocates a common Third World economic strategy and strongly supports NIEO. (See Manley, *Politics of Change*, pp. 131–132.) Jamaica signed the 1974 declaration for NIEO, which calls for closer regulation of the activities of multinational corporations, active associations of producer nations, increased foreign aid from the developed countries, and other arrangements to establish a more equitable economic development strategy for the Third World. (See Guy F. Erb and Valeriana Kallab, eds., *Beyond Dependency: The Developing World Speaks Out* [Washington, D.C.: Overseas Development Council, 1975], pp. 165–202; Richard N. Cooper, "A New International Economic Order for Mutual Gain," *Foreign Policy*, Spring 1977, pp. 66–120; and Roger D. Hansen, *Beyond The North-South Stalemate* [New York: McGraw-Hill, 1980], chap. 1.)

13. U.S., Congress, House, Committee on Foreign Affairs, *Caribbean Nations: Assessments of Conditions and U.S. Influence. Report of a Special Study Mission to Jamaica, Cuba, the Dominican Republic, and the Guantanamo*

Naval Base, January 3–12, 1979 (Washington, D.C.: Government Printing Office, 1979), pp. 8–9.

14. U.S., Congress, House, Committee on Foreign Affairs, Subcommittee on Inter-American Affairs, *Economic and Political Future of the Caribbean: Hearings*, 96th Cong., 1st Sess., July 24, 26, and September 20, 1979 (Washington, D.C.: Government Printing Office, 1979), p. 41. See also *Keesing's Contemporary Archives*, July 27, 1979, pp. 29746–748.

15. On Jamaica's external debt and debt-servicing burden, see U.S., CIA, National Assessment Center, *Non-OPEC LDCs: External Debt Positions*, ER 80–10030 (Washington, D.C., 1980), p. 65.

16. Ibid, p. 13.

17. *Latin American Weekly Report*, April 4, 1980, pp. 4–5.

18. L. Alan Eyre, "Quasi-Urban Melange Settlement: Cases from St. Catherine and St. James, Jamaica," *Applied Geography* 69 (January 1979): 95.

19. J. Daniel O'Flaherty, "Finding Jamaica's Way," *Foreign Policy*, Summer 1978, p. 143.

20. *Latin American Weekly Report*, May 2, 1980, p. 6.

21. *Area Handbook for Jamaica*, p. 280.

22. The PNP did introduce, however, a five-year plan in 1978 (see *Keesing's Archives*, July 27, 1979, p. 29747).

23. *Latin American Weekly Report*, April 4, 1980, p. 5.

24. Ibid.

25. House, Committee on Foreign Affairs, *Caribbean Nations*, p. 11.

26. *Latin American Weekly Report*, May 2, 1980, p. 6.

27. Ibid.

28. *Jamaica Newsletter* (a publication of the Jamaican Embassy in Washington, D.C.), January 1980, pp. 8–9.

29. The Manley government had previously suspended negotiations with the IMF in early 1977 and moved toward radical experimentation with the economy. By April 1977 this attempt had been discredited. (See O'Flaherty, "Finding Jamaica's Way," p. 148.)

30. See Richard F. Staar, ed., *Yearbook on International Communist Affairs, 1980* (Stanford: Hoover Institution Press, 1980), p. 486.

31. See House, Committee on Foreign Affairs, *Caribbean Nations*, pp. 10–11; and idem, *Economic and Political Future of the Caribbean*, pp. 32–33.

32. *Keesing's Contemporary Archives*, July 27, 1979, p. 29748.

33. Hansen, *North-South Stalemate*, chap. 1.

34. James Nelson Goodsell, "Cuba's Economic Report Card: 'F,' " *Christian Science Monitor*, May 9, 1980, p. 1.

35. See Graham Hovey, "Caribbean Nations Still in Focus," *New York*

Times, February 3, 1980, p. 5; and James Nelson Goodsell, "Carter's Caribbean Sea of Confusion," *Christian Science Monitor*, February 11, 1980, p. 12.

36. The response included the establishment of the Caribbean Contingency Joint Task Force in Key West, Florida, plus the resumption of surveillance flights over Cuba (See Szulc, "Radical Winds in the Caribbean," p. 56).

37. See Goodsell, "Castro 'Loses' in U.S., Caribbean Elections," *Christian Science Monitor*, November 12, 1980, p. 9. Also *Latin American Weekly Report*, November 9, 1980, p. 1, which describes Washington's satisfaction over the Jamaican elections.

38. There are currently fourteen active World Bank loans totaling approximately $195 million of which 71 percent is undisbursed; and seventeen active Inter-American Development Bank loans amounting to about $123 million, of which one-half have been disbursed. Other loans are from Sweden, Holland, Algeria, West Germany, and Canada. The Jamaican government is working closely with Venezuela and Mexico on other projects. (Embassy of Jamaica news release.)

8 | THE EASTERN CARIBBEAN

George Volsky

Before the late 1970s, the eastern Caribbean, a region of small, mostly poor islands, was almost as removed from the center stage of world politics as Micronesia. Yet for a brief period, these independent mini-states and self-governing colonies were drawn, albeit marginally, into the strategic competition between East and West.

Like the entire Caribbean region, the eastern part has for centuries been dominated politically and economically by the Western powers, first the European colonial nations and later the United States. The 1959 Cuban revolution had little impact on the eastern Caribbean, whose colonial administrations provided representative democracy of the kind that Cuba enjoyed only briefly after gaining independence at the turn of the century.

But in the late 1960s, the largely underdeveloped subregion was caught in the political turmoil caused by unfulfilled expectations generated by the end of the colonial rule. Although the three principal former colonial powers, Great Britain, France, and the Netherlands, continued to provide economic aid to the area after independence, as the United States increasingly did, the narrowly based economies of the eastern Caribbean islands could not support their growing populations.

The economic crisis of the mid-1970s and the entry of Cuba into the area's politics, chiefly as a result of an opening and encouragement given to Cuban President Fidel Castro by Michael Manley, then prime minister of Jamaica, fueled the turmoil. Western leaders who until that time ordinarily viewed the eastern Caribbean as one of the few remaining undeveloped and unspoiled vacation resorts in the world suddenly discovered its strategic importance. There was alarm in some quarters following the establishment in March 1979 of a pro-Cuban regime in Grenada, a tiny eastern Caribbean island-nation. Reports that Caribbean leaders other than Manley were considering Marxism as an answer to the area's economic problems increased this concern, as did the number of Caribbean states establishing diplomatic ties with Havana.

Until well into the second decade of the Cuban revolution, the Soviet Union never seriously challenged Western hegemony in the eastern Caribbean, possibly regarding such attempts as unrewarding if not foolhardy. But Soviet and Cuban propaganda encouraged anti-Western sentiments in the region, constantly repeating the theme that "Marxism is the wave of the future."

Even before Manley's October 1980 electoral defeat, which ended the socialist experiment in Jamaica, the pro-Cuba and pro-Soviet movement in the eastern Caribbean had faltered. Neither Havana nor Moscow, generous with rhetoric, provided what the area needed most: economic aid. The tougher anti-Marxist line adopted by the Carter and Reagan administrations reminded some Caribbean leaders that the days of American largesse were over. Washington, concerned with and strongly opposed to communist involvement in the area, indicated it would help only its faithful friends—and only those who put their economies in order. The area lowered its expectations, entering a seemingly less traumatic but more difficult period of national consolidation and of painful adjustment to the economic realities of the 1980s.

The Caribbean islands stretch 2,000 miles across the Atlantic, from the Bahamas to Guyana. Among the islands, Guadaloupe is an overseas department of France, which subsidizes its economy by paying high prices for Guadeloupan sugar, bananas, rum, and other agricultural products. Martinique, also a department of France, has 330,000 inhabitants, mostly black, and large sugarcane and banana plantations. Dominica, a poor former British colony with 80,000 inhabitants, gained independence in 1978. St. Lucia, which changed hands between France and Great Britain fourteen times, is a volcanic island with 120,000 inhabitants. With 250,000 persons living on 166 square miles, Barbados has the highest population density of any country in the Western Hemisphere. Its economy is based on sugar, light industry, and the tourist trade. Trinidad-Tobago has 1.2 million people, mostly blacks and East Indians, but also descendants of Chinese, Arab, and European immigrants. Petroleum, tourism, and agriculture (sugar, cocoa, copra, cattle) are the three principal economic sectors in Trinidad, the most industrialized nation in the Caribbean after Puerto Rico. Grenada is the smallest nation in the Western Hemisphere. It was occupied by the British from 1762 until independence in 1974. Also regarded as part of the eastern Caribbean, although located off the northern coast of Venezuela, are the prosperous Netherlands Antilles, consisting of Curaçao, Bonaire, and Aruba. Curaçao, a tax-free haven for foreign banks and investment companies, has one of the largest petroleum refineries in the world.

Nearly all Caribbean islands have developed a political system based on the European parliamentary model and the principle of one man, one vote. With the notable exception of Grenada, the thirty Caribbean political entities hold elections regularly and fairly, as evidenced by the October 1980 balloting in Jamaica. Even in the smallest mini-states the system seems to work. Turks and Caicos, a self-governing British colony with less than seven thousand people and 32 islands strung out from the Bahamas to Hispaniola, lost its prime minister in an airplane accident in 1980, and an election was called. The electorate gave eight of the eleven seats in the island's governing body to the opposition party. After the March 1979 pro-Cuban coup d'etat in Grenada, a series of elections shattered the Cuban notion of Marxism's "historical inevitability" in the Caribbean. Moderates won electoral victories in Antigua, Dominica, St. Kitts–Nevis, St. Lucia, and St. Vincent. Moreover, the larger states of Barbados and Trinidad-Tobago have become wary of Cuban activities. The Jamaican election, in which conservative leader Edward Seaga captured 52 of the 60 seats in the Parliament, confirmed the conservative mood and the steady trend away from socialism in the eastern Caribbean, where Grenada remained Cuba's only ally.

For a brief period after the Grenadian coup and the controversy a few months later over the presence of a Soviet combat brigade in Cuba, the eastern Caribbean ranked high on the Carter administration's foreign policy agenda. Recognizing that neither individually nor collectively did the Caribbean mini-states have major international significance, U.S. officials justified their concern by pointing out that more than half of the nation's oil imports travel through the Caribbean, where petroleum is transferred from supertankers to smaller ships for delivery to American ports; that in 1979, nearly nine million of the fourteen million tons of bauxite imported annually by the United States came from the Caribbean, chiefly from Jamaica; and that the area controls access to the Panama Canal and could become in unfriendly hands a bottleneck for maritime traffic, both commercial and military, between North and South America. These and other considerations, Washington officials argued, made the region strategically important for the United States.

Considering the Caribbean as the nation's southwestern defensive parameter, the Carter administration established the Caribbean Contingency Joint Task Force in Key West, Florida, in October 1979.

At the time, London, Paris, and the Hague, despite their vast commercial interests in the Carribbean, did not share U.S. fears. Neither were Caribbean leaders themsclves particularly alarmed over a possible Moscow-Washington confrontation in their area. Even the Caribbean allies of the United States contended that friendly relations with the Castro government were not tantamount to embracing communism. But the pragmatic leaders of the English-speaking Caribbean nations, mostly educated in the United States or Britain, are not above taking advantage of the East-West competition, like developing countries in other parts of the world. Facing the lack of foreign exchange to pay for increasingly expensive oil as well as unemployment and underemployment and the prospect of declining living standards in the 1980s, they have been prepared to look anywhere for answers to their problems.

Cuban Influence

Some saw Castro's revolutionary government as an example of how social ills could be solved, overlooking the fact that for many years Cuba has been receiving from the Soviet Union probably the highest annual per capita subsidy given on continuous basis to any country in the world. (In 1980 it was $300, half of Grenada's per capita gross domestic product and more than Haiti's.) "It is curious," observed Prof. Gordon K. Lewis in 1980, "that so many Caribbean groups accept the Cuban-Soviet model at the time when that very model is under severe scrutiny throughout the Socialist world itself." While Lewis viewed Cuba's revolutionary attraction as being of limited duration, he noted that "no one can underestimate the massive appeal of the Cuban event for the rest of the Caribbean. It is as much a cataclysm as the Haitian war of liberation in the period between 1791 and 1804. As the St. Domingue slave rebellion shattered the myth of white supremacy, so the Cuban revolution has shattered the myth of American supremacy."[1]

Another Caribbean scholar, Prof. Carl Stone, also foresaw a decline of Cuban influence in the region:

> To a considerable extent, the current fascination with Marxism by these vocal minorities represents a natural reaction to a virtual rediscovery of left political ideas suppressed over the years by a conservative orthodoxy. The fascination with leftist ideas, however, will prove to be short-lived unless the leftist regimes of the region convince the masses by policy successes that leftism as a direction for government policies produces

positive results over the long run after all the rhetoric and the promises have ceased to excite.

Stone predicted that eventually a new political mood will emerge in the Caribbean: the "flamboyance, demagoguery and excessive rhetoric that now predominate will give ground to greater emphasis on technocratic competence and skills and managerialism."[2] Other experts, even at the height of Cuba's activities in the area, also pointed out the limitations of Castro's power to influence the long-range dynamics of Caribbean development.

But even though their influence has diminished, Cubans are in the Caribbean to stay simply because they are part of the region. The emergence of Fidel Castro in Cuba improved Moscow's chances in the area and made the Caribbean a factor, albeit a small one, in its world power game with the United States. Even before Castro came to power, Moscow had not been unaware of Caribbean affairs. Before 1959, the Kremlin had used Havana as a center to control Caribbean communist parties, especially in the Spanish-speaking countries. The region's communist leaders used to report to and receive instructions from Blas Roca, the Stalinist secretary general of the Cuban Communist Party (which operated under different names between the 1930s and 1950s), or other Comintern and Cominform officials in Havana. But Soviet interest in the Caribbean was perfunctory. Moscow was apparently convinced that attaining power in America's backyard was impossible. The region's Communists, except for the Cuban party, were few in number and perennially divided into countless factions. The Kremlin's main insistence was on receiving regular expressions of obeisance to Stalin and vocal support for Soviet policies.

It was not until after the October 1962 missile crisis, when the United States in an agreement with the Soviet Union acquiesced to Castro's continuance in power, that Moscow began to perceive the potential of Cuba as a base for undermining the Caribbean status quo. Until then, Moscow had looked askance at Castro's activities in the Caribbean, regarded as "adventurism" by Blas Roca and his old-guard communist colleagues.

In 1947, as a University of Havana student, Castro had joined an abortive invasion of the Dominican Republic aimed at overthrowing Dominican dictator Rafael Leonidas Trujillo. Practically since his first day in power, Castro began to plot military intervention in the Caribbean countries. In the first seven months of 1959, invasions of Haiti, Nicaragua, the Dominican Republic, and Panama were organized by or carried out from Cuba. These amateurish military expeditions were led by officers of Castro's rebel army. Castro, his brother Raul, and Ernesto Che Guevara personally participated in their planning. After this series of failures, Castro, probably advised by Guevara (who late in 1959 wrote an essay entitled "Guerrilla Warfare," regarded in the 1960s as the manual for Marxist insurrection in developing countries), decided to broaden the scope of his foreign military activities and give them a stronger ideological content. In July 1960 he called on South Americans to rise in arms and make the Andes another Sierra Maestra (Castro's base of operations against Batista). The so-called Second Declaration of Havana of February 4, 1962, included the slogan, "The duty of every revolutionary is to make revolution." A year later, Cuba was actively supporting a rural guerrilla movement in Venezuela, which Castro regarded as the key to control of the Caribbean basin.

Castro has had many friends in the Caribbean. Moreover, Cubans have strong ethnic ties with the area. Many Cuban blacks are of Haitian and Jamaican descent, and thousands of Caribbean inhabitants once came to the island as temporary cane cutters. In January 1966, when the Latin American Solidarity Organization (LASO) was created in Havana, its members included representatives from Guadeloupe, Guyana, French Guiana, Haiti, Jamaica, Martinique, Puerto Rico, the Dominican Republic, Trinidad-Tobago, and Suriname. But LASO never took root, and by the early 1970s it seemed inoperative. In 1970, Trinidad-Tobago's Prime Minister Eric Williams urged the hemisphere to reconsider its political ostracism of the Castro government, a proposal endorsed by Mexico and Chile. At the same time, Jamaican Prime Minister Hugh Shearer suggested that the Organization of American States initiate new contacts with Cuba. In 1972, Guyana, Jamaica, Barbados, and Trinidad-Tobago established diplomatic relations with Cuba.

Since the early 1970s, Cuba has been making a concerted effort to woo Caribbean intellectuals through Casa de las Americas, a Havana-based cultural organization. Conceived in 1960 primarily as a vehicle for establishing ties with Latin American intellectuals, Casa de las Americas, according to Cuban Minister of Culture Armando Hart, later aimed at "bringing out the cultural identity of Latin America and the Caribbean, promoting their literature, plastic arts, music, theater, encouraging research, publications, documentations, and spreading and conserving the Latin American and Caribbean cultural heritage."[3] In 1980, among the twelve recipients of the Casa's annual literary awards were two Haitians and one Barbadan. Also in the same year, Casa de las Americas organized a meeting of Latin American and Caribbean writers in Havana.

Several months earlier, in December 1979, Havana had been the site of the Second Trade Union Conference for Unity and Solidarity of Caribbean Workers, attended by delegates from 28 unions in fifteen countries, including Antigua, the Dominican Republic, Dominica, Grenada, Guadeloupe, Guyana, and Jamaica.

In March 1980, the French government expressed concern about Cuba's growing influence in Martinique and Guadeloupe, then swept by strikes and street demonstrations. "International communism is on the march in the Caribbean, and Cuba is the Central American staging post for Soviet action," declared Minister for Overseas Departments and Territories Paul Dijoud. "France plans to halt this penetration together with the Western free nations."[4] Several days after Dijoud's statement, France sent 225 antiriot policemen to quell a violent strike in Martinique. Cuba denied any role in the labor and racial disorders in France's Caribbean possessions. While signing an economic and technical agreement with France late in March 1980, President Castro "pledged that he wouldn't fan discontent in the French Antilles."[5]

Haiti has been largely spared Cuba-inspired political agitation probably because of Castro's fear that Cuba might have to receive tens of thousands of Haitian immigrants. Even without his encouragement, Haitians have been landing in Cuba in increasing numbers, creating serious socioeconomic problems. Cuba, which is less than 50 miles from the eastern coast of Haiti, lies on the route of thousands of Haitians trying to get to the United States or the Bahamas. Haiti's population density is twice that of Cuba, whose much higher standard of living acts as a magnet to its impoverished neighbors. For a number of years, Cuban authorities have been helping Haitians leaving their country to continue their sea voyage, but the exodus has not been without problems for the Castro government. In 1979, according to Castro, 2,801 Haitians in 68 boats landed in just one area of Cuba. "The least we could do was help them so they could continue their journey," he said. "But the phenomenon is growing, and nobody knows where it might end." The Cuban leader blamed Haitians arriving in Cuba in boats with live animals aboard for a 1980 outbreak of African swine fever in eastern Cuba. The government has been forced to "take strict health measures because of risks involved for animals, plants, and even human beings."[6]

In the Dominican Republic, the other country on Hispaniola, Cuba's political involvement has recently been insignificant. There is no evidence that Cuba influenced the 1965 Dominican civil war, which was finally ended by U.S. military intervention. But defeated constitutionalist leader Francisco Caamaño Deño, head of one of the warring factions, sought asylum in Cuba and received help in organizing an armed group there. Several years later, Caamaño, with a score of Dominicans trained in Cuba, managed to land in his country, planning to lead a guerrilla movement and overthrow the government. He was promptly killed by Dominican troops, who appeared to know beforehand of the expedition's landing; and the insurrection collapsed. Cuba's role in this episode has not been fully explained.

The Dominican extreme left has weakened since the 1978 election of President Antonio Guzmán, fragmenting into a dozen minute, hostile groups. The powerful Dominican Revolutionary Party, which belongs to the West European socialist movement, has undercut the already limited appeal of Marxist pro-Cuban or pro-Chinese groups.

The Grenadian Revolution

There is some evidence that Cuba had contacts with Maurice Bishop prior to March 13, 1979, the day the young Grenadian and some fifty followers overthrew the government of Prime Minister Sir Eric Gairy. But Havana's interest in Grenadian affairs really began after the bloodless coup, which Jesus Montane Oropesa, leader of the Cuban delegation to its first anniversary celebration, called "one of the most important recent events in the Caribbean and America."[7] Whatever the longevity of the Bishop government and the historical importance of the Grenadian revolution, during its first two years in power, Bishop created a regime that in many ways resembled that of Cuba.

"Without the Cuban revolution of 1959 there could have been no Grenadian revolution," said Bishop on a visit to Havana in May 1980. "Certainly we in Grenada will never forget that it was the military assistance of Cuba in the first weeks that provided us with the basis to defend our revolution.... We look to the people of Cuba, we look to your revolution and your leadership to ensure that the revolutionary process in the Caribbean and Central American region continues to go forward with strength."[8]

But the size of Grenada points up the difference between the two revolutions. The 110,000 inhabitants of Grenada and the two tiny islands of Petit Martinique and Carriacou occupy an area of 133 square miles. Located in the southern part of the Windward Islands, close to Trinidad and Tobago and the Venezuelan coast, Grenada is only 21 miles in length. It gained independence from Great Britain in 1974 under Gairy, who rose to prominence in the early 1950s as a trade union leader.

A believer in voodoo and a man who repeatedly lectured the United Nations on unidentified flying objects, Gairy presided over a regime that combined peasant populism and the worst excesses of a one-man dic-tatorship; corruption, a personal secret police, and brutal abuse of power. He was opposed by a coalition of the urban establishment, the Commit-tee of 22 (which included churches, the Chamber of Commerce of St. George's, the capital, the Rotary and Lions clubs, and labor unions), and by a group of young middle-class radicals belonging to Bishop's New Jewel Movement. ("Jewel" stands for Joint Endeavor for Welfare, Edu-cation, and Liberation.) The swift coup, organized by members of the Jewel movement, was successful probably because it took place while Gairy was absent from the island.

Once in power, the Jewel regime quickly moved to neutralize the other anti-Gairy forces. According to Richard Jacobs, Grenada's ambas-sador in Havana, the Cuban and the Jamaican governments assisted the Bishop regime "in a very concrete way . . . within hours of the success of our revolution."[9] Apparently Cuba initially sent Grenada hundreds of Soviet-made AK-47 automatic rifles, which later became the standard equipment of the 1,500-man "people's revolutionary army." The army and a "people's militia" in the villages number about 2,000 men, propor-tionally the largest military contingent in the Americas. (Dominica, with a population of 80,000, has a defense force of only 30 men.) The Grena-dian revolutionary army received training mainly from Cuban instruc-tors, who are also advising a small, but growing security force. In May 1980, Grenada announced that it would send 500 soldiers to Namibia to fight alongside leftist guerrillas in that country.[10] It is not known whether this plan was carried out.

In addition to training regular forces, Cuban instructors in Grenada reportedly gave courses in terrorism, sabotage, and guerrilla warfare to hundreds of young radicals from neighboring island countries. The largest contingent was said to be from Trinidad, whose government ex-pressed concern over what it saw as the Grenada terrorism school.[11]

As a member of the Grenadian Parliament, Bishop had repeatedly stressed his allegiance to the principle of representative democracy and promised to hold free elections if he attained power. The tall, person-able, 35-year-old London-educated lawyer seemed to many to embody a new generation of Caribbean leaders. His victory over the Gairy regime was widely hailed in the area, which began to take notice of the small and poor island.

Like Fidel Castro twenty years earlier, Bishop reneged on his prom-ises to hold elections, instituting a one-party leftist dictatorship instead. He has ruled by staging frequent rallies, meetings, marches, and demon-strations, organized to maintain revolutionary fervor among his support-crs and to intimidate the opposition. The *Torchlight*, a semiweekly opposition newspaper that criticized Bishop's Cuban connection, was closed by the government in 1979.

At the same time, the Bishop government has earned a reputation for honesty in the management of the island's internal affairs. Schoolchildren have received free milk, roads have been built, and low-interest house repair loans have been available for the needy. Grenadian leaders have pledged to continue preserving the role of the private sector. They have started building roads and modernizing the fishing industry with Cuban assistance. Efforts have been made to increase exports of bananas, nutmeg, and cocoa, the island's chief products.

But it was the foreign policy of the Grenadian revolution that drew attention to the Bishop regime. United States–Grenadian relations began to deteriorate shortly after the March 1979 coup as Bishop's ties with Castro became progressively closer. Late in 1979, Cuba named Julian Torres Rizo, reportedly a senior officer of the General Directorate of Intelligence, as its first ambassador in Grenada. Rizo, whose mission occupies nearly half a city block in St. George's, was the first resident ambassador in that country.

The Cuban-Grenadian alliance has assumed an increasingly political character. Selwyn Strachan, one of the New Jewel Movement's founders and minister of labor, works, and communications, described it as a "socialist party, with the objective of bringing socialism to this country. . . . What Cuba had in 1959, after the revolution, was a dictatorship of the masses, just like what we have here."[12] Soon, Bishop and other Grenadian leaders were frequent and honored visitors to Havana, as were Cuban officials to St. George's. Grenada was the only Caribbean country to join Cuba in opposing the U.N. vote calling for the withdrawal of Soviet troops from Afghanistan.

The Cuban presence is plainly visible in Grenada. Murals of Che Guevara and other Cuban leaders adorn the island, and a portrait of Fidel Castro (as well as those of Nicaraguan revolutionaries and of Muammar Qadafi) decorate Bishop's office. At the Point Salinas International Airport, 350 Cubans are helping build a badly needed 5,000-foot runway. Cuban doctors and dentists work on the island, and Cuban technicians study its water resources.

The $70 million Salinas airport, which—according to Bishop—would increase tourism to the island and its fine beaches, will be one of the largest in the eastern Caribbean. In addition to commercial uses, the airport, to which Venezuela has also contributed financially, could be utilized as a refueling stop by Cuban and Soviet civilian and military airplanes flying between Havana and African and Soviet cities.

As Grenada gave every indication of following the lead of Cuba in international affairs, other island countries appeared to adopt a more cautious attitude toward the Bishop regime. In November 1980, Grenadian leaders charged that the government of Barbados was "attempting to lead the Caribbean community into a campaign against Grenada . . . Tom Adams, prime minister of Barbados, publicly demanded that the Grenadian government hold free elections, thus openly interfering in Grenadian affairs."[13] On March 13, 1981, during the celebration of the second anniversary of the coup d'etat, Bishop stated that the Caribbean should be declared a "zone of peace." "Grenada does not want to be the enemy of any country in the world, and it would like to have good relations with Washington," Bishop declared.[14]

In 1981, the Bishop government appeared to be having difficulties financing the Salinas airport construction when European credits for the project did not materialize. In addition, anti-American rhetoric has caused a decline in tourism, the prime source of hard currency. As a result, the government engaged an American public relations firm to counter what it said were misconceptions about Grenada's revolution and its relations with Cuba.

Whether Grenada can attract American tourists again without toning down its anti-U.S. rhetoric is debatable. But in the meantime, concern in Washington over the radicalization in the eastern Caribbean has receded. The Reagan administration was taking its time in re-examining American policy toward the area, which three years earlier has burst like a nova on the world and just as quickly disappeared from the sight of American policymakers. Those in Washington who continued to observe the area felt that its main problem was now economic and not political. Philip Habib, former undersecretary of state, visited the Caribbean in 1980. His still confidential report discussed the economic and social instability of the region and reportedly recommended a broadening of economic and political cooperation rather than increases in military aid.

This is also the general view of Prime Minister Seaga of Jamaica, who nevertheless warns that the danger of foreign, Marxist infiltration has not disappeared. "There is a Caribbean misconception that individual strength is sufficient to maintain a successful (democratic) party system," said Seaga in May 1981 in Miami.

> The misconception goes further: Alien ideologies, it is said, cannot infiltrate the political system; "it cannot happen here" is the familiar view.
> But it has happened! Alien ideologies have penetrated the political system of the Caribbean. At first the success was marginal, then it grew

stridently, led by the advocacy of Jamaica. It was only after a protracted struggle against the alien system, in which Jamaica again played a lead role, this time on the other side, that the political will of the people was summoned to decisively defeat the intruders.

Many lessons should have been learned from this struggle, which was enacted in a more vicarious manner in several other electoral contests in the region during that period.

The most important of these is no doubt the need for greater solidarity and fraternity of like-minded political parties in the region, because the misconception that political infiltration "cannot happen here" has been proven wrong, and the preconception that the democratic system is able "to take care of itself" is equally false.

The valid conception is that the infiltrators have lost the battle but we have not yet totally won the war.[15]

Notes

1. *Caribbean Review* 9, no. 1 (Winter 1980).
2. *Caribbean Life and Times* 1, no. 3 (1980).
3. *Granma*, February 24, 1980.
4. *Miami Herald*, March 14, 1980.
5. *Wall Street Journal*, April 1, 1980.
6. *Granma*, March 18, 1980.
7. Ibid., March 23, 1980.
8. Ibid., May 11, 1980.
9. Ibid., March 9, 1980.
10. *Miami Herald*, May 31, 1980.
11. *Trinidad Guardian* (Port-of-Spain), January 9, 1980.
12. *Socialist Voice* (Canada), December 24, 1979.
13. *Granma*, November 30, 1979.
14. Ibid., March 22, 1981.
15. *Miami Herald*, May 10, 1981.

9 | GUYANA

William E. Ratliff

The Jonestown massacre in November 1979 catapulted Guyana from the ranks of the least known to the company of the most misunderstood countries of the world. For most Americans, who saw weeks of grisly television and newspaper accounts of the Rev. Jim Jones's mass sacrifice, Guyana became synonymous with jungle slaughter and kinky cults. True, a few Americans had discerned Marxist Cheddi Jagan stalking the Caribbean from the nation's capital of Georgetown a decade before Fidel Castro planted his species of tropical communism in Havana. But that challenge had been met by international maneuvering, and Americans who had heard the name of the country in the years before Jonestown were as likely as not to confuse it with the African nations of Guinea or Ghana.

But ignorance and misunderstanding have hovered over the area since Christopher Columbus skirted its coast on his third voyage to the New World in 1498. In the words of one prominent historian, the region—settled by the Dutch in the sixteenth century and a British colony (British Guiana) from 1831 to 1966—was just that "swampy no-man's land between Venezuela and Portuguese Brazil."[1]

In many respects the Land of Many Waters (the Amerindian meaning of Guyana) has been shrouded in deep mystery and high romancé. Sir Walter Raleigh, Jiménez de Quesada, Francisco Orellana, and other explorers sought the fabled riches of El Dorado in Guyana and surrounding regions. William H. Hudson set his fantasy *Green Mansions* in the south of this land. And only a few score miles from the town of Adventure, where zoologist-author Gerald Durrell chased the capybara and cayman, Jones created his paradise for a new breed of American expatriates. But reality has been hard on romance in Guyana. The quests for El Dorado all failed; Rima, the mysterious bird-like girl in Hudson's novel, was burned to death by Indians in her magnificent tree;[2] and more than 900 died ritualistically in Jones's heavily armed, drug-soaked People's Temple outpost.

The Setting

Guyana is a domestically volatile nation strategically located next to oil-rich Venezuela and the explosive Caribbean islands. Its airfields reportedly have been used as stopover posts for Cuban troops being airlifted in Soviet planes to wars in Angola and other African countries. Within the borders of this Idaho-sized country—almost two-thirds of which is claimed by Venezuela on the west and Surinam on the east—are some of the largest bauxite reserves in the world.

Guyana is divided into four regions: (1) the coastal plain, where most of the people live and work in the towns, the sugar estates, and the rice fields; (2) the hilly area south of the plain, where bauxite is found around Linden and Kwakwani; (3) the highland region in the south and west, important for its forests, gold, diamonds, manganese, iron ore, and waterfalls; and (4) the rolling grasslands of the interior savannahs, the Rupununi, with its crops and cattle. The capital, and the country's main harbor, of Georgetown is the only city of any size, with a population of approximately 185,000; other towns are New Amsterdam (20,000), with its important harbor, and Linden (30,000), formerly MacKenzie, a mining center.[3]

Guyana is rich in many resources—from bauxite, diamonds, and gold to fertile land and forests—but the economy in the late 1970s and early 1980s was depressed. In 1980 the gross national product was approximately U.S. $570 million. There were food shortages, double-digit inflation, and increasing power blackouts. The national debt was estimated at U.S. $2 billion and rising rapidly. The balance of payments deficit for 1980 was approximately $122 million, resulting in a serious shortage of foreign exchange. Foreign exchange reserves, which stood at some $18.8 million in June 1980, have also been hit by major strikes in the sugar (1977–78) and bauxite (1979) industries. The cost of imported petroleum (used mainly to generate electricity) jumped from U.S. $18 million in 1973 to over $100 million in 1979. The government reported in early 1981 that real national economic growth in 1980 had been 2 percent and that production in the nation's three primary industries—bauxite, sugar, and rice—had fallen between 13 and 20 percent below target. A Guyanese academic told a reporter from the French daily *Le Monde* in December 1979: "It is only abroad, and then again outside the Caribbean, that people speak of Guyana's 'socialism.' We speak rather of bad management, corruption, and lack of planning."[4]

Although Guyana has increased its foreign trade with socialist countries in an effort to rely less on the United States and European powers, recent economic pressures have forced it to reconsider some ties with the nonsocialist world. Since 1978 the government has accepted loans and credits from the Inter-American Development Bank, the Royal Bank of Canada, the Caribbean Development Facility, and the International Monetary Fund. In February 1981 the World Bank approved a U.S. $23.5 million loan for industry and agriculture, part of which will be directed toward a billion-dollar project that may lead to the construction of a hydroelectric facility and aluminum smelter on the upper Mazaruni River.[5] To the hoots of opposition parties, the government reversed its position on foreign investment in the country and in 1979 published a major new code designed to encourage the inflow of foreign funds.

Ethnicity

Guyana is the only English-speaking country in South America. It has slightly more than 800,000 citizens, roughly the same as San Francisco. But the size of the population is less important than its racial composition and political orientation. Although precise figures cannot be ascertained, roughly 50 percent of the population is of East Indian descent, approximately 40 percent of African origin, and the remainder assorted Amerindian, Portuguese, Chinese, and racial mixtures. The first African slaves were taken to Guyana in about 1621 by the Dutch West India Company to work in the sugar plantation economy. A major shift in social structure occurred after the country became a British colony in 1831 and slavery was abolished in 1834. The importation of East Indians of all castes began in 1838; by 1891 East Indians are estimated to have constituted some 40 percent of the total population and 92 percent of the rural population. Limited importation of Portuguese laborers began in 1835 and of Chinese in 1853.[6] Today the Indo-Guyanese predominate in the agricultural sectors, particularly sugar production. The Afro-Guyanese dominate urban areas and supply the vast majority of bureaucrats, soldiers, and police. Racial rivalry is strong; large-scale violence erupted as recently as the early 1960s.

For the past 25 years, race has played a major role in politics, with the

Indo-Guyanese generally supporting the People's Progressive Party (PPP) headed by Cheddi Jagan and the Afro-Guyanese joining the People's National Congress (PNC) under Forbes Burnham. Recently these racial divisions have begun eroding in some respects, with significant crossovers in the major parties and the formation of a new party, the Working People's Alliance (WPA), which draws support irrespective of race or class. The major parties regularly denounce racism in what Guyanese analyst Ralph Premdas calls the formal or "clean campaign." At the same time, in the informal or "unclean campaign," grass-roots workers invoke long-standing negative stereotypes and reinforce the community solidarity of racial groups.[7] By and large religious divisions coincide with racial lines. Over 50 percent of the population is Christian, approximately 10 percent Muslim, and the remainder Hindu.

The presence of foreign religious cults in Guyana has further diversified the population, heightened racial tensions, and caused grave concern among Guyanese outside of the PNC. International attention was drawn to these cults in mid-November 1978 when a U.S. congressman and his party were murdered while investigating Jonestown and when this event led Jim Jones to order the mass suicide of the community. But for Guyanese, the Jonestown phenomenon was more than a horror story of a fanatical cult in the wastelands. Jones had bypassed Guyanese customs and imported weapons, drugs, and a powerful radio transmitter, forming what the PPP called a "state within a state." Many in Guyana are concerned that the Burnham government has encouraged such settlements to provide shock troops to "prop up the PNC." In mid-1980 the primary cult involved was the black House of Israel, led by the American Edward "Rabbi" Washington, which has allegedly been used to intimidate and assault opposition groups in the country.[8] The Christian Refugee Team International proposal in early 1980 to resettle several thousand Hmong tribesmen from Laos near the Jonestown site was opposed by opposition parties who feared that the anticommunist Laotians might be used as agents of the PNC.

Political Parties and Politics

British Guiana was granted limited representative government in 1928. In 1953 a new constitution providing for universal adult suffrage, a bicameral legislature and a ministerial system was adopted. The country has had two major political parties since the 1950s: the PPP and the PNC. The latter was a breakaway group from the former. The WPA was launched as a political party in 1979, although it had been around for several years as a pressure group; by 1980 it had become a significant political force in the country.

The PPP emerged from the Political Affairs Committee (PAC), formed in 1946. It was led by Indo-Guyanese Cheddi Jagan, a U.S.-trained dentist, and his American wife, Janet Rosenberg, a Marxist who had been active in political circles in the United States. Other prominent PAC members were Indo-Guyanese Ram Karran and J. P. Kachmansingh and Afro-Guyanese Martin Carter, Ashton Chase, and Sydney King. Although some early activists wanted the PPP to declare itself a communist party, it was decided to give the new entity a broader base to increase its electoral appeal. Looking for a black leader with greater public support than any on the committee, the PAC's attention fell on labor leader Linden Forbes Sampson Burnham, a prominent student with degrees from the University of London. Thus Burnham, who was elected president of the Bar Association of Guyana in 1949, became a founding member of the PPP, taking the position of chairman, while Cheddi Jagan retained the top post of leader of the party. Clinton Wong, of Chinese descent, was selected as senior vice-chairman.

The PPP's primary objectives, enshrined in the constitution adopted at the first party congress in April 1951, were to pursue national self-determination and independence, to transform the new country into a socialist nation, and to work for the eventual political union with other Caribbean territories. Independence was won fifteen years later, and during the next decade many steps were taken to socialize the new state. The objective of uniting Guyana with other Caribbean countries was modified to a call for unified action among independent nations.

The new party won 51 percent of the vote in 1953 but, because of the single-member district electoral system, took 18 of the 24 seats in the legislature. This was the peak of the party's popular support. This remarkable electoral success was preceded and followed by complications that prevented the party from ever again winning a clear majority of the popular vote in a national legislative election.

The first setback, precipitated by PPP leaders themselves, came only a couple of months after Jagan and his ministers assumed power. The PPP conducted such an aggressive nationalistic and semisocialistic program that the British colonial government suspended the constitution and removed the PPP from office, charging in a "white paper" that there was evidence of a "communist plot" to "turn British Guiana into a state subordinate to Moscow."[9] The report of the British Constitutional Commission in 1954 further charged that PPP leaders Cheddi Jagan, Janet Jagan, Sydney King, Rory Westmaas, Brindley Benn, and Martin Carter "accepted unreservedly the 'classical' doctrines of Marx and Lenin, were enthusiastic supporters of the policies and practices of modern Communist movements, and were contemptuous of social democratic parties."[10] A number of PPP leaders were imprisoned for some months in the wake of the constitutional suspension. Burnham and several other party leaders were classified as "socialists," although their equal determination to achieve national independence was duly noted.[11]

A second problem was less evident at the time but more consequential in the long run. As Georgetown's New World magazine noted in 1963, even at the time of the 1953 election the PPP was not so much a "homogeneous unit" as a "coalition . . . The coalition represented an advance along the road to unity, it was not a unity."[12] Despres notes that even before the 1953 election the more radical Jaganite wing of the PPP had worked secretly to gain control of the party. Burnham was considered too opportunistic, too lax in his Marxism, and too willing to concede too much in pursuit of Caribbean unity. Immediately after the election, disputes over parliamentary leadership and ministerial portfolios emerged; and eventual compromises pleased neither side. The Jaganites formulated an elaborate plan for dumping Burnham, according to Despres, and in 1955 the party split. For a brief period two PPPs coexisted simultaneously: a smaller faction led by Burnham and a larger group headed by Jagan and including, for a short time, several of the PPP's top Afro-Guyanese leaders—King, Carter, Westmaas, and Benn.[13]

The colonial government permitted legislative elections again in 1957; Jagan's PPP, still with considerable Afro-Guyanese backing, won 47.5 percent of the vote and 9 of 14 seats. But Burnham's PNC took 25.5 percent of the vote and three Georgetown seats, starting the movement toward the racial politics that marked the 1960s and 1970s.

Over the next two years most of the Afro-Guyanese remaining in Jagan's PPP left the party and shattered the prospects for an integrated, multiracial, nationalist organization under Jagan's control. Evidently disillusioned by several events in 1956—Khrushchev's "secret speech" denouncing Stalin, the Soviet repression in Hungary, and Jagan's speech at the PPP congress—Carter and Westmaas retired from politics.[14] King left the PPP but continued his political activities, first as an independent, then within the PNC, and again as an independent—now calling himself Eusi Kwayana—forming several new organizations, including the Association for Social and Cultural Relations with Independent Africa (ASCRIA). Benn withdrew from the PPP in 1969.

The years 1968 and 1969 marked a turning point for the PPP. Its Afro-Guyanese support all but gone, Jagan evidently decided that without the broad multiracial backing sought fitfully from late PAC days, he might as well give the PPP a clearer political stance. The party committed itself openly to Marxism-Leninism at its congress in August 1968. In June 1969 Jagan turned up at the international conference of communist

and workers' parties in Moscow. Jagan moved to align the PPP unequivocally with the Soviet Union, and in turn, Soviet leaders recognized the
PPP as a bona fide communist party. Jagan dutifully condemned the
Chinese Communist Party and approved the Soviet-bloc invasion of
Czechoslovakia. This move, which PPP leaders had not approved,
provoked serious and open conflict within the party. Veteran leaders
who protested were demoted or purged. Party leaders subsequently
stated that the process of transforming the PPP into a Leninist party
began in 1969.[15]

A second crisis erupted in 1975–76 over the direction, especially the
domestic direction, the party was taking. Former organizing secretary
Balchand Persaud was expelled, and three prominent party members
and their followers resigned: Harry Lall, former PPP leader in parliament and head of the PPP-controlled Guyana Agricultural and General
Workers' Union; Halim Majeed, chairman of the PPP youth group, the
Progressive Youth Organization, along with six senior youth leaders;
and Ranji Chandisingh, the party's top theoretician and editor of the
PPP theoretical journal, *Thunder*. Other prominent PPP leaders resigned or were expelled—among them Lalbachan Lalbahadur and Vincent Teekah. Forbes Burnham encouraged this dissension by making
two PPP defectors—Chandisingh and Teekah—ministers in the PNC
government. Teekah, who had become a member of the Guyanese Parliament for the PPP in 1969, was assassinated on October 25, 1979, in
Georgetown; and the only witness, an American, was hurriedly flown
out of the country.[16]

Yet despite its internal problems, the PPP is one of only two pro-
Soviet communist parties in Latin America to have fared consistently
well in free or even partially free elections. Since 1973, when the other
(in Chile) was declared illegal, it has been the only one.[17]

As Jagan's PPP lost its Afro-Guyanese support in the late 1950s,
Burnham's fortunes began to rise. He formed the PNC in the mid-1950s
by merging his faction of the PPP with the United Democratic Party, an
organization of the Afro-Guyanese middle class. In the years that followed, the PNC leadership and membership became largely Afro-
Guyanese, leaving the PPP increasingly Indo-Guyanese. The PNC
came within 2 percentage points of the PPP in the popular vote in the
1961 legislative election, but Jagan's party ended up with 20 of 35 legislative seats. The PNC took 11.

The British found it increasingly difficult to withhold independence
from Guyana. British and American concern over the possibility of a
communist government emerging under Jagan, compounded by economic difficulties and severe racial unrest in Guyana, led the British to

introduce a new system of proportional representation in a unicameral legislature before the 1964 election.[18] In 1964 the PPP took 45.88 percent of the popular vote and 24 of 53 legislative seats; the PNC, with 40.5 percent of the vote, won 20 legislative seats and assumed the leadership of the country in coalition with the recently formed, more conservative United Front, which won 7 seats.

The PNC has remained in control ever since—through independence in May 1966, the formation of a cooperative republic in 1970, and the adoption of a socialist constitution in October 1980. The PPP has charged that the 1968, 1973, and oft-postponed 1980 elections were fraudulent; outside observers have tended to agree. PNC representation in the 53-seat assembly has increased from 30 (to 19 for the PPP) in 1968 to 37 (to 14 PPP) in 1973 to 41 (to 10 PPP) in 1980.[19] Probably most Guyanese, whomever they support, would agree with WPA leader Clive Thomas's 1979 statement: "We believe the government will never change through elections."[20]

Two other leftist parties exist in Guyana, though only one is of any significance. The WPA was formed in the mid-1970s as a pressure group. Founding members included Eusi Kwayana's ASCRIA; the Indian Political Revolutionary Associates, led by Moses Bhagwan; the Ratoon group of intellectuals, led by Clive Thomas and Walter Rodney; and the Working People's Vanguard Party (WPVP), led by Brindley Benn. Benn and the WPVP—a long-lived but minuscule group representing a pro-Chinese position after Jagan's open swing toward the Soviet Union in 1969—withdrew from the WPA before the latter became a party in 1979.

Recent Party Policies and Relations

Forbes Burnham's primary concerns over the past three decades have been Guyanese independence, the nation's position among Third World states, the development of a productive, socialist-oriented society, and his own position as prime leader of the country.

Guyanese independence was more granted than won when the British moved out, and, as noted below, many of Burnham's critics charge that he has allowed "imperialist" forces to limit national sovereignty. Burnham, however, sought to emphasize Guyana's independence by adopting an active role in the nonaligned movement. A major move in this direction came in 1972 when he hosted a meeting of the nonaligned foreign ministers in Georgetown, the first official meeting of the movement in the Western Hemisphere. He has also emphasized both independence and nonalignment by nationalizing several major foreign economic holdings in Guyana—the North American–owned Demerara Bauxite Company (Alcan) in 1971, the Reynolds Metal Company in 1975, and the British Booker holdings in 1976, thus bringing 80 percent of the nation's goods and services under government control. And Burnham has been moderately successful in maintaining a nonaligned position with respect to the United States, the Soviet Union, Cuba, and other powers, despite periodic tilts in one direction or the other, as detailed below.

Domestic policies have been a still greater concern. Guyanese government leaders, such as Minister of Economic Development Desmond Hoyte at the August 1979 PNC Congress, speak in lofty terms of economic efficiency and productivity, of cooperatives and socialism promoting the dignity and welfare of the masses. But simple economic indicators suggest that little has been achieved along these lines, and critics of the government are not optimistic about the immediate future. The PNC has indicated that the state must increasingly "intervene actively in the affairs of its people" in order to promote individual and national progress, convictions that are included in the socialist constitution adopted in October 1980.[21] But other parties have long objected to the growing bureaucracy and the PNC's strong-arm tactics in dealing with opposition groups.

Burnham's longest-standing critics are the Jagans, their party, and national organizations under PPP control—the Progressive Youth Organization, the Women's Progressive Organization, and the Guyana Agricultural and General Workers' Union. Some of the problems in Guyana under PNC rule, Jagan says, are "lack of democracy, bureaucratic-administrative and police-military methods of rule, denial of human rights and civil liberties, militarization of politics and industrial relations, refusal to establish democratic management and workers' control at state enterprises, non-recognition of truly democratic mass organizations, political and racial discrimination in the allocation of jobs, lands, credit, houses and consumer goods at state outlets, political patronage, corruption and extravagance."[22] The PNC, he concludes, "is unwilling to surrender its narrow party interests and wants to stay in power and retain its privileges at all costs."[23] The PPP termed the killing of WPA leader Walter Rodney in mid-1980 "a political act of the ruling party to get rid of a very strong voice of opposition."[24] The PNC has tried to mute Jagan's criticism by denying newsprint to the PPP organ, *Mirror*. The official reason in early 1980 was the "shortage of foreign exchange," but Guyanese authorities also refused to allow into the country a gift of five tons of newsprint donated to the PPP by sympathetic editors in the Caribbean.[25]

The PPP took part in the December 1980 election because, it claimed, the election provided an opportunity for Burnham's critics to put their case before the people. Jagan concluded that the PPP won "an overwhelming victory" in the election, but that his party's triumph had been taken away by a "combined military coup" under the army, police, and PNC.[26] At the end of 1979 Jagan warned: "We of the PPP do not want it, the people of Guyana do not want it, but if the government continues in the way it is going, then civil war in the country is inevitable."[27] In early 1981 the PPP called on party members to "step up mass agitation at home on all fronts and intensify the isolation of the regime internationally."[28] The PPP warned that 1981 would bring worsening social conditions and a sharpening of contradictions between the ruling PNC and the masses. According to the PPP, social improvement would come only with the removal of the PNC and the establishment of a broadly based National Patriotic Front government.[29] In April 1981 Jagan, as he has done since 1977, called upon Burnham to resign and urged the formation of "a genuine assembly of all popular and democratic social, political and other organizations."[30]

When the WPA became a party in 1979, its leaders pledged to use Marxism-Leninism to create "a classless society in which human exploitation, coercion and want are at an end." Thomas said in late 1979 that the alliance is "definitely leftist and as socialist as the PPP, but not linked to any international bloc, as they are." The WPA wants a two-year transitional government that will end the economic crisis by redistributing income, undertaking land reform, renegotiating the foreign debt, defining the economic role of the private sector, and stopping the growth of the public sector.[31]

The WPA has been under heavy government pressure since its formation as a party. Three WPA leaders, including historian Rodney, were charged with arson in mid-1979 after the burning of government and PNC buildings. In February 1980, the WPA charged that the PNC government had armed the House of Israel and called for an international commission of inquiry to investigate the violence committed by government security and paramilitary organizations.[32] A number of WPA members were detained by immigration officials in 1980, one instance drawing particular attention. Cheddi Jagan, also on a plane from which a WPA official was removed, protested loudly on the WPA leader's behalf.[33] In mid-June 1980 Rodney was killed when a bomb exploded in his car in Georgetown. The WPA refused to participate in the 1980 elections; some of its members were arrested while campaigning for abstention. The party claimed that up to 70 percent of the Guyanese people boycotted the voting and that PNC support has fallen to about 10 percent.³⁴ In November 1979 Thomas denied that WPA members were arsonists or even being armed, but he warned: "If the government drives us underground, that would change the ground rules."³⁵

International Communist Contacts

Guyanese contacts with communist nations have been complicated by the competition and conflict between Burnham's PNC and Jagan's communist party.

The PNC. Forbes Burnham's relations with the communist bloc and the Third World have varied greatly during his years as prime minister. Between 1964, when he took office, and 1970, when he proclaimed the establishment of a cooperative republic, ties with the Third World were limited and contacts with the communist states were nonexistent. During the 1970s, however, Burnham sought to establish a place for himself in the nonaligned world and to expand his contacts with the socialist countries. On the one hand, he contributed U.S. $50,000 to support "freedom fighters" in southern Africa at the 1970 conference of the non-aligned nations in Lusaka and promised a contribution every year thereafter. He reiterated his support for the struggle in southern Africa in April 1980 on a trip to Mozambique and Botswana. In 1972 Burnham hosted the first major nonaligned meeting ever held in Latin America and in September 1979 spoke passionately and at length on behalf of the movement at the nonaligned conference in Havana.³⁶

During the 1970s he also worked to establish fruitful relations with the communist world, with some success. Trade with socialist countries increased dramatically between 1970 and the end of the decade, though in 1978 it still did not exceed Guyana's trade with Great Britain—just over 25 percent of the nation's total. Whereas Georgetown had no diplomatic ties with the communist world in 1970, it had relations at the ambassadorial level with Cuba, the Soviet Union, China, and six other communist countries in 1979.

Burnham has found the Soviet Union only cautiously receptive to his overtures, perhaps in part because Guyana's pro-Soviet communist party, the PPP, is often in open opposition to PNC policies. The Guyanese prime minister made contact with the Soviet Union in 1970, but no Soviet ambassador was admitted to Georgetown until 1976, after the PPP had ended a three-year boycott of the national parliament. Cuban use of Guyana's airport while sending troops to Angola was a major concession to Soviet policy in the mid-1970s. But on trips to Moscow—most recently in 1979—Burnham has never been given the levels of aid hc has wanted. Relations with Moscow have deteriorated somewhat in the past two years. Shortly after the Jonestown massacre the Guyanese government revealed that contacts had gone on for a year between Soviet secret police agents and the People's Temple leadership. Some consideration had been given to moving the Jonestown residents to the Black Sea, and more than U.S. $7 million of People's Temple funds had been deposited in foreign bank accounts open to Soviet leaders.[37] In late 1979 and early 1980 Burnham noted with concern "the great power competition and interest in the Caribbean."[38]

Guyana established diplomatic relations with Cuba in December 1972 and limited trade and aid followed. Fidel Castro visited Georgetown in 1973, and Burnham took his first of several trips to Havana in 1975.[39] During the mid-1970s, Guyana gave diplomatic support in the United Nations to the Soviet-Cuban policy in Africa in addition to providing refueling stations for planes transporting Cuban troops to Africa.[40] In 1978, the Guyanese government launched political education programs that reflected Cuban influence, and Cuba sent one hundred or so advisers to Guyana. An apparent cooling of Guyanese-Cuban relations in early 1980 was followed by improving relations in early 1981. Contacts at the foreign-minister level were followed by trade and other agreements. Havana supports Guyana's territorial claims against Venezuela. One Venezuelan congressman charged that Cuban troops were located in Guyana.[41]

Guyana established diplomatic relations with the People's Republic of China in June 1972, and in 1975 Burnham was the first elected chief of state from the Commonwealth Caribbean to visit the PRC. The Chinese have given interest-free loans and other aid to Guyana since 1972.[42]

The PPP. Cheddi Jagan's sympathies for the Soviet Union long predated his decision to ally the PPP formally with the Soviet bloc at the 1969 Moscow meeting of communist and workers' parties. Indeed, Jagan told delegates to the Moscow meeting that his participation was "like a homecoming" to an "ideological family," adding that "not only theory, but practice has taught us that this is where we belong."[43] The PPP leader chided the PNC in the early- and middle-1970s for not developing closer relations more quickly with the Soviet Union and for maligning the Soviets in official government statements with references to "two superpowers" and "two imperialisms." The PPP's ties to the Soviet Union came up in parliament in January 1979 when a legislator reminded Jagan that the Georgetown *Daily Chronicle* had called him "a Moscow puppet." Jagan replied: "Called me a Moscow puppet? I am glad for that. I'm not ashamed of being a Moscow puppet, if you want to put it that way, because Moscow stands for socialism, for democracy, for proletarian internationalism. It helps liberation movements, not like you puppets of the CIA, of imperialism." Several days later, in a letter to the *Chronicle*, he went on: "Let me say that neither the PPP nor I take orders from Moscow. We can state categorically that at no time has any attempt been made to give us orders."[44]

Jagan repeatedly criticized Burnham for not improving relations more quickly with Cuba. In 1976 he even said that the Guyanese government should ask Cuban troops to defend the homeland if threatened by neighboring countries with territorial claims.[45] The Indo-Guyanese leader hosted the Caribbean anti-imperialist conference in August–September 1973 in Georgetown and attended a number of meetings in Havana, among them the conference of Latin American communist and workers' parties in 1975 and the conference of communist parties of the Caribbean subregion in 1977. The report of the Central Committee at the PPP's 1979 congress stated that communists in Latin America are in the "frontline" of the revolutionary struggle and continued: "Socialist Cuba is a bastion of peace, democracy and progress in an area ridden with crises. We must defend the Cuban Revolution as a principled duty, and as a prerequisite for the attainment of our freedom, and the freedom of all peoples fighting against imperialism."[46]

Socialist and communist leaders have received the vast majority of votes in every Guyanese election since the mid-1950s, a decade before the country was given its independence by Great Britain. And yet there is little reason to believe that the majority of the Guyanese people have any strong preference for socialism, much less Cuban- or Soviet-style communism. Poverty and race count for much more. Burnham and Jagan have gotten votes because they have built up large, racially oriented constituencies and made promises attractive to a poor people. They have pledged to improve the lot of their supporters and have frequently attributed any failures to their domestic political opponents or a real or alleged international enemy. Not infrequently, particularly at the local levels, it has been suggested that racial groups must stick together to promote their presumed common interests.

The WPA has tried with some success to break into this scene with a more racially neutral, radical socialism, but the new party finds pressures applied on all sides. The PNC openly suppresses and harasses the WPA, while the PPP, despite a degree of surface support, is no more enthusiastic about the new group than the Burnhamites.

The two principal parties are essentially the creatures of their top leaders. Burnham has flipped from fairly conservative in the 1960s to fairly radical (in many respects) in the 1970s, and there is reason to believe that he could flop back again if the right opportunities arose. Burnham's position is particularly flexible—even vulnerable, despite his control of the state apparatus—for he lacks firm international backing from a major power. He maintains active relations with the United States, Great Britain, the Soviet Union, Cuba, even the People's Republic of China, but none of these governments is very enthusiastic about him and for some he is decidedly a second choice. Jagan has been more consistently tied to Soviet-style solutions and international alignments. In power, he would almost certainly ask for—and receive—much more active Soviet and Cuban participation in the affairs of the country. The WPA, on the other hand, is not (at least yet) a one-man party. For that reason—and because it is so new on the scene, though some of its leaders are not—the WPA has less mass appeal. As yet the WPA lacks significant international support, despite ties to certain radical movements in neighboring countries and an undeniable appeal to Havana.

Prospects for stability and constructive development in Guyana are not good. Indeed, under present conditions of economic crisis, actual and potential racial confrontation, domestic ideological demagoguery, territorial disputes with Venezuela and Suriname, Caribbean radicalism, and increasing big-power rivalry in the area, Guyana is everyone's target and a virtual model of instability.

Notes

1. J. H. Parry, *The Establishment of the European Hegemony, 1415–1715* (New York: Harper & Row, Harper Torchbook, 1961), p. 105.

2. In *Candide*, Voltaire informs us that Raleigh "came very near" to El Dorado. Candide found it, of course, in Peru.

3. *Guyana in Brief* (Georgetown: Guyana Information Service, 1979), pp. 7–11.

4. Pierre-Michel Thivolet, *Le Monde* (Paris), December 4, 1979, tr. in *Manchester Guardian*, December 23, 1979.

5. Thivolet, *Le Monde*, December 4, 1979; *Quarterly Economic Review* (London), fourth quarter 1980, p. 26; James Nelson Goodsell, *Christian Science Monitor*, March 27, 1979; and Muhamad Hamaludin, *Financial Times*, December 7, 1979.

6. Roy Arthur Glasgow, *Guyana: Race and Politics Among Africans and East Indians* (Hague: Martinus Nijhoff, 1970), pp. 25, 29–30, 70, 73, 79–80, 85–87.

7. Ralph Premdas, *Party Politics and Racial Division in Guyana*, Studies in Race and Nations, vol. 4, study 4 (Denver, 1972–1973).

8. Washington's real name is David Hill. On the use of the House of Israel by the PNC, see Thivolet, *Le Monde*, December 4, 1979; and the PPP organ *Mirror*, December 3, 1978, and May 6 and November 18, 1979. On November 25, 1979, the *Mirror* editorialized: "Who sends thugs to break up meetings and demonstrations, to throw chemically dangerous liquids at speakers, to attack with broken bottles, sticks and paling staves? It is common knowledge that the PNC and their House of Israel henchmen are responsible for these acts of violence, which continue to this day."

9. Leo A. Despres, *Cultural Pluralism and Nationalist Politics in British Guiana* (Chicago: Rand-McNally, 1967), p. 209.

10. Kenneth M. Glazier, "Guyana," in Witold S. Sworakowski, ed., *World Communism: A Handbook, 1918–1965* (Stanford: Hoover Institution Press, 1973), p. 180.

11. See Robert H. Manley, *Guyana Emergent* (Cambrigde, Mass.: Schenkman Publishing Co., 1979), p. 6.

12. Quoted in Peter Newman, *British Guiana* (London: Oxford University Press, 1964), p. 82.

13. Despres, *Cultural Pluralism*, chap. 5.

14. Ibid., pp. 217–20.

15. Lynn Ratliff, "Guyana," in Richard F. Staar, ed., *Yearbook on International Communist Affairs, 1970* (Stanford: Hoover Institution Press, 1971), pp. 426–30; Brian Wearing, "Present Political Situation," in Brian Irving, ed., *Guyana: A Composite Monologue* (Hato Rey, Puerto Rico: Inter-American University Press, 1972), p. 33; and *Mirror*, March 28, 1976.

16. William Ratliff, "Guyana," in Richard F. Staar, ed., *Yearbook, 1977, Yearbook, 1978,* and *Yearbook, 1980,* pp. 459–62, 387, and 364–65, respectively; and *New York Times,* June 15, 1980.

17. William Ratliff, *Castroism and Communism in Latin America* (Washington, D.C.: American Enterprise Institute, 1976), pp. 65–66.

18. The role of the American Central Intelligence Agency in Burnham's victory is discussed in Ronald Radosh, *American Labor and United States Foreign Policy* (New York: Random House, 1969), pp. 393–405; and summarized in Manley, *Guyana Emergent*, pp. 57–58. For the PPP version, see Cheddi Jagan, *The Role of the CIA in Guyana and Its Activities Throughout the World* (Georgetown: New Guyana Co., 1967).

19. The PNC won 169 of 205 local council seats in 1980; the PPP took 35 and the United Front, 1.

20. Quoted by Lew Wheaton in an Associated Press story from Georgetown, released in the United States on November 4, 1979. As early as March 1971 Carl Blackman, the prominent Afro-Guyanese editor of the *Sunday Graphic*, told me that under no circumstances could he imagine Burnham allowing an election that would remove him from office.

21. Desmond Hoyte, *A Socialist Economy Through Agricultural, Industrial*

and *Technical Development* (Georgetown: Guyana Printers, 1979); and Mohamed Shahabbuddeen, *The New Guyana Constitution: Philosophy and Mechanics* (Georgetown: Guyana Printers, 1979?).

22. *Mirror*, May 6, 1979.

23. Cheddi Jagan, "Acute Problems of Guyana," *World Marxist Review*, December 1979, pp. 54–56; and *Mirror*, editorial, December 9, 1979.

24. *Intercontinental Press* (New York), June 30, 1980.

25. *Quarterly Economic Review*, first quarter 1980, p. 33.

26. Agence France Presse, December 17, 1980. Some British and other observers also charged numerous cases of fraud perpetrated by the PNC government (*Latin America Regional Report, Caribbean*, January 16, 1981).

27. Quoted in *Kingston Daily Gleaner* (Jamaica), October 30, 1979.

28. *Latin America Weekly Report*, January 23, 1981.

29. *Guyana Chronicle* (Georgetown), January 5, 1981.

30. CANA radio (Bridgetown), April 25, 1981.

31. Lew Wheaton, AP dispatch, November 4, 1979.

32. *Latin America Weekly Report*, March 14, 1980.

33. Ibid., March 21, 1980.

34. *Latin America Regional Report, Caribbean*, January 16, 1981.

35. Quoted by Lew Wheaton, AP dispatch, November 4, 1979.

36. Manley, *Guyana Emergent*, p. 91; and Burnham, *To Build a New World* (Georgetown?: Guyana Ministry of Information, 1979).

37. *Washington Post*, February 1, 1979.

38. *Latin America Weekly Report*, February 1, 1979.

39. Manley, *Guyana Emergent*, p. 69.

40. Ronald E. Jones, "Cuba and the English-speaking Caribbean," in Cole Blasier and Carmelo Mesa-Lago, eds., *Cuba in the World* (Pittsburgh: University of Pittsburgh Press, 1979), p. 140.

41. *Advocate News* (Bridgetown), January 13, 1981; and *Latin America Weekly Report*, January 23, February 27, 1981.

42. Manley, *Guyana Emergent*, pp. 68–69; and William Ratliff, "Communist China and Latin America," *Asian Survey*, October 1972, pp. 857–58.

43. *International Meeting of Communist and Workers' Parties* (Prague: Peace and Socialism Publishers, 1969), p. 610.

44. *Daily Chronicle* (Georgetown), January 9, 14, 1979.

45. *Washington Post*, March 13, 1976.

46. Jagan, "Report of the Central Committee," pp. 4–5; and *Mirror*, August 8, 1979.

10 | CONCLUSION

Robert Wesson

The Caribbean and Central America are deeply troubled, as the preceding studies make amply clear; and their peoples furnish ready recruits for radical or revolutionary movements. It is a field of opportunity for Soviet foreign policy and correspondingly presents difficult problems for the United States.

The basic misfortune of the area is that its countries are small, weak, and poor to very poor. They are economically dependent to a high degree, mostly relying precariously on a few agricultural exports or tourism. Of the countries considered here, Jamaica and Guyana have bauxite, Panama has the canal, and Guatemala may have consequential oil deposits. Only for Panama has the geographic advantage much raised the general economy. Otherwise, natural resources are modest. Agricultural potentials are limited, and people crowd the land in various island nations and El Salvador, while populations are growing rapidly. Industrial development is scanty. Per capita incomes are low, generally well below those of most countries of South America.

The potential for discontent is raised by a high degree of inequality, particularly in the Central American countries, where small elites hold both political power and the lion's share of property. Racial divisions contribute to inequality and to political tensions. In Guatemala, for example, the battle of the guerrillas has ethnic and racial overtones, as the radicals try to lead the Indians to rebel against their condition as plantation workers. In Guyana, those of African background stand against and generally dominate those of East Indian origin, while in many places class differences correlate with skin pigmentation.

In these conditions, one would not expect to find honest, legalistic governments exercising power under constitutional restraints and with full responsibility to the people. Rather remarkably, some islands, with Jamaica in the lead, have retained democratic institutions implanted during prolonged British rule. On the mainland, Costa Rica is proud to be a beacon of freedom and democratic government amid authoritarian regimes; indeed, it is the only Latin American country with a deep and mature democratic tradition. Otherwise, military oligarchies prevail in Central America; the Somoza dictatorship has been replaced by a new authoritarianism that pays more attention to the economic needs of the people than did the former ruler but allows even less political rights.

Under these conditions, extremism flourishes, and bullets make politics, often to the exclusion of ballots. Politics is strongly ideological, and opposing parties have little understanding of the virtues of compromise. There are formidable leftist, near-communist, or communist parties or movements, opposed (or in various countries repressed) by rightist forces. The parties of discontent, to the extent that they are committed to radical change, are almost inevitably anti-American because the United States has generally supported stability and the status quo. On the one hand, it is intellectually easy to equate the United States with the oppressive and unjust social order; on the other hand, it is politically attractive to do so because American interests represent a conspicuous foreign presence. Discontent becomes anticapitalism because the dominant power is capitalist and the most visible foreign intrusion is economic, while anticapitalism, expressed as Marxism, merges into a welter of antiforeign or "anti-imperialist" causes.

This condition invites the Soviet Union to present itself as a champion of economic and political liberation; and its opportunities are greatly increased by the fact that it has a base and willing surrogate in Cuba. Fidel Castro invited himself and his country into the Soviet camp in 1961, and his policies have not always pleased his Soviet mentors and protectors. But Castro's deviation has mostly been to be a more zealous revolutionary than the more cautious Soviet leaders. In particular, he has been prone to promote guerrilla uprisings, while the Soviet Union was content to let staid Latin American communist parties play a careful game on behalf not of revolution but of Soviet foreign policy. But this has increased rather than diminished the utility of Cuba for the spread of the Soviet system. It adds ginger to the movement and enables the Soviet Union to sponsor subversive activism in the Caribbean and Central America indirectly, with minimal risk and commitment.

With these advantages, it is not remarkable that the anti-U.S., pro-

Cuban or pro-Soviet cause has marked up some successes, as detailed in the preceding essays. It is perhaps chiefly because of the fracturing of radical movements that they have not been more successful. The radicals of the Sandinista party took over a broad popular movement to end forty years of one-family rule, and for the first time the United States faces a decidedly unfriendly government in the region most subject to its influence, Central America. The capture of Grenada by a few dozen pro-Castroites caused the United States political embarrassment disproportionate to the island's size and intrinsic importance. A terrorist and guerrilla threat to El Salvador for a time seemed to occupy most of the political and diplomatic energies of the American administration in a world beset by far larger troubles, from inflation to the nuclear arms race.

Yet the United States can hardly afford to neglect the area or to permit foreign-supported, anti-American movements to advance freely. There is little to gain, perhaps, but much to lose in the area. In the day of missiles, it still has strategic importance, dominating the southern approaches to Mexico and the United States and the waterway between the oceans. Politically, any setback in the area represents a loss of hemispheric influence by the United States. Perhaps most of all, the United States cannot escape a considerable degree of moral responsibility for Central America, which was long within its sphere of influence and where U.S. predominance—or the idea of predominance—persists, as it does not in South America. It would be pleasant if the United States could point to the region as a relatively stable and prosperous exception to the political disorder and poverty prevalent in much of the Third World, thanks to beneficent influence of this country.

More or less communistic movements, however, are successful not only in places where they may be able to seize power, as in Grenada. They are everywhere able to score some victories by destabilizing politics and making moderate or reformist solutions more difficult. They cannot be blamed basically for poverty and tyranny in the area; it was poor and (in the older independent area of Central America) subject to nasty politics long before Lenin, much less Castro. But they make progressive improvement more difficult in many ways. They increase tensions, heighten ideological antagonisms, and confuse issues. They raise a specter of total change, which the upper and middle classes generally oppose with great passion. The example of Cuba, in which a large part of the population lost their homes and livelihood if not lives, makes the communist threat seem serious. It provides holders of power and wealth with a rationale for yielding nothing and treating brutally those who propose serious change.

The narrow rigidity of ruling groups, on the other hand, pushes moderates into revolutionary movements and drives them to accept the proffered assistance of external powers prepared to support the attack on the status quo. Where communism is at issue, questions of the shape of society are not to be decided by the formality of placing marked papers in boxes. Even in Costa Rica, the control of major trade unions by communists raises political temperatures and impedes the normal workings of the system. If, in case of major economic difficulties, the communist party should capture a large part of the electorate, Costa Rica's proud democracy would certainly stumble and might well fall.

Leftist, Marxist, or procommunist politics also contribute to the economic distress that makes fertile soil for revolutionary or communist movements. In an atmosphere of tension, uncertainty, and distrust for private enterprise, foreign and domestic capital either stays away or flees. Despite low wage levels, few corporations put plants in Central America except to serve a protected local market. A large fraction of the middle and upper classes left Jamaica during the Manley years, taking much of their property with them; and few are likely to return unless the new policies of Seaga are more successful than can reasonably be expected. Civil conflict in El Salvador has likewise led to the flight of both people and capital to the security of Miami and Los Angeles. The proper functioning of any economy requires security and predictability, values the region markedly lacks and qualities that not only communist but socialist parties effectively destroy.

In this very difficult situation, the United States cannot well adopt a simple policy of supporting friendly powers against subversive movements. This has various drawbacks. The regimes supported are relieved of the necessity to improve themselves and the lot of their people to the extent that they can count on the backing of the United States, while shoring up irresponsible governments only postpones problems and may permit them to become worse. It increases their dependency on the United States, reinforces anti-Americanism, and enables the communists to present themselves as national liberators. It means a more or less permanent burden for the United States, as unpopular governments needing help from this country are likely to continue to need it indefinitely.

No less important, the support of more or less reprehensible governments has a diplomatic and political cost that may be disproportionate to possible positive gains. Conflicts in Central America use up diplomatic capital; the Reagan administration felt it necessary to send a special envoy, Vernon Walters, on a tour of Latin American capitals to beg for sympathy for U.S. policy in El Salvador; he did not get much. Bolstering the status quo in Central America inevitably causes friction with Mexico, a country far more important than all Central America together and a country determined to maintain some image of revolutionism. It was in protest against U.S. aid to the government of El Salvador that President López Portillo hugged Fidel Castro and called him "dearest friend." The American administration felt that it had to persuade European governments of the importance of the antiguerrilla struggle in El Salvador, which they tended to find not only remote but trivial compared with Poland, the Persian Gulf, the debate over missiles, and so forth. Remote or not, El Salvador moved tens of thousands of Europeans to stage anti-U.S. demonstrations and doubtless lessened their acceptance of NATO defense measures.

It is equally important that support for unsavory dictatorships or governments widely believed to be such is repugnant to many Americans and offers a handle for protest by many disposed against administration policies. American foreign policy needs broad backing in order to be effective, with congressional support on the big questions; and any course that is widely viewed as narrow, antipopular, or immoral is a heavy burden. If an important number of Americans are alienated from the general principles of security policy by unhappiness over actions taken in regard to El Salvador or Guatemala, it is a poor trade-off. What happens on American campuses is important for the long-term strength of the United States.

It is thus essential to uphold vital interests in ways broadly acceptable to Latin America, to U.S. allies, and to the American people. This means halting foreign-supported subversion without championing a status quo that is unpromising and unacceptable to a large part of the people, preventing hostile revolutionary action without supporting unsavory oligarchic or dictatorial regimes. The governments that most need U.S. aid against communist-led undermining are unfortunately apt to be oppressive and of doubtful legitimacy. The United States assumes a large moral cost in backing a government like that of Guatemala, although the leftist forces that would like to replace it might be no more of an improvement than the Sandinistas have been an improvement over the Somocistas. A Costa Rica, on the other hand, presents no problems.

Yet it is difficult for the United States to sponsor an alternative enlightened, democratic, moderate, or centrist regime prepared to respond to the needs of the people in a legal way. Enlightened centrist forces are usually weak to nonexistent; the United States cannot create them, and if they existed, there might be no feasible means of lifting them to power. Democracy seems an unlikely political outcome in most of the region; it is somewhat miraculous that it has prevailed recently in Costa Rica, Jamaica, and lesser islands. Military rule or dictatorship of some degree has been the almost invariable condition of Central America, except for Costa Rica but including Panama. The recently independent former British colonies in the Caribbean have thus far not exchanged the Anglo-Saxon civilian for the Hispanic military tradition. But the experience of Guyana shows that democratic institutions are not reliable, and the case of Grenada makes clear that leftist dictatorship is a real possibility.

This complicates the navigational problems of the U.S. attempt to steer between hazards on the left and problems on the right: the middle, moderate way of democracy is evidently full of reefs. Free elections do not necessarily solve anything except the desire for free elections, and it may be argued that democratic institutions for which the people are unprepared may break down valid anticommunist forces and open the doors to disorder and radicalism. The failure of democracy in Argentina, Brazil, Chile, and Uruguay, the most modernized countries of Latin America, is relevant in this regard. In Central America, the example of Guatemala is discouraging. Following the fall of the Ubico dictatorship in 1944, that country entered the most democratic period of its history. But the organization best prepared to take advantage of the sudden freedom to organize and politicize the worker and peasant masses was the communist party. Political tensions rose, and the country was overtaken by inflation and economic woes. In 1954 the armed forces refused to countenance the arming of militias and, with the encouragement of the United States, overthrew the elected president.

It is not clear, moreover, how far democratic institutions are consonant with the economic growth that is generally accepted as not only desirable per se but the basic answer to radicalism. Costa Rica has relatively prospered with democratic government and has possibly the highest standard of living of the countries considered here, but it is unique. Jamaica under Manley hardly showed that democracy was the way to prosperity, but under Seaga it may present a different picture. The semidemocratic regime of Guyana has given no cause for optimism.

The most successful Third World economies, at least in terms of raising the total national product, are uniformly authoritarian, with strong governments moderated by fairly consistent adherence to legality and a constitutional order. They include in this hemisphere Mexico, where the governing party is completely dominant but observes democratic forms, and Brazil, ruled by a military establishment moving cautiously in the direction of democracy. The other outstanding examples are South Korea, Taiwan, and Singapore, under military or single-party rule, and Hong Kong, a British crown colony with substantial autonomy. These countries, especially the Asian (which have registered the more spectacular growth rates) have succeeded in maintaining relatively free market economies with moderate taxation and favorable conditions for productive enterprise, with minimal interference of Marxist-Leninist ideology and communist or radical parties or movements.

It is not clear, however, that any of these countries has found a long-term answer to the problems of political and economic development of the poorer majority of mankind or that they teach lessons that the United States could apply elsewhere, particularly in the Central American–Caribbean region. The problems of stability with change are especially acute in this area, and the questions posed for American foreign policy are correspondingly difficult. Much intelligence, forebearance, resolution, and sober judgment will be necessary to meet them.

CONTRIBUTORS

THOMAS P. ANDERSON is Professor at Eastern Connecticut State College. A graduate of Loyola University, he has published two books on El Salvador, including *Matanza: El Salvador's Communist Revolt of 1932*, and a score of articles.

W. RAYMOND DUNCAN is Distinguished Teaching Professor and Director of Global Studies at SUNY-Brockport. His most recent book is *Latin American Politics: A Developmental Approach* (Praeger Publishers, 1976). He is editor of *Soviet Policy in Developing Countries* (Ginn-Blaisdell, 1970) and *Soviet Policy in the Third World* (Pergamon, 1980) and coeditor with James Nelson Goodsell of *The Quest for Change in Latin America* (Oxford, 1970). He has written numerous articles and essays on Latin American politics and Cuban foreign policy.

JAMES NELSON GOODSELL has been Latin American correspondent of the *Christian Science Monitor* for many years. He has an M.A. from Mexico City College and a Ph.D. from Harvard and has lived and traveled widely in many Latin American countries. He has received several awards and citations for coverage of Latin American affairs and has published books on Cuba, Puerto Rico, Venezuela, and Nicaragua.

WILLIAM M. LEOGRANDE teaches political science at American University. He received his Ph.D. in Latin American studies from the University of Syracuse. He has published dozens of articles and several monographs, mostly on Cuban politics and foreign relations, and is active as a foreign policy consultant.

NEALE J. PEARSON is Associate Professor of Political Science at Texas Tech University. He received his Ph.D. from the University of Florida. He has written many articles for journals and books on Latin America, especially on peasant groups, trade unions, and revolutionary organizations.

DANIEL L. PREMO is an Associate Professor of Political Science and History at Washington College. He served with the United States Information Agency in Guatemala and Colombia from 1958 to 1965 and has traveled extensively throughout Mexico and Central America. He has been a contributor to the Hoover Institution's *Yearbook on International Communist Affairs* since 1973, authoring country profiles on Colombia, Guatemala, and Peru.

WILLIAM E. RATLIFF (Ph.D., University of Washington) is Research Fellow of the Hoover Institution and staff writer of the *Peninsula Times Tribune* (Palo Alto, Calif.). His publications include *Castroism and Communism in Latin America*, chapters in several books, and numerous articles on Latin American affairs.

GEORGE VOLSKY, Miami-based correspondent for the *New York Times* covering Cuba, the rest of the Caribbean, and Florida, is Research Associate at the Center for Advanced International Studies, University of Miami, and consultant on Cuban affairs for various research organizations, including the Hoover Institution and the RAND Corporation. Born in Poland, he was educated at the Jagiellonian University in Cracow and the London School of Economics. He lived in Cuba from 1947 to 1961 and visited the country recently. He is a regular contributor to the *Yearbook on International Communist Affairs*. He wrote the chapters on Cuba in the American Assembly's *United States and the Caribbean* and in the *Encyclopedia of Developing Nations*. He is currently working on a history of the Communist Party of Cuba, to be published by the Hoover Institution.

ROBERT WESSON is Professor of Political Science at the University of California, Santa Barbara, and Senior Research Fellow at the Hoover Institution. He has spent many years in various activities in Latin America, mostly in Costa Rica. He earned his Ph.D. from Columbia University and has published numerous books on Soviet and communist politics and foreign policy.

INDEX

174 | Index

Manley Michael (continued)
117, 122–23, 132; foreign policy of,
117–24 passim, 131; and IMF negotiations, 120, 122, 123–24, 129; political
model of, 121–22, 128. See also Jamaica
Martell, Juan José, 69
Martínez, Angel Guadalupe, 69
Martinique, 131–32, 136, 137
Marxism-Leninism and Marxist-Leninist
movements, xiii, 161–62; in Cuba, 6,
33–35; in Caribbean, 9–10, 44–46, 134–
38; in Nicaragua, 11, 53–60 passim; in
Central America, 102–14; in El Salvador, 62, 63, 66–70; in Guatemala, 78–
80, 82–84, 91; in Jamaica, 117–19, 123–
24, 126; in Guyana, 147–48, 152–53,
155–56. See also individual movements
and parties by name
Mayorga Quirós, Román, 64, 65
Mazarumi River, Guyana, 145
Melgar Castro, Juan Alberto, 101
Méndez Montenegro, Julio César, 79
Mesa-Lago, Carmelo, 36
Mexico, 4, 53, 76, 85, 161, 164; and U.S.
policy, ix, xiv, 3, 162–63; role in region,
16, 24; foreign policy of, 18, 22, 30, 130;
and Cuba, 40–41, 136
Middle East, xiii–xiv, 6–7, 20
Mira Valverde, Manuel, 104, 105
Mirror (Guyana), 151
Missile crisis of 1962, 35–36, 47, 135
Mongolia, 8
Monroe, Trevor, 123
Monroe Doctrine, Roosevelt "corollary"
to, xi
Montane Oropesa, Jesus, 138
Morales Erlich, Antonio, 65
Montes, César, 91
Moscow Olympics, boycott of, 111
Movimiento Popular de Liberacion
Cinchonero (Honduras), 108
Murphy, John, 110

Namibia, 139
Napoleón Duarte, José, 12, 62, 65, 71,
106
National Association of Salvadoran Education, 63
National Autonomous University of Honduras, 101, 107, 108

National Committee for the Defense of
Sovereignty and Peace (Panama) 111
National Council on Legislation (Pan-
ama), 101
National Democratic Union (El Sal-
vador), 62–69 passim
National Federation of Workers in Pub-
lic Administration (Costa Rica) 104
National Institute for Agrarian Reform
(Guatemala), 89
Nationalist Party (Honduras), 101
National Liberation Movement
(Guatemala), 77, 85, 90
National Liberation Party (Panama), 112
National Opposition Union (El Salvador),
62
National Organized Anticommunist
Movement (Guatemala), 79, 80
National Peasant Federation (Costa
Rica), 104
National Revolutionary Movement (El
Salvador), 62, 64, 68, 69, 70
National University (El Salvador),64
National University (Panama), 110
Nativi, Tomás, 108
NATO, xiii, 163
Netherlands, 130, 131, 134, 143
Netherlands Antilles, 133
New Anticommunist Organization
(Guatemala), 79, 80
New International Economic Order, 22,
120, 128
New Jewel Movement (Greneda), 9, 27,
46, 139–41
Nicaragua, 8, 18, 52–60, 86, 87, 94, 135,
160; U.S. policy toward, xi, 3, 20, 29,
53, 163; leftist movements in, xiii, 11–
12, 13–14, 91; Sandinista revolution and
government, 1, 11–12, 54–60, 106; socioeconomic and demographic
characteristics, 2, 14, 15, 53, 54, 73–75,
95–99 passim; Soviet and Cuban roles
in, 4, 5, 7, 12–17 passim, 23, 41–43, 47,
125; regional influence, 13, 19, 30, 85;
non-Cuban and non-Soviet aid to insurgents, 30; history, 52–54; aid to other
insurgent movements, 70, 84. See also
Sandinistas and Sandinista National
Liberation Front
Nixon, Richard M., xii, 110

Reagan, Ronald, administration of, xiv, 119, 141; Caribbean and Central American policy of, 2–4, 113, 132, 162–63; and El Salvador 3–4, 71; and Cuba, 38; and Guatemala, 55, 59–60, 86–87
Rebel Armed Forces (Guatemala), 13
Remón, José Antonio, 99
Revolutionary Coordination of the Masses (El Salvador), 67–69
Revolutionary Democratic Front (El Salvador), 12, 13, 28, 68–69, 70
Revolutionary Directorate (Cuba), 34
Revolutionary Military Coordination (El Salvador), 68
Revolutionary Movement of the People (Costa Rica), 103, 106
Revolutionary Party (Guatemala), 90, 93
Revolutionary Party of Central American Workers (Honduras), 104
Rizo, Julian Torres, 140
Roa, Raul, 109
Robelo Callejas, Alfonso, 57, 58
Roca, Blas, 135
Rodas Alvarado, Modesto, 100
Rodney, Walter, 150, 151, 152
Rodríguez Ruiz, José Napoleón, 69
Romania, 8, 17, 125
Romero, Carlos Humberto, 12, 62, 63, 64
Romero y Galdánez, Oscar Arnulfo, 28, 63–67 *passim*
Roosevelt, Franklin D., xii
Roosevelt, Theodore, xi, 31–32
Royo, Aristides, 19, 21–22, 100, 103, 110
Ruiz, Henry, 56, 57

St.Kitts-Nevis, 10, 133
St. Lucia, 8, 10, 22, 132, 133
St. Vincent, 8, 10, 133
Salazar, Jorge, 58
Salvadoran Democratic Front, 68
Samayoa, Salvador, 69
San Carlos, University of (Guatemala), 28, 81
Sandinistas and Sandinista National Liberation Front, 11–12, 43, 53, 103, 161; U.S. policy toward, 3, 42, 58, 59; aid from other countries to, 28, 30, 41–43, 55, 58, 59, 106, 109–10; and other insurgent movements, 30, 71, 85; politics of government, 54–60,160; leaders, 56–57. *See also* Nicaragua

Sandino, Augusto Cesar, 53
Sandoval Alarcón, Mario, 77, 85
San Pedro Sula, Honduras, 95
San Salvador, El Salvador, 66
Seaga, Edward, 10, 141–42; victory of, in Jamaica, xiii, 4, 117, 118, 122–24, 127, 133; and Cuba, 45, 46; and United States, 118; economic problems confronting, 120, 125–26, 162, 164. *See also* Jamaica
Secret Anticommunist Army (Guatemala), 81–82, 85
Serrano Pinto, Germán, 105
Shafik Handal, Jorge, 65, 67, 70
Shearer, Hugh, 136
Social Christian Party (El Salvador), 69
Social Democratic Party (Costa Rica), 98
Social Democratic Party (Guatemala), 81, 91
Socialist Party (Costa Rica), 103, 105
Socialist Student Front (Honduras), 107
Socialist Workers' Organization (Costa Rica), 103
Solano, César, 107
Somoza Debayle, Anastasio, 4, 19, 53, 54, 86, 99, 106, 110, 160; overthrow of, xiii, 2, 11–12, 30, 42–43, 54–55, 58, 59. *See also* Nicaragua
Somoza Debayle, Luis, 53
Somoza García, Anastasio, 53
Soviet Union, *see* Union of Soviet Socialist Republics
Spanish-American War, ix, 31
Spiegler, Otto, 77
Standard Fruit/Castle and Cook Company, 105, 107
Strachan, Selwyn, 140
Summit Meeting of Nonaligned Countries, Sixth, 18–19
Suriname, 7, 8, 10, 136, 156

Teekah, Vincent, 149
Tegucigalpa, Honduras, 95
Third World: Soviet relations with, 2, 21–22, 24, 29
Thomas, Clive, 150, 152, 153
Tirado López, Victor Manuel, 56, 57
Tito, Josip Broz, 21
Torchlight, (Grenada), 140
Torrijos Herrera, Omar, 4, 99–100, 103, 109–12 *passim*